T0320162

Innovation and Economic Development

Innovation and Economic Development

The Impact of Information and Communication Technologies in Latin America

Edited by

Mario Cimoli

Economic Commission for Latin America and the Caribbean (ECLAC), Chile and University of Venice (Ca' Foscari), Italy

André A. Hofman

Economic Commission for Latin America and the Caribbean (ECLAC), Chile

Nanno Mulder

Economic Commission for Latin America and the Caribbean (ECLAC), Chile

IN ASSOCIATION WITH THE UNITED NATIONS ECONOMIC COMMISSION FOR LATIN AMERICA AND THE CARIBBEAN (ECLAC)

Edward Elgar
Cheltenham, UK • Northampton, MA, USA

Published by
Edward Elgar Publishing Limited
The Lypiatts
15 Lansdown Road
Cheltenham
Glos GL50 2JA
UK

Edward Elgar Publishing, Inc.
William Pratt House
9 Dewey Court
Northampton
Massachusetts 01060
USA

A catalogue record for this book
is available from the British Library

Library of Congress Control Number: 2010922143

Mixed Sources
Product group from well-managed
forests and other controlled sources
www.fsc.org Cert no. SA-COC-1565
© 1996 Forest Stewardship Council

ISBN 978 1 84980 241 3

Printed and bound by MPG Books Group, UK

Contents

Contributors

Claudio Aravena is Researcher at the Economic Development Division at the Economic Commission for Latin America and the Caribbean (ECLAC) in Santiago, Chile.

Marc Badia-Miró is Lecturer in the Department of Economics and Business in the Universitat Oberta de Catalunya, Barcelona, Spain.

Nauro F. Campos is Professor of Economics at Brunel University, Uxbridge, West London, United Kingdom.

Marco Capasso is Post-Doctoral Researcher at the Faculty of Geosciences and Utrecht School of Economics, Utrecht University, the Netherlands.

Carolina Castaldi is Assistant Professor at the Eindhoven Centre for Innovation Studies (ECIS), Eindhoven Technology University, the Netherlands.

Mario Cimoli is Director of the Division of Production, Productivity and Management at the Economic Commission for Latin America and the Caribbean (ECLAC) in Santiago, Chile and Professor of Economics at the University of Venice (Ca' Foscari), Italy.

Nelson Correa is a Researcher at the Economic Commission for Latin America and the Caribbean (ECLAC) in Santiago, Chile.

Mariela Dal Borgo is a PhD Student in Economics at the University of Warwick, Coventry, United Kingdom.

Gaaitzen J. De Vries is a Post-Doctoral Researcher at the Groningen Growth and Development Centre and Faculty of Economics and Business of the University of Groningen, the Netherlands.

Giovanni Dosi is a Professor of Economics and Coordinator of the Laboratory of Economics and Management (LEM) at the Scuola Superiore Sant'Anna, Pisa, Italy.

Esther Dweck is Associate Professor at the Institute of Economics, Federal University of Rio de Janeiro (IE/UFRJ), Brazil.

Fabio Freitas is Associate Professor of Economics and, presently, coordinator of the graduate programme in economics of the Institute of Economics of the Federal University of Rio de Janeiro (IE/UFRJ), Brazil.

José Jofré González is an Economic Analyst at the Department of Studies on Prices of the National Statistics Institute, Chile.

André A. Hofman is Director of the *Revista CEPAL Review* of the Economic Commission for Latin America and the Caribbean (ECLAC) in Santiago, Chile.

Christian Hurtado is Head of the Department of Studies on Prices of the National Statistics Institute, Chile.

Dale W. Jorgenson is Samuel W. Morris University Professor at Harvard University, Cambridge, MA, United States.

David Kupfer is Associate Professor at the Institute of Economics, Federal University of Rio de Janeiro (IE/UFRJ), Brazil and Coordinator of the Research Group on Industry and Competitiveness.

Nanno Mulder is an Economic Affairs Officer at the Division for International Trade and Integration of the Economic Commission for Latin America and the Caribbean (ECLAC) in Santiago, Chile.

Mary O'Mahony is Professor of Economics at the Birmingham Business School, University of Birmingham, United Kingdom.

Marcel Timmer is Professor of Economic Growth and Development and Director of the Groningen Growth and Development Centre (GGDC), Faculty of Economics and Business, University of Groningen, the Netherlands.

Bart Van Ark is Professor at the University of Groningen, the Netherlands and Chief Economist of the The Conference Board based in New York, United States.

Khuong Minh Vu is Assistant Professor at the Lee Kuan Yew School of Public Policy, National University of Singapore.

Foreword

The rapid development and spread of information and communication technologies (ICT) can bring about major economic and social progress. ICT represents a breakthrough both as a general purpose technology and as a techno-economic paradigm characterized by falling prices of micro-electronics, computers, software, telecom devices, control instruments, computer-aided biotechnology and new materials. This paradigm has the potential to foster structural change, productivity growth and economic and social development.

However, the benefits of ICT for Latin America and the Caribbean may be small owing to the 'digital gap' and to the large internal divides that exist within the Latin American and Caribbean region as compared with advanced countries. This is illustrated by underdeveloped infrastructures and the resulting gaps in access to, and use of, ICT, in particular by those with low incomes and little education, those living in rural areas and small and micro-enterprises. Low skills levels and the lack of training and programmes adapted to local needs and conditions, poor legislation and inadequate regulation and use of multiple technical standards are also manifestations of the digital gap. These shortcomings may reduce the potential of ICT and dilute its contribution to development in the region.

Following the Summit of Heads of State and Government from Latin America and the Caribbean and from the European Union in Rio de Janeiro in 1999, and based on its own experience in promoting convergence of regulation and policies among the European Union member states, the European Commission created the Alliance for the Information Society (@LIS) under its external cooperation programmes. @LIS aims to extend the benefits of the information society to all and reduce the digital divide throughout Latin America and the Caribbean. The first @ LIS programme ran from 2002 to 2007, and was executed in part by the Economic Commission for Latin America and the Caribbean (ECLAC), after countries in the region requested support in the definition and adoption of strategies for the construction of the information society.

Within @LIS, ECLAC has coordinated the Plan of Action for the Information Society in Latin America and the Caribbean (eLAC) (2005–07 and 2008–10), which is geared towards promotion of the information society in Latin America and the Caribbean. eLAC is a 'metaplatform' from which to coordinate public and private initiatives, build national strategies in specific areas and deepen knowledge on key issues in order to improve the design, implementation and evaluation of policies. As part of this effort, ECLAC coordinated an ambitious research effort designed to shed more light on the economic impact of ICT in the region. The present book is the fruit of that research.

This book analyses the relationship between ICT diffusion patterns, productivity and economic growth in Latin America after 1990 using two different conceptual approaches: growth accounting and evolutionary economics. It incorporates contributions from ECLAC analysts and distinguished international scholars representing both perspectives.

The two approaches have different theoretical backgrounds. Growth accounting is based on neoclassical growth theory and analyses whether economic growth is attributable to the accumulation of labour, ICT capital and non-ICT capital, or technological advances and improvements in the organization of production, also referred to as multi-factor productivity. Evolutionary economics is based on evolutionary and heterodox perspectives and captures a broad set of factors affecting growth patterns and the role of ICT, such as technological paradigms, firm and sector heterogeneity and cumulative learning. The evolutionary approach delves into the 'black box' of technical progress, explaining its development and the characteristics of technological learning. It starts from a historical interpretation of technical and organizational change, and considers persistent asymmetries among countries in the production system to account for stubborn technological gaps and national institutional diversities.

The book concludes that the two approaches are complementary in their analysis of the role of ICT in economic growth, productivity and structural change in Latin America. Although they start from different premises, both arrive at similar conclusions: ICT has had a positive impact on economic growth and productivity since 1990 in Latin America, but its contribution is indeed smaller than in industrialized economies. The book also emphasizes the marked heterogeneity among Latin American countries as regards the incorporation of technology and ICT into the economic structure. The countries' uneven progress is partly attributable to path dependence (that is, differences in their initial stock of resources, capabilities and institutions) and to rates of investment in ICT and other physical and human capital.

The book identifies several opportunities for affording ICT a more dynamic role in structural change and productivity growth, as well as challenges in this regard. Expediting the adoption of ICT and fostering more efficient use of these technologies should be an essential ingredient in any development strategy aimed at promoting structural change and productivity growth in the region.

In 2009, the European Union launched the @LIS2 programme (2009–12) for Latin America and the Caribbean, with three goals: to stimulate research within the region and with Europe; to support the harmonization of regulatory processes; and to promote an inclusive political dialogue and exchange of experiences. ECLAC is coordinating this effort in five strategic areas: e-Government, e-Health, e-Inclusion, e-Government and regional integration, and productivity impact and innovation for growth. In this last area, ECLAC is building a detailed, sector-by-sector database for the largest economies in the region. Known as LA-KLEMS, this database is intended to contribute to refining policy evaluation of the contribution made by ICT to economic growth and development.

Alicia Bárcena, Executive Secretary
Economic Commission for Latin America and the Caribbean (ECLAC)

Introduction and synthesis

Mario Cimoli, André A. Hofman and Nanno Mulder

Information and communication technologies (ICT) are spreading fast across Latin America and the Caribbean. Despite an overall persistent digital gap with advanced economies, where ICT diffuse at even higher rates, mobile phone penetration is approaching levels of some advanced countries and an increasing part of the population is using the Internet. This phenomenon has brought about profound economic and social changes in the region, which so far have largely gone unmeasured. Indeed, policy-makers, entrepreneurs, scholars, political parties and other social actors have raised concerns with regard to the real contribution of ICT to economic growth and productivity in the region. But, can a significant economic impact of ICT be expected in a context in which most countries in the region are only ICT users and few produce these technologies? And if there is an impact, how does it relate to that in other parts of the world? Common intuition suggests that there should still be some impact of the use of ICT as a source of innovation, encouraged by the high penetration rate of some aspects of ICT.

ICT represent a major breakthrough as a general-purpose technology (GPT) or a techno-economic paradigm (TEP), boosting productivity and economic growth (see Chapters 1 and 2; Helpman, 1998). A GPT or TEP are well-structured bodies of knowledge that are progressively modified and improved over time, with at least one artefact driving the entire technological process through successive price reductions and technical improvements. Technological paradigms are associated with the progressive realization of the innovative opportunities arising from individual technologies. The constant advances made in technical and physical characteristics of semiconductors, microprocessors, hard disk drives, storage systems, graphics and video devices constitute one of the main set of parameters on which the ICT paradigm is developed and diffused. Moore's Law, projecting a doubling of transistors on microchips every 18 to 24 months is the baseline for how the technical characteristics of semiconductors have developed and advanced over the last three decades. Each techno-economic paradigm constitutes a redefinition and requires new infrastructure for disseminating the technologies throughout the economic system. At the same time, the dominant characteristics of the industry are reshaped through the process of developing and diffusing new products.[1] The ICT infrastructure assumes a more intangible form and incorporates digital telecommunications (cable, fibre optics, radio and satellite), Internet/electronic mail, flexible use and electricity networks, thereby redefining the interaction with pre-existing well-established infrastructures. The falling price of microelectronics devices, computers and the new equipment in telecommunication, control instruments, computer-aided biotechnology and new materials pushes the reorganization in the industry and production activities. In short, the ICT techno-economic paradigm is associated with a profound process of structural change.

Most empirical work on the impact of ICT has focused on developed countries, and hence, there still is an open question regarding the economic benefits of ICT diffusion in developing economies such as those in Latin America. In this context, the Economic Commission for Latin America and the Caribbean (ECLAC) has undertaken an ambitious research effort to measure the economic effects of ICT in the region. With the financial support of the Information Society programme (@LIS – Alliance for the Information Society) of the European Commission, ECLAC has been in the forefront of the debate on this issue in Latin America. ECLAC has commissioned multiple studies both to in-house analysts as well as distinguished scholars inside and outside Latin America and the Caribbean. This book is the fruit of this work, with ten chapters offering both theoretical and empirical contributions to the debate of the contribution of ICT to economic development in Latin America. One distinguishing feature of the present book is the use of two different approaches to measure the economic effects of these technologies: the neoclassical growth accounting approach and the evolutionary-structuralist approach. Both approaches have in common the pivotal importance of technical progress, productivity and structural transformation in economic growth, which are part of the main messages of ECLAC.

The book concludes that both approaches are complementary in their analysis of the role of ICT in economic growth, productivity and structural change in Latin America. This book identifies several opportunities and challenges for bringing about a more dynamic role for ICT in the process of structural change and productivity growth. The ten chapters show that countries in Latin America are at different stages in terms of the incorporation of technology and ICT in their economic structure. The countries' heterogeneous advances can be explained in part by their path dependence (differences in their initial stock of resources, capabilities and institutions) and investment rates of ICT and other physical and human capital. Accelerating the adoption and efficient use of ICT is essential to any strategy of structural change and productivity growth.

A new ECLAC project on ICT, growth and productivity, entitled LA KLEMS, will further analyse the causality between ICT, productivity gains and the dynamics of the production structure. Emphasis will be placed on a number of productivity determinants, such as the application of knowledge to economic activities, the diversification of the production structure, gender, age and level of educational attainment characteristics of the work force and so on. Moreover, more studies will look into the necessary elements that must be in place in the society as a whole, the economic system, infrastructure and industry to adapt to the new processes and products that these technologies engender. The evolutionary approach of technological changes and economic development will be particularly useful in this respect to deepen our understanding of how the region reacts to and engages in the diffusion of these technologies in the economic and social spheres.

Before presenting in more detail the conclusions of the different chapters of the book, we will review first the theoretical and empirical similarities and differences of the two main approaches of the book.

1 TWO APPROACHES: NEOCLASSICAL GROWTH ACCOUNTING AND THE EVOLUTIONARY-STRUCTURALIST APPROACH

The ten chapters in this book follow two different but complementary theoretical approaches. The first is growth accounting, which is a nonparametric index number approach embedded in a neoclassical production theory framework. It assesses how much of an observed rate of change of an output can be accounted for by the rate of change of combined inputs and a residual that is considered a proxy of multi-factor productivity (MFP) or the rate of technological change (Solow, 1957; Denison, 1962; Jorgenson and Griliches, 1967).[2] Growth accounts provide a static conceptual framework within which the interaction between variables can be analysed and micro-results can be aggregated to unique macro-outcomes, both of which are relevant for the study of structural change and policy evaluation (Lipsey et al., 2005; Timmer et al., Chapter 3 this volume). The standard theory has several underlying assumptions. First, it supposes that agents and firms are rational and can change their choice of production factors at no cost. Second, factor markets are characterized by perfect competition, so that the payment received by each factor equals its marginal product. Moreover, market participants are price-takers who can only adjust to quantities but cannot individually influence market prices. Third, growth accounting assumes Hicks-neutral technological progress, meaning that this progress affects all inputs proportionally. Fourth, the production function exhibits constant returns to scale. Over time, growth accounting has become more sophisticated, in part by relaxing one or several of the above assumptions (OECD, 2001).

A key question analysed in growth accounting is whether economic growth is attributable to the accumulation of factors' inputs or to technological advances and the organization of production, which is also referred to as multi-factor productivity. Growth accounting exercises may serve different purposes such as explaining differences in growth rates between countries, illuminating the process of convergence and divergence, assessing the role of structural change, technical progress and calculating potential output losses. However, growth accounting cannot provide a full causal explanation. It deals with 'proximate' rather than 'ultimate' causality and records the facts about growth components: it does not explain the underlying elements of policy or circumstances, national or international, but it does identify which issues need further explanation (Hofman, 2000).

Growth accounts assume that technological progress is exogenous. The traditional framework of growth accounting introduced by Solow and Kuznets in the 1970s follows a Cobb-Douglas production function with constant returns to scale. This model is also adopted in Chapter 5 and 6 of this study. Solow showed how to weight the contribution of the rate of increase in inputs – labour (i.e. persons engaged) and capital (i.e. the stock of capital) – to arrive at a simple estimate of MFP growth as a residual. Solow and Kuznets, who supposed the same and constant quality for all types of labour and all types of capital, attributed most of economic growth in advanced countries in the 1950s and 1960s to the increase in Solow residual or a proxy of MFP.

A new framework of growth accounting was developed by Jorgenson and Griliches from 1967 onwards, which yields different results (Jorgenson, 2009). In contrast to the classical Solow model, these authors accounted for quality changes in labour and capital inputs. They showed that over time, quality changes explained most of the Solow residual. In other words, with this new framework, economic growth in the 1950s and 1960s was no longer attributed to MFP but to quality-adjusted factor accumulation. With regard to labour, university-educated persons increased their share in the work force over time at the expense of workers with only primary school education in many countries. As the skills and productivity of the former, proxied by their wage, are higher than that of the latter, the overall 'quality' of the labour force improved. Quality-adjusted labour services are measured by weighting different categories of labour input (i.e., hours worked) by their wage rate.

The new accounting framework is a very useful tool to analyse the impact of the ICT revolution on economic growth and productivity, and is adopted in several chapters of this book (1, 3 and 4). This framework demonstrates that the investment in ICT has contributed considerably to the growth of capital services, overall economic growth and productivity over the past two decades in many countries, even though the invested amounts have been relatively small compared with other types of assets. This proportionally large contribution originates from the fact that the 'rental price' of ICT, used to weight the contribution of different types of capital, is much higher than that of other assets for two reasons. First, the prices of these assets decline rapidly over time, which is a 'burden' to the investor, as investing today means forgoing the opportunity of investing tomorrow at a lower cost. Second, depreciation rates of ICT are also very high at around 30 per year (full depreciation in three to three-and-a-half years). A fast-declining price combined with a high depreciation rate make up for a high user cost of capital or rental price, which is a proxy of the annualized price of using a capital input and comparable to the wage rate for labour. The high user cost of ICT capital gives a relatively large weight to this asset in the overall growth of capital services, which itself is a weighted average of the growth rates of the net capital stock of each asset, using its user cost as weight. This approach is followed in Chapters 1, 3 and 4 of this book, showing that the share of ICT services in overall capital services has strongly increased in all parts of the world since the mid-1990s (Chapter 1). In the European Union and the United States, ICT accounted for half and almost two-thirds of the capital contribution to economic growth, respectively, between 1995 and 2005 (Chapter 3). As expected in Latin America, the ICT share was much smaller at around one-fifth of the total capital contribution to growth in the same period (Chapter 4).

The new framework also shows that MFP or technological progress has increased after 1995 as a result of the ICT revolution, in particular in the United States. In this country, the productivity improvement between 1995 and 2000 was attributed mostly to ICT investment and productivity gains in ICT producers. The productivity boom from 2000 to 2008 is somewhat different, and can be attributed to the benefits of the reorganization of business processes alongside investments in hardware and software in previous years (Brynjolfsson and Saunders, 2009).

The second approach in this book is referred to as the evolutionary-structuralist (E-S) approach. The E-S approach explains the development and the characteristics of a technological learning path. It starts from an historical interpretation of technical change and organizational change, assuming that technologies and organizational structures and behaviours tend to co-evolve. It identifies persistent asymmetries among countries in the production system in order to account for those processes by which technological gaps and national institutional diversities can jointly reproduce themselves over rather long spans of time. In this regard, ICT are analysed as a force of technical progress that may change the actual technological trajectory, and thereby the techno-economic paradigm of the economy.

The E-S approach differs in various aspects from the neoclassical growth accounting approach. First, the former approach can be characterized as an 'endogenous account of change', whereas the second is an 'exogenous account of change'. The E-S approach enters the 'black box' of technical progress and analyses its microeconomic dimensions. Technology is observed through its embodiment in physical and human capital, infrastructure, the legal system, social norms and practices, and so on. The E-S theories try to incorporate many facets of the microeconomics of innovation, treating the economic, social and political structure of an economy explicitly. Institutions are considered to co-evolve with technology. The firm occupies a specific point in input space with options to move to another point but only at a significant cost and under uncertainty (Lipsey et al., 2005).

The notions of 'techno-economic paradigm' or 'regime' allow the inclusion of the economic and institutional dimensions. At the micro-level, technologies are incorporated in particular institutions and firms, whose capabilities are fundamental in shaping the rates and directions of technological advance. Firms, however, are not the sole repositories of technologies. More ample socioeconomic and institutional settings shape the availability of existing technologies within each paradigm. Perez (2002) emphasized the process of establishment of new techno-economic paradigms; technological factors are deeply intertwined with social ones:

> Each technological revolution, originally received as a bright new set of opportunities, is soon recognized as a threat to the established way of doing things in firms, institutions and society at large. The new techno-economic paradigm gradually takes place as a different 'common sense' for effective action in any area of endeavour. But while competitive forces, profit seeking and survival pressures help diffuse the changes in the economy, the wider social and institutional spheres where change is also needed are held back by strong inertia stemming from routine, ideology and vested interests. . . . It is thus that the first 20 or 30 years of diffusion of each technological revolution lead to an increasing mismatch between the economy and the social and regulatory systems. (Perez, 2002, p. 26)

The E-S approach illustrates well that the paradigm-based theory of innovation and production is highly consistent with the evidence for Latin America on the cumulative nature of the production and adoption of ICT (Chapters 2, 7 and 8). Compared with developed economies, Latin American countries show a large gap in terms of capabilities to produce and diffuse ICT. The process of adoption and adaptation of ICT depends in part on the specificities of domestic innovation systems. In turn, the building of production and innovation systems is closely linked to the borrowing, imitation and adaptation of established technologies from more advanced economies. The empirical evidence suggests that technological progress linked to ICT in Latin American countries requires building indigenous skills within firms, sectors and institutions. Some sectors have clearly benefited from the incorporation of ICT and expanded their participation in international markets. Others, however, have been constrained in their productive use of these technologies due to limited capabilities.

Both approaches emphasize the importance of innovation and technological progress for economic growth. Even though the neoclassical mainstream approach to growth accounting simplifies the description of the innovative process, it allows for sophisticated quantitative modelling with strong internal analytical consistency. In contrast, the E-S approach describes in more detail the microeconomic dimensions of the innovative process, but is less suitable for modelling purposes.

Despite their theoretical differences, a certain convergence can be observed in the empirical analysis of the neoclassical and E-S approaches over the past decade (Castellacci, 2007, 2009). First, over the last two decades, growth accounting exercises have incorporated explicitly the heterogeneity of economic units (firms, sectors, countries), deviating from the representative agent assumption underlying the standard neoclassical model. As evidenced by the EU KLEMS project described in Chapter 3, individual sectors or factors of production have quite different productivity behaviour. Moreover, some growth accounts model the competition and selection process among heterogeneous units (based on minimum thresholds). Second, growth accounts have integrated the interaction of different levels of analysis. For example, in the EU KLEMS project, the analysis of firm-level data has complemented sectoral growth accounting by adding the possibility of studying the effect of entry and exit of firms on productivity. Third, recent research has greatly enriched growth accounting by relaxing certain key assumptions, which are not present in the E-S framework, such as Hicks-neutral technological progress, constant returns to scale, perfect competition and the exogenous character of technological change (Hulten, 2009). In sum, recent trends in growth accounts have provided a major step toward giving a more realistic description of the true economic environment of heterogeneity, competition and selection. It should be kept in mind that these growth accounts continue to be embedded in a standard neoclassical framework with a great potential for modelling, but with assumptions that in general continue to differ from the E-S models.

Both approaches in this book support the view that the ICT revolution is far from having expressed its full potential yet in Latin America. Technological revolutions display long diffusion processes, because they entail co-evolution and co-adaptation of new technologies, new organizational forms, new institutions, and new consumption patterns:

> The eventual supplanting of an entrenched techno-economic regime involves profound changes whose revolutionary nature is better revealed by their eventual breadth and depth of the clusters of innovation that emerge than by the pace at which they achieve their influence. Exactly because of the breadth and depth of the changes entailed, successful elaboration of a new 'general purpose' technology requires the development and coordination of a vast array of complementary tangible and intangible elements: new physical plant and equipment, new kinds of workforce skills, new organizational forms, new forms of legal property, new regulatory framework, new habits of mind and patterns of taste. (David, 2001, p. 53)

The well-known claim by Robert Solow about seeing computers everywhere but in productivity statistics (Solow, 1987) captured the amazement of economists for not being able to immediately observe the gains from a new technological revolution. In fact, if one takes into account the existence of powerful retardation factors, then the paradox is not a paradox anymore. The way productivity gains diffuse across countries and industries is a painstaking process that needs adaptation of economic activities, institutional and social setting to the new paradigm. In the interpretation of David (2001), we are only starting to observe the real gains from the current ICT-based techno-economic paradigm in Latin America.

2   MAIN CONCLUSIONS BY CHAPTER

The book starts out with two introductory chapters on neoclassical growth accounting and the E-S approach, respectively. The first chapter by Dale Jorgenson and Khuong Minh Vu on 'Latin America and the world economy' analyses the impact of investment in ICT on the recent resurgence of growth in Latin America and the world economy using growth accounting. They describe the growth process of the world economy in seven regions, including Latin America, and 14 major economies during the period 1989–2005. In this period, global economic growth was led by the industrialized countries and Developing Asia, and experienced a strong resurgence after 1995. Growth of world output is allocated between input growth and (multi-factor) productivity, with the former accounting for the bulk of economic growth. Among the inputs, investment in tangible assets, including ICT equipment and software, was the most important source of growth. However, non-ICT investment predominated. The contribution of labour input was next in magnitude with hours worked outweighing labour quality. The contributions of ICT investment increased in all regions, but especially in industrialized economies and Developing Asia. After the dot-com crash of 2000, ICT investment in the industrialized countries moderated but continued to expand in the developing world, especially in Asia. The contribution of ICT investment to economic growth more than doubled after 1995 in Developing Asia, Latin America, Eastern Europe, North Africa and the Middle East and Sub-Saharan Africa.

Differences in per capita output levels are mainly explained by differences in per capita input, rather than variations in productivity. This can be explained by the fact that technology can be easily transferred from industrialized countries to the developing regions, while the investment in capital and labour inputs requires more time and greater effort. Outdated production techniques must give way to newer methods that incorporate the modern technologies, especially those that use ICT. Latin American productivity remained above world levels, albeit with stagnant productivity growth throughout the period 1989–2005. All Latin American economies had a substantial shortfall in GDP per capita, relative to world levels, due to large gaps in input per capita and stagnation in productivity growth. Chile and Mexico made some headway in reducing this gap during the period 1989–2005, largely through investment in non-ICT assets.

The second introductory chapter, entitled 'Technical change and economic growth: some lessons from secular patterns and some conjectures on the current impact of ICT' by Carolina Castaldi and Giovanni Dosi discusses the link between patterns of technological change and economic development taking an evolutionary-structuralist perspective. They argue that economic development depends on the emergence of new techno-economic paradigms or regimes. The current paradigm is driven by ICT, which are still at an early stage of diffusion, particularly for developing regions such as Latin America. For these regions, the new techno-economic paradigm represents both an opportunity and a threat. The pervasiveness of these new technologies makes their adoption a development necessity, independently from the countries' patterns of comparative advantage. The catch-up in ICT investment for developing countries is crucial to foster their 'national absorptive capacity', in part for foreign-generated knowledge. While latecomers have the potential to achieve high economic growth rates, this potential is only realized if local enterprises are able to recognize, exploit and internalize the knowledge underlying the new technologies. ICT infrastructures and corporate organizations, promoted by governmental policies, play a crucial role in the latter process.

To promote a virtuous ICT-based growth path for developing countries, the authors argue that policy-makers need to carefully balance several trade-offs and complementarities through different policies. The ultimate success or failure of these policies will depend on their combination with different institutional arrangements, to the extent they enhance learning processes by individuals and organizations, on the one hand, and selection processes, including market competition, on the other. The trajectory of several countries points to a variety of country- and sector-specific policies. First, governments have to increase opportunities for scientific and technological innovation by ensuring a rapid expansion of the number of qualified engineers and the strengthening of graduate education. Second, governments need to stimulate technological learning and penalize rent-seeking behaviours. Third, the public sector can promote the patterns of information distribution and interaction across economic actors. Finally, firms need high rates of physical and intangible investment and the progressive integration of production design, marketing and research activities.

After the two introductory chapters, the book continues with four chapters using growth accounting to assess the role of ICT in economic growth and productivity outside and inside Latin America. In Chapter 3, Marcel Timmer et al. compare the productivity performance of the European Union (EU) and the United States from 1980 to 2005, using growth accounts and a detailed database that distinguish between gross output and various inputs referred to as KLEMS (capital K, labour L, energy E, materials M and service inputs S), and MFP. A key advantage of the EU KLEMS database is that it moves beyond the aggregate economy level to examine the productivity performance of individual industries and their contribution to aggregate growth. Its theoretical framework is the same as Chapter 1. Previous studies have demonstrated that there is enormous heterogeneity in output and productivity growth across industries, so analysts should focus on the industry-level detail to understand the origins of the European growth process. The EU KLEMS database covers 25 EU countries (EU-25), as well as Japan and the United States.

Compared with the EU, in the United States economic growth accelerated much more and the contribution of MFP was much larger from the 1980–95 to the 1995–2005 period. Trends in MFP explain most of the growth differentials between the two economies: while contributing 1.0

and 0.7 per cent to market economy GDP growth during 1980–95 in the EU and the United States, respectively, the trend accelerated to 1.7 per cent in the United States, but declined to 0.4 per cent in the EU after 1995. This slowdown in MFP growth is recorded almost everywhere across the EU, with the exception of Finland and the Netherlands where it has improved since 1995. In France, MFP growth in the market economy has remained stable, but it slowed sharply in Germany and in the United Kingdom. In Italy and Spain, MFP growth was even negative, reflecting the lack of technology and innovation spillovers and market rigidities, in particular in services industries. When decomposing growth by industry, it seems that market services are mostly responsible for the divergent performance of the EU, both among themselves as well as relative to the United States.

The overall contribution of capital services to growth has not changed, but the distribution has shifted somewhat from non-ICT capital to ICT capital. However, compared with the United States the shift towards ICT has generally not been as pronounced. Notably, when comparing the ratio of capital to labour contributions to growth in the EU, there are signs of declining capital intensity in the regions. This development is in sharp contrast to the US trend in capital intensity since 1995.

According to Timmer et al., the potential for a recovery in the EU's productivity growth will to a large extent depend on its capability to transform the economy towards one that makes more productive use of its resources. Much will depend on the capacity of markets to facilitate the reallocation of resources to industries that show rapid productivity growth. However, it is difficult to predict which industries will be the most productive in the future, as technology and innovation trends are inherently difficult to forecast. A productive use of a larger input from skilled employment and the exploitation of ICT investments in service industries appear the most successful policy avenues for a European productivity revival.

Chapter 4 moves the analysis from advanced countries to Latin America and the Caribbean. In this chapter ('ICT investment in Latin America: does it matter for economic growth?'), Gaaitzen De Vries et al. present a first attempt to estimate investment in ICT and assess its contribution to economic growth in five Latin American countries (Argentina, Brazil, Chile, Costa Rica and Uruguay). Investment in computer hardware and communication equipment is estimated using a commodity-flow method, which traces domestically produced and imported ICT goods to their final destination: exports, consumption and investment. Investment in software is approximated using a fixed-effects panel data model. Their findings suggest, not surprisingly, that ICT investment in Latin America has been substantially below that in the United States and Europe, with the exception of Chile, whose ICT investment efforts are approaching European levels. ICT investment shares as a percentage of GDP increased in the 1990s; they bounced back temporarily after 2000, except in Costa Rica. Similar patterns are observed in the European Union and the United States, but here investments in new technologies are much higher.

De Vries et al. use a standard growth accounting framework to estimate the contribution of ICT investment to economic growth in these countries. The average annual contribution of ICT capital to growth from 1995 to 2004 ranges from 0.21 percentage points in Brazil to 0.62 percentage points in Chile. This finding indicates that Latin America has not been excluded from the ICT revolution, but the differences across countries are huge. ICT adopters can be divided into two clusters. The first cluster includes Chile and Costa Rica, which invested substantially in computers, communication equipment and software. In the second cluster are Argentina, Brazil and Uruguay, which invested relatively little in new technologies.

In Chapter 5 ('Growth, productivity and information and communications technologies in Latin America, 1950–2005'), Claudio Aravena et al. take a longer time perspective and include more countries than the previous chapter, but analyse the role of ICT only indirectly as an explanatory factor of multi-factor productivity growth. This study includes ten countries in Latin America (Argentina, Bolivarian Republic of Venezuela, Bolivia, Brazil, Chile, Colombia, Costa Rica, Ecuador, Mexico and Peru). In the past half-century, these countries experienced periods of strong growth, especially in 1950–73, and periods of crisis. A persistent characteristic has been the very strong fluctuations in their growth pattern. The chapter presents the stylized facts on per capita GDP growth in the region. It employs a standard methodology of growth accounting, explaining economic growth by labour and capital accumulation, and estimating multi-factor productivity as a proxy for technical progress and other not identified growth factors. The authors find positive growth rates for individual factors of production for all the periods in Latin America, but MFP is negative in 1980–90 and 1998–2005. In the decades before the crisis of the 1980s, capital was the main factor that explained economic growth. This began to change afterwards however, as a lower level of factor accumulation was coupled with a decrease in the relative contribution and labour became the leading contributor to GDP growth. This difference in performance is even more striking in the case of MFP.

This chapter also presents an econometric analysis of panel data to explain the behaviour of MFP and quantify the role of efficiency and the economic cycle, together with the impact of ICT dissemination on MFP performance. A fixed-effects panel data model is used with the following explanatory variables: the variability of the real exchange rate, macroeconomic instability and an index of economic reforms; for ICT, an index has been estimated to measure their adoption in the country's economic structure on the basis of five representative variables: fixed telephones, mobile telephones, personal computers, number of television sets and number of Internet users. The results obtained suggest that the efficiency variables of the economy, exchange-rate variability, macroeconomic instability and especially the reform index are the most important group for explaining the productivity dynamics in the countries of the region during the period 1960–2005. Therefore, the results suggest that the volatility of Latin American economies recorded in the 1980s was the main cause of the negative performance of productivity. Although it was possible to significantly relate the evolution of factor productivity to a set of ICT variables, these variables proved to play only a limited role in explaining MFP. Isolating the contribution of ICT to economic growth seems more promising when these assets are incorporated into capital services, as done in the previous chapter.

An even broader approach with a comparison among different regions in the world, again embedded in growth accounting, is taken in Chapter 6 ('The impact of information and communication technologies on economic growth in Latin America in comparative perspective') by Nauro Campos. He contributes to the econometric literature on the macroeconomic impacts of ICT with an emphasis on the comparative experience of Latin America. The central question is therefore: how econometrically robust is the effect of ICT diffusion in terms of long-term per capita economic growth rates? The author intends to improve upon the sizable literature on this issue by: (1) putting together a comprehensive dataset encompassing more than 150 developed and developing countries covering the period from 1960 to 2004; (2) presenting simple Granger-causality evidence that supports the view that causality flows from ICT diffusion to economic growth (and surely not the other way around); and (3) estimating, using panel data techniques, the effects of ICT for all countries as well as for each regional group (that is, OECD, Latin America, Asia, Middle East, Africa and transition economies). One major and recurring concern of the existing literature refers to the robustness of the econometric estimates, driven mainly by the twin facts that although (1) endogeneity has proved an important and difficult source of bias, (2) the standard solutions to deal with it have been shown to be equally sensitive to other equally severe sources of bias (more specifically, the resulting system generalized methods of moments [GMM] estimates in relatively small and heterogeneous samples unfortunately also tend to be fragile). The results are encouraging as they suggest that reverse causality bias does not seem to be sufficiently severe in the five-year averages panel design adopted.

Overall, the estimates show that the effect of ICT on growth is positive, statistically significant and reasonably robust to different measures of ICT, different econometric estimators, different specifications (standard aggregate production and endogenous growth frameworks), as well as different ways of measuring key control variables. The impact of ICT on growth in Latin America is found to be smaller than that in the OECD and Asian countries, but larger than the impact in Middle Eastern, African and transition economies. In terms of suggestions for future research the author echoes the literature in pointing to the need to tackle an important source of omitted variable bias by putting forward indexes of economic reforms (quality of institutions and of the regulatory framework) as well as to try to construct composite indexes of ICT that better reflect their multifaceted nature.

The following two chapters take an evolutionary-structuralist approach to technical change. In Chapter 7 ('ICT, learning and growth: an evolutionary perspective'), Mario Cimoli and Nelson Correa analyse the impact of the ongoing ICT revolution on economic growth. Using an E-S approach they argue that: first, countries can be unequivocally ranked according to their efficiencies in the ICT space and second, there is not a significant relationship between these technological gaps and international differences in the expenditure on ICT. Moreover, the positive ICT impact on labour productivity seems to be higher for developed countries than for developing ones. All these findings support the thesis that the capabilities to promote structural changes and proactive innovation systems are crucial determinants for the development and full exploitation of ICT. The configuration of production and innovation systems is closely linked with the borrowing, imitation and adaptation of established technologies from more advanced economies.

In a specific comparison of Latin American countries with industrialized economies, Cimoli and Correa show that in the former a large gap exists with respect to their capabilities for absorbing and diffusing ICT. Empirical evidence suggests that establishing proper technological dynamism in Latin American countries is impossible without first achieving major changes and the sequential construction of widening opportunities for firms, sectors and institutions, including indigenous skills in a set of 'core' technologies and production capacities. The overlap between the ICT impact and the configuration of Latin American production and innovation systems have diffused opportunities on the one hand, and raised barriers on the other. Some sectors and activities have clearly benefited from the incorporation of ICT and expanded their participation in international markets. Others have been constrained in creating capabilities and acceding to these technologies.

The next contribution from the E-S school is Chapter 8 ('ICT and knowledge complementarities: a factor analysis on growth'), in which Marco Capasso and Nelson Correa investigate the influence of the use of ICT on economic growth. Most of the literature dealing with the relation between ICT and growth is based on the channels of capital or labour skills. Instead, this chapter focuses on the role that ICT play as a complement to a country's knowledge base. Using a principal factor model, they build a knowledge indicator that defines the value for the stock of knowledge of each country and year. The factor procedure is used to estimate a 'golden proportion' linking ICT use to other knowledge proxies, that is, the number of publications in technical and scientific journals, enrolment in tertiary education and expenditure on research and development. When an economy complies with this proportion, the knowledge level exerts its maximum influence on GDP growth. The golden proportion can thus be seen as an ideal state for which the complementarity between the ICT use and knowledge proxies works best in producing GDP. The phenomenon is illustrated by introducing both the knowledge indicator and the distance from the best optimal complementarity proportion as regressors in a classical GDP growth function, estimated through a panel data regression for 73 countries. By putting together the results of the growth model and the relation between ICT use and knowledge, it is possible to isolate the effect of ICT use on economic growth through the knowledge channel.

For several Latin American economies, the current level of ICT use is above this golden proportion. Nevertheless, an increase in the use of ICT will still produce a positive impact on knowledge and economic growth. However, the magnitude of this positive impact depends on the current level of ICT use with respect to the ICT level predicted by the golden proportion. In other words, if the increased ICT use drives the country to a position that is closer to the golden proportion, then ICT use will better complement the other knowledge proxies, and the corresponding increase in GDP will be higher. In contrast, a country whose ICT use level is already relatively high compared with the other knowledge proxies would benefit less from a further increase in ICT use.

The final two chapters of the book look into the diffusion aspects of ICT. In Chapter 9 ('A dynamic input–output simulation analysis of the impact of ICT diffusion in the Brazilian economy'), Fabio Freitas et al. use an input–output methodology to evaluate the size and the structural characteristics of the ICT-producing sectors and to analyse the impact of different scenarios of ICT diffusion in the Brazilian economy in 2003. The authors estimate that there was an incipient ICT diffusion in the Brazilian economy both in demand and production sides. On the demand side, first, the shares of ICT-producing sectors in total gross output, value-added, employment and final demand components were small. Second, the forward linkages of the ICT industries in Brazil were remarkably low compared with both the United States indicators and with the average forward linkage in the Brazilian economy. On the production side, in spite of the incipient demand, it was observed that the share of ICT in total imports is significant.

This chapter also presents the simulation results of two different scenarios. The first assumes different growth rates for ICT sectors with an unchanged pattern of international trade and the second assumes a different import substitution/penetration hypothesis in relation to the reference scenarios. The results of the model suggest different ICT diffusion trajectories for the Brazilian economy.

In the final chapter, Chapter 10 ('The relative impact of the regulatory framework on the diffusion of ICT: evidence from Latin America'), Nauro Campos analyses the importance of privatization and deregulation for the diffusion of information and communication technologies in Latin America. The ICT as a general-purpose technology have a potential comparable with those that underpinned the Industrial Revolution of the middle of the nineteenth century. Indeed, fixed and mobile phones, personal computers and the Internet have diffused rapidly in the past ten or 15 years with massive (and still imperfectly understood) productivity, growth and welfare implications. One argument is that privatization and de-regulation have played a major role in this process although, to date, there have been few efforts to understand and assess their relative importance.

This chapter tries to fill this gap. It provides the first comprehensive assessment of the determinants of ICT diffusion. In this chapter, the diffusion processes of four ICT (fixed and mobile phones, personal computers and the Internet) is studied and the author examines a comprehensive set of potential determinants (i.e., economic, political, technological and the institutional and regulatory framework dimensions) using a unique yearly panel dataset of 35 Latin American and Caribbean economies between 1989 and 2004. The ordinary least squares (OLS) fixed effects estimates support a ranking of determinants with human capital and per capita GDP as main factors, followed in decreasing order of importance by the effectiveness of the regulatory framework (degree of competition in the domestic market and various characteristics of regulatory agencies), technical aspects (e.g., average price of call for phones, bandwidth for Internet and speed for computers) and political variables (democracy and durability of the regime). This ranking varies a little depending on the type of ICT. The general ranking holds for fixed and mobile lines (although human capital is more important than per capita income for the latter), while in the case of PCs the share of the services sector on GDP is more important than level of human capital and technical factors are more important than regulatory and political aspects. Finally, the rise in Internet users seems to depend on levels of human capital, per capita income, regulation and technical aspects, while political factors matter little.

NOTES

1. In general, each techno-economic paradigm strongly influences the behaviour of the relative costs, supply and pervasiveness of new technologies and the organization of production activities. In particular: '(i) clearly perceived low – and descending – relative cost, (ii) apparently unlimited supply (for all practical purposes), (iii) obvious potential for all-pervasive influence in the productive sphere, and (iv) a generally recognized capacity, based on a set of interwoven technical and organizational innovations, to reduce the costs and change the quality of capital equipment, labour and products' (Perez, 1985, p. 444).

2. A general equation is: $Y = AF(L, K_{Non\text{-}ICT}, K_{ICT})$, where Y denotes the output and L the labour input in hours. Capital inputs are decomposed by $K_{Non\text{-}ICT}$ and K_{ICT}, which denote non-ICT and ICT capital goods, respectively. Rewriting the equation, we obtain:

$$\Delta \ln Y = \bar{v}_L \Delta \ln L + \bar{v}_{K\_Non\text{-}ICT} \Delta \ln K_{Non\text{-}ICT} + \bar{v}_{K\_ICT} \Delta \ln K_{ICT} + \Delta \ln A$$

where $\bar{v}$ denotes average value shares of input i in nominal output and $v_L + v_{K\text{-}Non\text{-}ICT} + v_{K\text{-}ICT} = 1$. Each element on the right-hand side indicates the proportion of output growth accounted for by growth in labour, capital *Non-ICT* and *ICT* and multi-factor productivity, respectively. This output decomposition assumes that factor markets are perfectly competitive, according to which each input is remunerated by its marginal product and prices correspond to their rate of substitution. Moreover, constant returns to scale are assumed (since $v_L + v_{K\text{-}Non\text{-}ICT} + v_{K\text{-}ICT} = 1$). The growth rate of output is a weighted average of growth rates of capital and labour services and the contribution of each input is its weighted growth rate. The contribution of MFP, the growth rate of the augmentation factor A, is the difference between growth rates of output and inputs.

REFERENCES

Brynjolfsson, Erik and Adam Saunders (2009), *Wired for Innovation: How Information Technology is Reshaping the Economy*, Cambridge, MA: The MIT Press.

Castellacci, Fulvio (2007), 'Evolutionary and New Growth Theories: Are they Converging?', *Journal of Economic Survey*, **21**(3), 585–627.

Castellacci, Fulvio (2009), 'Theoretical Models of Heterogeneity, Growth and Competitiveness', *NUPI Working Paper*, No. 763, Oslo: Norwegian Institute of International Affairs.

David, P.A. (2001), 'Understanding Digital Technology's Evolution and the Path of Measured Productivity Growth: Present and Future in the Mirror of the Past', in E. Brynjolfsson and B. Kahin (eds), *Understanding the Digital Economy*, Cambridge, MA: MIT Press.

Denison, Edward F. (1962), 'The Sources of Economic Growth in the United States and the Alternatives Before Us', *The Economic Journal*, **72**(288), 935–8.

Helpman, Elhanan (ed.) (1998), *General Purpose Technologies and Economic Growth*, Cambridge, MA: The MIT Press.

Hofman, André A. (2000), *The Economic Development of Latin America in the Twentieth Century*, Cheltenham, UK and Northampton, MA, USA: Edward Elgar.

Hulten, C. (2009), 'Growth Accounting', *NBER Working Paper Series*, No. 15341, Cambridge, MA: NBER.

Jorgenson, Dale W. (ed.) (2009), *The Economics of Productivity*, The International Library of Critical Writings in Economics, No. 236, Cheltenham, UK and Northampton, MA, USA: Edward Elgar.

Jorgenson, Dale W. and Zvi Griliches (1967), 'The Explanation of Productivity Change', *Review of Economic Studies*, **34**(99), 249–80.

Lipsey, R.G., K. Carlaw and C. Bekar (2005), *Economic Transformations: General Purpose Technologies and Long Term Economic Growth*, Oxford: Oxford University Press.

OECD (2001), *Measuring Productivity: OECD Manual – Measurement of Aggregate and Industry-Level Productivity Growth*, Paris: OECD.

Perez, C. (1985), 'Micro-electronics, Long Waves and World Structural Change: New Perspectives for Developing Countries', *World Development*, **13**(3).

Perez, C. (2002), *Technological Revolutions and Financial Capital*, Cheltenham, UK and Northampton, MA, USA: Edward Elgar.

Solow, Robert M. (1957), 'Technical Change and the Aggregate Production Function', *The Review of Economics and Statistics*, **39**(3), 312–20.

Solow, R. (1987), 'We'd better watch out', *New York Times Book Review*, 12 July.

1. Latin America and the world economy*

Dale W. Jorgenson and Khuong Minh Vu

1 INTRODUCTION

The purpose of this paper is to analyze the impact of investment in information and communication technologies (ICT) equipment and software on the recent revival of growth in Latin America and the world economy. The crucial role of ICT investment in the growth of the US economy has been thoroughly documented and widely discussed.[1] Jorgenson (2001) has shown that the remarkable behavior of ICT prices is the key to the understanding of the US growth resurgence since 1995. This behavior can be traced to developments in semiconductor technology that are widely understood by technologists and economists.

Jorgenson (2003) has shown that the growth of ICT investment jumped to double-digit levels after 1995 in all the G7 economies – Canada, France, Germany, Italy, Japan and the United Kingdom, as well as the United States.[2] These economies account for nearly half of world output and a much larger share of world ICT investment. The surge of ICT investment resulted from a sharp acceleration in the rate of decline of prices of ICT equipment and software. Jorgenson (2001) has traced this to a drastic shortening of the product cycle for semiconductors from three years to two years, beginning in 1995.

Our methodology for analyzing the sources of growth is based on the production possibility frontier (PPF),[3] which describes efficient combinations of outputs and inputs for the economy as a whole, which takes the form:

$$Y = A.f(K, L), \qquad (1.1)$$

where Y is aggregate output, K and L are inputs of capital services and labor services, and A is a 'Hicks-neutral' augmentation of aggregate inputs.

The standard framework can be extended to highlight compositions of the capital and labor inputs as:

$$Y = A.f(K(K_{ICT}, K_n), L(H, L_Q)), \qquad (1.2)$$

where K_{ICT} and K_n are capital services from ICT assets and non-ICT assets, respectively, H is total hours worked, and L_Q is labor quality, defined as the ratio of labor input to hours worked.

Under the assumption that product and factor markets are competitive, the extended framework (1.2) implies the following decomposition:

$$\Delta \ln Y = \bar{v}_{K_{ICT}} \Delta \ln K_{ICT} + \bar{v}_{K_n} \Delta \ln K_n + \bar{v}_L \Delta \ln H + \bar{v}_L \Delta \ln L_Q + \Delta \ln A$$
$$(1.3)$$

where each v represents the input share of the subscripted input; a bar over the shares indicates a two-period average. That is, the output growth ($\Delta \ln Y$) can be decomposed into contributions of ICT capital ($\bar{v}_{K_{ICT}} \Delta \ln K_{ICT}$), non-ICT capital ($\bar{v}_{K_n} \Delta \ln K_n$), labor hours worked ($\bar{v}_L \Delta \ln H$), labor quality ($\bar{v}_L \Delta \ln L_Q$) and total factor productivity growth ($\Delta \ln A$).

The output data for our growth accounts are compiled from World Development Indicators (WDI) (2008). The input data are drawn from the following sources:

- the Total Economy Growth Accounting Database provided by the Groningen Growth and Development Centre for the data on employment and hours worked;[4]
- the EU KLEMS dataset for the data on capital and labor services for countries of the European Union and Japan;[5]
- the data from Digital Planet reports published by the World Information Technology and Services Alliance (WITSA).

We construct estimates of investment in ICT and labor quality as follows:

- We update the data from Jorgenson (2003) for the US and Canada and use the data from the EU KLEMS dataset for Japan and 14 European countries: Austria, Belgium, Czech Republic, Denmark, Finland, France, Germany, Hungary, Italy, Netherlands, Slovenia, Spain, Sweden, and United Kingdom. For all other economies we estimate their ICT capital stock data based on the data on ICT expenditures from the WITSA Digital Planet reports[6] and data on ICT penetration from WDI.
- To estimate ICT capital services we assume the hedonic price indices for computer hardware, computer software and telecommunication

equipment in these countries follow the same patterns observed for the US. Additional details on our methodology are presented in Jorgenson and Vu (2006).

Our data sample consists of 110 economies, which account for over 95 per cent of the world GDP and ICT expenditures. For analysis, we divide the 110 economies into seven economic regions:

1. G7 (seven largest industrialized economies): Canada, France, Germany, Italy, Japan, United Kingdom, United States;
2. non-G7 (15 non-G7 industrialized economies): Australia, Austria, Belgium, Denmark, Finland, Greece, Ireland, Israel, Netherlands, New Zealand, Norway, Portugal, Spain, Sweden, Switzerland;
3. Developing Asia (16 economies): Bangladesh, Cambodia, China, Hong Kong, India, Indonesia, Malaysia, Nepal, Pakistan, Philippines, Singapore, South Korea, Sri Lanka, Taiwan, Thailand, Vietnam;
4. Latin America (19 economies): Argentina, Bolivia, Brazil, Chile, Colombia, Costa Rica, Ecuador, El Salvador, Guatemala, Honduras, Jamaica, Mexico, Nicaragua, Panama, Paraguay, Peru, Trinidad and Tobago, Uruguay, Venezuela;
5. Eastern Europe and the former Soviet Union (14 economies): Albania, Bulgaria, Croatia, Czech Rep., Estonia, Hungary, Latvia, Lithuania, Poland, Romania, Russia, Slovakia, Slovenia, Ukraine;
6. Sub-Saharan Africa (28 economies): Benin, Botswana, Burkina Faso, Cameroon, Central African Rep., Chad, Congo Rep., Côte d'Ivoire, Ethiopia, Gabon, Ghana, Guinea, Kenya, Madagascar, Malawi, Mali, Mauritius, Mozambique, Namibia, Niger, Nigeria, Senegal, South Africa, Swaziland, Tanzania, Togo, Uganda, Zambia;
7. North Africa and Middle East (11 economies): Algeria, Egypt, Iran, Jordan, Lebanon, Mauritania, Morocco, Syria, Tunisia, Turkey, Yemen.

In Section 2 we describe the growth of the world economy, seven economic regions, the G7 economies, China and India, which belong to the Developing Asia group, and the seven major economies of Latin America during the period 1989–2005.

We have subdivided the period 1989–2005 into 1989–95, 1995–2000, and 2000–05 in order to focus on the response of ICT investment to the accelerated decline in ICT prices in 1995 and the impact of the dot-com crash of 2000. World economic growth has undergone a powerful revival since 1995. The GDP growth rate jumped more than a full percentage point from 2.67 per cent during 1989–95 to 3.80 per cent in 1995–2000 and

3.82 per cent in 2000–05. We can underscore the significance of more rapid growth by pointing out that GDP growth of 2.67 per cent doubles world output by four times in a century, while 3.80 per cent doubles output more than five times per century.

In Section 3 we allocate the growth of world output between input growth and productivity. Our most astonishing finding is that input growth greatly predominates! Productivity growth accounted for just about one-fifth of the total during 1989–95, while input growth accounted for about four-fifths. Similarly, input growth contributed almost three-quarters of growth from 1995–2000 and more than three-fifths from 2000–05. The only departure from this worldwide trend was the revival of economic growth in Eastern Europe after 1995, driven by a rebound from the productivity collapse of 1989–95.

In Section 3 we distribute the growth between investments in human capital and tangible assets, especially ICT equipment and software. The world economy and all seven regions experienced a surge in investment in ICT after 1995. The soaring level of US ICT investment after 1995 was paralleled by jumps in ICT investment throughout the industrialized world. The contributions of ICT investment to growth in Developing Asia, Latin America, Eastern Europe, North Africa and the Middle East and Sub-Saharan Africa more than doubled after 1995, beginning from much lower levels.

The contribution of ICT investment to growth of the world economy has moderated substantially since the dot-com crash of 2000. However, the contribution of ICT investment has continued to rise for Developing Asia, Latin America, Eastern Europe, North Africa and the Middle East and Sub-Saharan Africa. The contributions of non-ICT investment and labor input to world growth declined after the dot-com crash, but total factor productivity growth rose substantially, reflecting considerable increases in four groups: Developing Asia, Eastern Europe and the former Soviet Union, Sub-Saharan Africa and North Africa, and the Middle East.

In Section 4 we present levels of output per capita, input per capita and productivity for the world economy, the seven economic regions, the G7 economies and the seven major economies of Latin America. We find that differences in per capita output levels are explained more by differences in per capita input than variations in productivity. Taking US output per capita in 2000 as 100.0, world output per capita was 25.8 in 2005. Using similar scales for input and productivity, world input per capita in 2005 was 49.8 and world productivity was 51.9. Section 5 concludes the paper.

2 WORLD ECONOMIC GROWTH, 1989–2005

In order to set the stage for analyzing the impact of ICT investment on the growth of the world economy, we first consider the shares of world product and growth for the seven regions, the G7 economies and seven major economies of Latin America presented in Table 1.1. Following Jorgenson (2001), we have chosen GDP as a measure of output.

The G7 economies accounted for slightly under half of world product from 1989–95. The GDP growth rates of these economies – 2.14 per cent for 1989–95, 3.11 per cent from 1995–2000 and 2.06 per cent during 2000–05 – lagged considerably behind world growth rates for these periods. The G7 shares in world growth were 40.0 per cent during 1989–95 and 39.1 per cent from 1995–2000, but only a meager 24.2 per cent during 2000–05. This led to a decline of almost five percentage points in the G7 share of world product from 49.7 per cent in 1989–95 to 44.9 per cent during 2000–05.

During 1989–95 the US accounted for 22.2 per cent of world product and 44.7 per cent of G7 product. The US share of G7 output rose to 46.3 per cent from 1995–2000 and 48.1 per cent during 2000–05. After 1995 Japan fell from its ranking as the world's second largest economy to third largest after China, but remained second among the G7 economies. Germany dropped from fourth place before 1995, following the US, China and Japan, to fifth place after 1995, ranking behind India as well. However, Germany retained its position as the leading European economy. France, Italy and the UK were considerably smaller, but similar in size. Canada was the smallest of the G7 economies.

The US growth rate jumped from 2.44 per cent during 1989–95 to 4.29 per cent in 1995–2000, before subsiding to 2.76 per cent from 2000–05. The period 2000–05 includes the dot-com crash of 2000, the shallow US recession of 2001, and the recovery that followed, while the period 1995–2000 encompasses the ICT-generated investment boom of the last half of the 1990s. The US share in world growth exceeded its share in world product only during 1995–2000. The remaining G7 economies had lower shares of world growth than world product throughout the period 1989–2005.

The 16 economies of Developing Asia generated only about a fifth of world output before 1995, but 23.9 per cent from 1995–2000 and a stunning 27.6 per cent after 2000! The burgeoning economies of China and India accounted for 61.1 per cent of Asian output during 1989–95, 64.5 per cent in 1995–2000 and 68.7 per cent after 2000.[7] The economies of Developing Asia grew at 7.64 per cent before 1995, 5.97 per cent from 1995–2000 and 7.15 per cent after 2000. These economies generated an astounding 56.7 per cent of world growth during the remarkable revival

Table 1.1 The world economy: % shares in size and growth by group, region and major economies

Group	Period 1989–95 GDP Growth	Period 1989–95 Average Share GDP	Period 1989–95 Average Share Growth	Period 1995–2000 GDP Growth	Period 1995–2000 Average Share GDP	Period 1995–2000 Average Share Growth	Period 2000–05 GDP Growth	Period 2000–05 Average Share GDP	Period 2000–05 Average Share Growth
World (110 economies)	2.67	100.0	100.0	3.80	100.0	100.0	3.82	100.0	100.0
G7 (7)	2.14	49.7	40.0	3.11	47.9	39.1	2.06	44.9	24.2
Developing Asia (16)	7.64	19.7	56.7	5.97	23.9	37.6	7.15	27.6	51.8
Non-G7 (15)	2.06	9.3	7.2	3.65	9.1	8.7	2.32	8.7	5.3
Latin America (19)	2.94	8.4	9.2	2.97	8.2	6.4	2.39	7.8	4.9
Eastern Europe (14)	–6.44	7.6	–19.0	1.96	5.5	2.8	5.23	5.5	7.5
Sub-Saharan Africa (28)	1.51	2.1	1.2	3.44	2.0	1.9	4.23	2.1	2.3
N. Africa and M. East (11)	3.80	3.2	4.6	3.96	3.3	3.5	4.51	3.4	4.0

Economy	Period 1989–95 GDP Growth	Period 1989–95 GDP Share Group	Period 1989–95 GDP Share World	Period 1989–95 Growth Share Group	Period 1989–95 Growth Share World	Period 1995–2000 GDP Growth	Period 1995–2000 GDP Share Group	Period 1995–2000 GDP Share World	Period 1995–2000 Growth Share Group	Period 1995–2000 Growth Share World	Period 2000–05 GDP Growth	Period 2000–05 GDP Share Group	Period 2000–05 GDP Share World	Period 2000–05 Growth Share Group	Period 2000–05 Growth Share World
G7															
Canada	1.44	4.0	2.0	2.7	1.1	4.07	4.0	1.9	5.2	2.1	2.50	4.2	1.9	5.1	1.2
France	1.46	7.7	3.8	5.2	2.1	2.76	7.5	3.6	6.6	2.6	1.48	7.4	3.3	5.3	1.3
Germany	2.74	10.5	5.2	13.4	5.3	1.99	10.4	5.0	6.7	2.6	0.74	9.8	4.4	3.5	0.9

Italy	1.39	7.6	3.8	2.0	1.89	7.2	3.5	4.4	1.7	0.64	6.8	3.1	2.1	0.5
Japan	2.09	17.8	8.9	7.0	0.96	17.0	8.1	5.3	2.1	1.42	15.9	7.1	11.0	2.7
United Kingdom	1.53	7.8	3.9	2.2	3.18	7.7	3.7	7.9	3.1	2.31	7.8	3.5	8.7	2.1
United States	2.44	44.7	22.2	20.4	4.29	46.3	22.1	63.9	25.0	2.76	48.1	21.6	64.3	15.6
G7	2.14	100.0	49.7	40.0	3.11	100.0	47.9	100.0	39.1	2.06	100.0	44.9	100.0	24.2
Seven major Latin American economies (LA7)														
Argentina	4.88	12.2	1.0	1.9	2.54	12.7	1.1	10.9	0.7	1.97	12.5	1.0	10.3	0.5
Brazil	1.84	37.9	3.2	2.2	2.22	36.0	3.0	26.8	1.7	2.16	35.1	2.7	31.8	1.6
Chile	7.55	3.3	0.3	0.8	4.07	3.9	0.3	5.3	0.3	4.29	4.2	0.3	7.5	0.4
Colombia	4.35	7.5	0.6	1.0	0.91	7.5	0.6	2.3	0.1	3.37	7.3	0.6	10.2	0.5
Mexico	2.09	23.2	1.9	1.5	5.31	24.0	2.0	42.9	2.8	1.80	25.1	2.0	18.9	0.9
Peru	3.57	3.5	0.3	0.4	2.46	3.5	0.3	2.9	0.2	4.08	3.6	0.3	6.2	0.3
Venezuela	3.87	4.3	0.4	0.5	0.75	4.2	0.3	1.1	0.1	2.28	3.9	0.3	3.8	0.2
LA7	2.88	87.7	7.3	7.8	2.99	87.6	7.2	91.1	5.9	2.31	87.7	6.9	84.8	4.2
Latin America	2.94	100.0	8.4	9.2	2.97	100.0	8.2	100.0	6.4	2.39	100.0	7.8	100.0	4.9
China and India in the Developing Asia group														
China	10.26	37.2	7.4	28.6	8.27	42.6	10.2	58.9	22.2	9.11	47.2	13.1	60.2	31.2
India	5.17	23.9	4.7	9.0	5.63	21.9	5.2	20.7	7.8	6.72	21.5	5.9	20.2	10.4
China and India		61.1	12.1	37.6		64.5	15.5	79.6	29.9		68.7	19.0	80.4	41.7

Source: Authors' calculations.

of 1989–95! Developing Asia's share in world growth declined to 37.6 per cent during 1995–2000, below the G7 share of 39.1 per cent, but recovered to 51.8 per cent during 2000–05. China alone accounted for more than a quarter of world growth during the period 1989–2005.

The 15 non-G7 industrialized economies generated 9.3 per cent of world output during 1989–95. However, these economies had lower shares in world growth than world product throughout the period 1989–2005. Their shares in world output dropped to 9 per cent during 1995–2000 and 8.7 per cent after 2000.

All of the economies of the Eastern Europe group experienced a decline in output during 1989–95 after initiating the transition from socialism to a market economy. Collectively, these economies reduced world growth by 19 per cent during the period 1989–95, lowering their share of world product by more than two percentage points from 7.6 per cent during 1989–95 to 5.5 per cent in 1995–2000 and in 2000–05. However, the growth share of this group has tended to rise, from 2.8 per cent in 1995–2000 to 7.5 per cent in 2000–05.

Sub-Saharan Africa, which includes 28 economies, has a world output of about 2 per cent, which ranked with Canada. Growth shares in the economies of Sub-Saharan Africa lagged behind their shares in world product before 2000 but showed an increasing trend, from 1.2 per cent in 1989–95 to 1.9 per cent in 1995–2000, to 2.3 per cent in 2000–05.

The 11 economies of North Africa and the Middle East, taken together, were comparable in size to France, Italy or the UK. The economies of North Africa and the Middle East had a share in world growth of 4.6 per cent during 1989–95, well above their 3.2 per cent share in world product. During 1995–2000 their share in world growth fell to 3.5 per cent, still above the corresponding share in world product of 3.3 per cent. This trend continued with a growth share of 4.0 per cent and a product share of 3.4 per cent after 2000.

Now we examine the output and growth shares of the Latin American group in a greater detail. During 1989–95 the 9.2 per cent share of the Latin American economies in world growth exceeded their 8.4 per cent share in world product. However, their growth shares were below their output shares after 1995, and these shares both experienced declining trends: their growth share declined to 6.4 per cent during 1995–2000, and to 4.9 after 2000, while their output shares dropped to 8.2 per cent during 1995–2000, and to 7.8 per cent after 2000.

The subgroup of the seven largest Latin American economies, which together account for more than 87 per cent of the group output, experienced similar declining trends observed above for the entire group.

Brazil and Mexico were responsible for more than 60 per cent of Latin

American GDP throughout the period 1989–2005. However, the shares of these two major Latin American economies in world product fell below their growth shares, leading to gradual declines in their product shares from 5.1 per cent in 1989–95, to 5.0 during 1995–2000 and 4.7 per cent after 2000. It is worth noting that the growth of Mexico compared with other major Latin American economies was more correlated with the performance of the US economy. During 1995–2000, Mexico's growth surged to 5.31 per cent from 2.09 per cent during 1989–95, and fell to 1.8 per cent after 2000. Among the seven major Latin American economies, only Chile managed to have its world growth share not below its output share throughout 1989–2005.

3 SOURCES OF WORLD ECONOMIC GROWTH

In this section we allocate the sources of world economic growth among the contributions of capital and labor inputs and the growth of productivity. About 40–50 per cent of world growth can be attributed to the accumulation and deployment of capital and another 25–30 per cent to the use of labor input. We find that productivity, frequently described as the primary engine of economic growth, accounted for only 20–35 per cent of growth.

Our second objective is to explore the determinants of the growth of capital input, emphasizing the role of investment in information and communication technologies.

Our third objective is to analyze the determinants of the growth of labor input, focusing on the role of investment in human capital. We have divided labor input growth between the growth of hours worked and labor quality, where quality is defined as the ratio of labor input to hours worked. Labor quality growth captures the impact of changes in the composition of labor input. These arise, for example, through increases in the education and experience of the labor force. The contribution of labor input is the sum of the two components, weighted by the share of labor in output. Finally, productivity growth is the difference between the rate of growth of output and the contributions of capital and labor inputs.

The contribution of capital input to world economic growth before 1995 was 1.31 per cent, 49.2 per cent of the growth rate of 2.66 per cent. Labor input contributed 0.88 per cent or 33 per cent of growth, while productivity growth was 0.47 per cent per year or 17.7 per cent of growth. During 1995–2000 the contribution of capital input climbed to 1.73 per cent, 45.5 per cent of output growth of 3.80 per cent, while the contribution of labor input rose to 1.19 per cent, 31 per cent of growth. Productivity increased to 0.89 per cent per year or 23.4 per cent of growth.

After 2000, world growth continued at an accelerated rate of 3.82 per cent. The contribution of capital slightly declined to 1.59 per cent or 44.6 per cent of growth. The contribution of labor fell to 0.93 per cent or 24.2 per cent of growth. More rapid growth was maintained by a jump in productivity growth to 1.31 per cent per year or 34.2 per cent of the growth of output. We arrive at the astonishing conclusion that the contributions of capital and labor inputs greatly predominate over productivity as sources of world economic growth throughout the period 1989–2005, although the share of productivity has been rising.

We have divided the contribution of capital input to world economic growth between ICT capital and non-ICT capital inputs. The contribution of ICT almost doubled after 1995 from less than a quarter of the contribution of capital input during 1989–95 to about a third from 1995–2000. The share of ICT in the contribution of capital input receded to slightly less than a third after the dot-com crash of 2000. However, it is important to emphasize that the contribution of non-ICT investment was more important throughout the period 1989–2005.

We have divided the contribution of labor input between hours worked and labor quality. Hours worked was the major source of the contribution of labor input to economic growth throughout the period 1989–2005. The contribution of hours rose from 0.47 per cent before 1995 to 0.85 per cent during 1995–2000, but fell back to 0.58 per cent after 2000. The contribution of labor quality declined steadily from 0.41 per cent before 1995 to 0.34 per cent during 1995–2000 and to 0.35 per cent after 2000.

After 1995, world economic growth jumped by more than a full percentage point. The contribution of capital explained 36.9 per cent of this acceleration, while productivity growth accounted for a 36.6 per cent share and labor contributed 26.5 per cent. The jump in ICT investment of 0.27 per cent was by far the most important source of the increase in capital. This can be traced to the more rapid rate of decline of ICT prices after 1995 analyzed by Jorgenson (2001). The substantial increase of 0.37 per cent in the contribution of hours worked offset the decline in the contribution of labor quality.

Table 1.2 presents the contribution of capital input to economic growth for the G7 economies, divided between ICT and non-ICT. Capital input was the most important source of growth before and after 1995. The contribution of capital input before 1995 was 1.29 per cent or three-fifths of the G7 growth rate of 2.14 per cent. The capital contribution of 1.66 per cent from 1995–2000 was 53 per cent of the higher growth rate of 3.11 per

Table 1.2 Sources of output growth

Periods: **Period 1989–95** | **Period 1995–2000** | **Period 2000–05**. Within each period — Sources of Growth (% ppa): Capital (ICT, Non-ICT), Labor (Hours, Quality), TFP.

Group	GDP Growth	ICT	Non-ICT	Hours	Quality	TFP	GDP Growth	ICT	Non-ICT	Hours	Quality	TFP	GDP Growth	ICT	Non-ICT	Hours	Quality	TFP
World	2.66	0.28	1.03	0.47	0.41	0.47	3.80	0.54	1.19	0.85	0.34	0.89	3.82	0.42	1.17	0.58	0.35	1.31
*Growth Share**	*100.0*	*10.5*	*38.8*	*17.8*	*15.3*	*17.7*	*100.0*	*14.3*	*31.2*	*22.2*	*8.8*	*23.4*	*100.0*	*11.0*	*30.6*	*15.1*	*9.1*	*34.2*
G7	2.14	0.39	0.90	0.08	0.36	0.42	3.11	0.74	0.92	0.58	0.27	0.60	2.06	0.39	0.73	0.07	0.29	0.59
	100.0	*18.1*	*41.8*	*4.0*	*16.6*	*19.6*	*100.0*	*24.0*	*29.5*	*18.6*	*8.7*	*19.3*	*100.0*	*18.7*	*35.2*	*3.3*	*14.1*	*28.7*
Developing Asia	7.64	0.18	2.24	1.62	0.48	3.12	5.97	0.35	2.44	1.07	0.43	1.68	7.15	0.52	2.41	1.03	0.42	2.76
	100.0	*2.3*	*29.3*	*21.3*	*6.2*	*40.9*	*100.0*	*5.9*	*40.8*	*17.9*	*7.1*	*28.2*	*100.0*	*7.3*	*33.8*	*14.4*	*5.9*	*38.6*
Non-G7	2.06	0.29	0.76	0.21	0.37	0.44	3.65	0.56	0.97	1.33	0.26	0.53	2.32	0.39	1.04	0.78	0.12	−0.01
	100.0	*14.1*	*36.6*	*10.3*	*17.9*	*21.1*	*100.0*	*15.3*	*26.5*	*36.5*	*7.1*	*14.6*	*100.0*	*16.8*	*44.6*	*33.6*	*5.3*	*−0.4*
Latin America	2.94	0.12	0.63	1.27	0.43	0.50	2.97	0.30	0.80	1.41	0.38	0.09	2.39	0.35	0.60	1.28	0.38	−0.22
	100.0	*4.0*	*21.4*	*43.1*	*14.6*	*16.9*	*100.0*	*10.1*	*26.8*	*47.4*	*12.8*	*2.9*	*100.0*	*14.8*	*25.2*	*53.5*	*15.7*	*−9.2*
Eastern Europe	−6.44	0.10	−0.17	−1.54	0.41	−5.24	1.96	0.27	−0.62	−0.37	0.40	2.27	5.23	0.41	−0.28	0.08	0.57	4.45
	100.0	*−1.5*	*2.7*	*23.8*	*−6.3*	*81.3*	*100.0*	*13.9*	*−31.5*	*−18.9*	*20.2*	*116.2*	*100.0*	*7.9*	*−5.4*	*1.5*	*11.0*	*85.0*
Sub-Saharan Africa	1.51	0.18	0.26	1.89	0.62	−1.44	3.44	0.33	0.60	1.81	0.46	0.25	4.23	0.49	1.03	1.19	0.45	1.06
	100.0	*12.0*	*17.4*	*125.0*	*40.8*	*−95.1*	*100.0*	*9.5*	*17.4*	*52.6*	*13.3*	*7.2*	*100.0*	*11.7*	*24.4*	*28.1*	*10.7*	*25.1*
N. Africa and M. East	3.80	0.11	0.92	1.87	0.64	0.26	3.96	0.19	1.01	1.79	0.56	0.41	4.51	0.26	0.93	1.88	0.56	0.89
	100.0	*2.8*	*24.2*	*49.1*	*16.9*	*7.0*	*100.0*	*4.9*	*25.4*	*45.3*	*14.1*	*10.3*	*100.0*	*5.8*	*20.6*	*41.6*	*12.3*	*19.7*

Table 1.2 (continued)

Group	Period 1989–95						Period 1995–2000						Period 2000–05					
	GDP Growth	Capital ICT	Capital Non-ICT	Labor Hours	Labor Quality	TFP	GDP Growth	Capital ICT	Capital Non-ICT	Labor Hours	Labor Quality	TFP	GDP Growth	Capital ICT	Capital Non-ICT	Labor Hours	Labor Quality	TFP
G7																		
Canada	1.44	0.49	0.27	0.08	0.55	0.05	4.07	0.94	0.77	1.08	0.21	1.07	2.50	0.44	1.15	1.22	0.18	-0.50
	100.0	*34.0*	*18.7*	*5.5*	*38.1*	*3.6*	*100.0*	*23.1*	*18.9*	*26.6*	*5.2*	*26.2*	*100.0*	*17.8*	*46.1*	*48.8*	*7.2*	*-19.9*
France	1.46	0.22	0.62	-0.32	0.64	0.31	2.76	0.44	0.53	0.43	0.49	0.88	1.48	0.24	0.63	0.06	0.29	0.27
	100.0	*14.9*	*42.2*	*-22.3*	*43.7*	*21.5*	*100.0*	*15.8*	*19.1*	*15.5*	*17.6*	*32.0*	*100.0*	*16.0*	*42.3*	*4.3*	*19.3*	*18.0*
Germany	2.74	0.23	1.08	-0.05	-0.01	1.49	1.99	0.50	0.88	0.00	-0.10	0.71	0.74	0.24	0.44	-0.36	0.26	0.15
	100.0	*8.5*	*39.6*	*-1.9*	*-0.5*	*54.3*	*100.0*	*25.2*	*44.3*	*0.0*	*-5.1*	*35.5*	*100.0*	*32.2*	*59.9*	*-48.6*	*35.9*	*20.6*
Italy	1.39	0.18	0.68	-0.53	0.21	0.85	1.89	0.35	0.81	0.51	0.18	0.04	0.64	0.06	0.83	0.54	-0.06	-0.74
	100.0	*12.7*	*48.5*	*-37.9*	*15.4*	*61.3*	*100.0*	*18.7*	*43.0*	*26.9*	*9.4*	*2.2*	*100.0*	*9.7*	*130.2*	*84.8*	*-9.1*	*-115.6*
Japan	2.09	0.28	1.68	-0.28	0.37	0.04	0.96	0.39	0.72	-0.64	0.57	-0.08	1.42	0.16	0.41	-0.19	0.22	0.83
	100.0	*13.3*	*80.2*	*-13.2*	*17.7*	*1.9*	*100.0*	*40.0*	*74.6*	*-66.1*	*59.6*	*-8.0*	*100.0*	*11.4*	*28.4*	*-13.4*	*15.3*	*58.3*
United Kingdom	1.53	0.48	0.61	-0.78	0.51	0.70	3.18	0.93	0.77	0.68	0.51	0.30	2.31	0.52	0.58	0.59	0.52	0.11
	100.0	*31.5*	*40.0*	*-50.9*	*33.7*	*45.7*	*100.0*	*29.3*	*24.1*	*21.3*	*15.9*	*9.5*	*100.0*	*22.5*	*25.0*	*25.5*	*22.4*	*4.6*
United States	2.44	0.50	0.73	0.58	0.37	0.25	4.29	0.99	1.11	1.13	0.19	0.87	2.76	0.53	0.88	-0.01	0.34	1.01
	100.0	*20.7*	*29.9*	*24.0*	*15.0*	*10.3*	*100.0*	*23.1*	*25.9*	*26.3*	*4.4*	*20.3*	*100.0*	*19.3*	*31.9*	*-0.4*	*12.4*	*36.7*

Note: * The italic number below each growth source is its percentage share in output growth.

Source: Authors' calculation.

30

cent. After 2000 the capital contribution fell to 1.11 per cent or 54 per cent of the substantially lower G7 growth rate of 2.06 per cent.

Labor input growth contributed 0.44 per cent to growth of the G7 economies before 1995, 0.85 per cent in 1995–2000, but only 0.36 per cent after 2000. Hours worked predominated during 1995–2000, contributing 0.58 per cent, while labor quality rose at 0.27 per cent. Growth contribution of hours was only 0.08 per cent before 1995 and 0.07 per cent after 2000, while the labor quality contribution was 0.36 per cent and 0.29 per cent, respectively. Productivity accounted for 0.42 per cent before 1995, 0.60 per cent during 1995–2000, and 0.59 per cent after 2000. Productivity share ranged from less than 20 per cent before 1995 to 29 per cent after 2000.

The powerful surge of ICT investment in the US after 1995 is mirrored in jumps in the growth rates of ICT capital through the G7. The contribution of ICT capital input for the G7 nearly doubled from 0.39 during the period 1989–95 to 0.74 per cent during 1995–2005, before receding to 0.39 per cent after 2000. The contribution of non-ICT capital input predominated in all three sub-periods, but fell slightly throughout 1989–2005. This reflected more rapid substitution of ICT capital input for non-ICT capital input in response to swiftly declining prices of ICT equipment and software after 1995.

In Developing Asia the contribution of capital input steadily increased from 2.41 per cent before 1995 to 2.79 per cent in 1995–2000, and to 2.94 per cent after 2000. The contribution of labor input fell from 2.1 per cent during 1989–95 to 1.5 per cent during 1995–2000, and to 1.46 after 2000. The significant slowdown in the Asian growth rate from 7.64 per cent before 1995 to 5.97 per cent during 1995–2000 can be traced almost entirely to a sharp decline in productivity growth from 3.12 to 1.68 per cent. Similarly, the revival of growth to 7.15 per cent during 2000–05 can be attributed to higher productivity growth of 2.76 per cent. Productivity explained 40.9 per cent of Asian growth before 1995, 28.2 per cent in 1995–2000 and 38.6 per cent after 2000.

For China productivity accounted for a major share in growth: 44.4 per cent in 1989–95, 40.7 per cent in 1995–2000, and 42.2 in 2000–05; the contribution of capital growth surpassed productivity after 1995, rising from 27.3 per cent in 1989–95 to 44.4 per cent in 1995–2000, to 44.5 per cent in 2000–05.

For India productivity also played an important role at around 40 per cent in 1989–95 and 2000–05, and 30 per cent in 1995–2000. However, relative to China, labor accounted for a larger share in growth after 1995.

The first half of the 1990s was a continuation of the Asian Miracle, analyzed by Krugman (1994), Lau (1999) and Young (1995). This period was dominated by the spectacular rise of China and India and the continuing emergence of the Gang of Four – Hong Kong, Singapore, South Korea and Taiwan. However, all Asian economies, except the Philippines, had growth rates in excess of the world average of 3.80 per cent. The second half of the 1990s was dominated by the Asian financial crisis but, surprisingly, conforms much more closely to the 'Krugman thesis' attributing Asian growth to input growth more than productivity.

The 'Krugman thesis' was originally propounded to distinguish the Asian Miracle from growth in industrialized countries. According to this thesis, Asian growth was differentiated by high growth rates and a great predominance of inputs over productivity as the sources of growth. In fact, the peak of productivity growth in Developing Asia, absolutely and relatively, was during the Asian Miracle of the early 1990s! Moreover, growth in the world economy and the G7 economies was dominated by growth of capital and labor inputs, not productivity.

The pattern of economic growth in the 15 non-G7 industrialized economies was similar to G7 growth before 2000 with a sharp acceleration after 1995. However, the non-G7 economies maintained a higher growth rate after 2000, while the G7 economies reverted to pre-1995 growth rates. The contribution of capital and labor inputs are major sources of growth throughout the period 1989–2005. Non-G7 productivity growth climbed from 0.44 per cent before 1995 to 0.53 per cent in 1995–2000, before falling to −0.01 per cent after 2000. Productivity accounted for 20 per cent of growth before 1995, 16 per cent from 1995–2000 and nearly zero after 2000.

The impact of investment in ICT equipment and software in the non-G7 economies nearly doubled from 0.29 per cent before 1995 to 0.56 per cent during 1995–2000, before receding to 0.39 per cent after 2000. This provided a substantial impetus to the acceleration in non-G7 growth rates in the face of sharply declining productivity growth. Non-ICT investment explained an important part of the growth acceleration. However, the increased contribution of hours worked from 0.21 per cent before 1995 to 1.33 in 1995–2000 and 0.78 per cent after 2000 also played a major role.

The collapse of economic growth in Eastern Europe and the former Soviet Union during 1989–95 can be attributed to a steep decline in productivity during the initial transition from socialism. This was followed by a modest revival in both economic growth and productivity growth from 1995–2000, bringing many of the transition economies back to 1989 levels of output per capita. The contribution of capital input declined until 2000 even as the contribution of ICT investment jumped from 0.10 per cent before 1995 to 0.27 per cent in 1995–2000 and 0.41 per cent after 2000. Hours worked declined sharply during 1989–95 and continued to fall during 1995–2000 before showing a negligible growth in 2000–05, while labor quality steadily improved throughout 1989–2005.

Latin America's growth was rather stable during 1989–95 and 1995–2000 (2.94 and 2.97 per cent, respectively) before falling to 2.39 per cent after 2000. The contribution of labor input was 1.70 per cent before 1995, 1.79 from 1995–2000 and 1.66 per cent after 2000, accounting for the lion's share of regional growth. The contribution of capital input shifted toward ICT, but remained relatively weak. Nonetheless, the contribution of ICT investment in Latin America more than doubled, jumping from 0.12 per cent before 1995 to 0.30 per cent in 1995–2000 and 0.35 after 2000. Productivity collapsed after 1995, falling from 0.50 in 1989–95 to 0.09 in 1995–2000, to a negative 0.22 per cent after in 1995–2000.

Chile was the only Latin American economy to experience growth that exceeded the world average in all the three periods from 1989 to 2005. Economic growth in Brazil and Mexico, the two largest Latin American economies, languished below the world average throughout in 1989–2005, except that Mexico's growth surged above the world average during 1995–2000, which coincided with the boom of the US economy. Labor input greatly predominated as a source of economic growth for all major Latin American countries except for Chile, which had substantial contributions from capital input. All the seven major Latin American countries except for Chile experienced productivity growth collapse in at least one of the three periods: Argentina and Venezuela in 1995–2000 and 2000–05; Mexico in 1989–95 and 2000–05; Colombia and Peru in 2000–05; Brazil in 2000–05. For the entire Latin American group as well as its subgroup of seven major economies, there was a declining trend of productivity growth!

Productivity in Sub-Saharan Africa collapsed during 1989–95, running at −1.44 per cent, before recovering to 0.25 per cent in 1995–2000 and rising sharply to 1.06 per cent after 2000. As in Latin America, the contribution of labor input predominated throughout the period 1989–2005. Productivity in North Africa and the Middle East rose from 0.26 per cent before 1995 to 0.41 per cent in 1995–2000 and 0.89 per cent after 2000. In Sub-Saharan Africa and North Africa and the Middle East, growth of capital and labor inputs greatly predominated over productivity as a source of economic growth.

4   WORLD OUTPUT, INPUT AND PRODUCTIVITY

The final step in analyzing the world growth resurgence is to characterize the evolution of levels of output, input and productivity for the world economy, the seven economic regions, the G7 economies, the seven major Latin American economies and China and India.

We construct the levels of output, input and productivity for each economy based on the production function (1.1) presented in Section 1: $Y = A.f(K, L)$.

The productivity computed as $A = Y/f(K, L)$ is the amount of output produced by a unit of combined labor and capital inputs and it relates to the efficiency of the economy.[8]

The levels of per capita output, per capita input and productivity are computed using the following guidelines:

- The output is measured in 2000 PPP$.
- The combined input $f(K, L)$ is computed as $f(K, L) = K^{s_K} * L^{s_L}$, where s_K and s_L are the shares in current output of capital and labor input, respectively. The capital input K is converted from its value in current US$ to 2005 PPP$ by using the aggregate capital investment deflator (to get the value in 2005 US$) and the PPP exchange factor in 2005. The labor input L is estimated as the product of hours worked and the labor quality index and a similar constant for all countries.
- The level of productivity is computed as the ratio between the levels of per capita output and per capita input.

Taking the US levels of output, input and productivity in 2000 as 100.0, we compute the levels of output, input and productivity for each of the 110 economies in the years of interest.

In Table 1.3 we present levels of output per capita when the transition from socialism began in 1989, at the start of the worldwide ICT investment boom in 1995, at the beginning of the dot-com crash in 2000 and at the end of the period covered by our study in 2005. We also present input per capita and productivity for these years.

Differences in per capita output levels are mainly due to differences in per capita input, rather than disparities in productivity. Taking US output per capita in 2000 as 100.0, world output per capita was a relatively modest 18.5 in 1989. Using similar scales for input and productivity, world input per capita in 1989 was a considerable 41.4 and world productivity a more substantial 44.8. The level of world output advanced to 20.0 in 1995, jumped to 22.6 in 2000, and leapt again to 25.8 in 2005, reflecting impressive progress in mobilizing world inputs. World productivity edged upward modestly to 46.1 in 1995, 48.1 in 2000 and then 51.9 in 2004.

It is not surprising that world productivity is closer to US levels than world input per capita. As globalization has proceeded, technologies have

Table 1.3   Levels of output and input per capita and productivity (US = 100 in 2000)

Group	Output Per Capita				Input Per Capita				Productivity			
	1989	1995	2000	2005	1989	1995	2000	2005	1989	1995	2000	2005
World	18.5	20.0	22.6	25.8	41.4	43.3	47.1	49.8	44.8	46.1	48.1	51.9
G7	69.2	75.3	85.2	91.7	77.6	82.1	90.2	94.5	89.2	91.6	94.4	97.1
Developing Asia	5.7	8.1	10.2	13.8	20.7	24.8	28.8	34.1	27.3	32.8	35.5	40.6
Non-G7	56.5	61.5	71.4	76.7	64.5	68.9	78.1	84.0	87.6	89.3	91.4	91.3
Latin America	18.4	19.8	21.3	22.2	30.0	31.5	34.0	35.8	61.5	62.8	62.6	62.1
Eastern Europe	27.0	19.3	21.7	28.9	33.8	34.1	34.2	35.8	80.1	56.7	63.5	80.7
Sub-Saharan Africa	5.2	4.8	5.1	5.5	20.1	20.2	20.9	22.1	25.9	23.9	24.2	25.1
N. Africa and M. East	11.3	12.4	13.8	15.7	23.3	25.3	27.6	30.4	48.5	49.0	49.9	51.6
G7												
Canada	66.9	68.0	79.5	85.8	79.0	80.1	88.8	98.2	84.6	84.9	89.5	87.3
France	62.4	66.5	75.0	78.1	68.2	71.3	76.9	79.0	91.6	93.3	97.5	98.8
Germany	58.7	66.8	73.2	75.7	77.8	80.9	85.6	87.8	75.5	82.6	85.6	86.2
Italy	61.5	66.2	72.2	73.4	59.3	60.6	73.2	69.5	93.5	98.4	98.6	95.1
Japan	65.3	72.7	75.4	80.3	77.7	86.2	89.8	91.7	84.1	84.3	84.0	87.5
United Kingdom	62.2	67.1	77.9	85.5	75.5	78.1	89.3	97.5	82.4	85.9	87.2	87.7
United States	79.7	85.5	100.0	109.4	84.5	89.3	100.0	104.0	94.3	95.7	100.0	105.2
G7	69.2	75.3	85.2	91.7	77.6	82.1	90.2	94.5	89.2	91.6	94.4	97.1

Table 1.3 (continued)

Group	Output Per Capita				Input Per Capita				Productivity			
	1989	1995	2000	2005	1989	1995	2000	2005	1989	1995	2000	2005
Seven Major Latin American Economies (LA7)												
Argentina	26.5	33.3	36.0	36.8	42.1	41.1	45.0	47.3	63.0	80.9	79.8	77.7
Brazil	19.9	20.3	21.2	21.7	30.9	31.3	32.6	33.3	64.5	64.8	65.2	65.0
Chile	16.4	23.3	26.7	30.9	34.3	40.0	45.6	51.0	47.7	58.3	58.6	60.7
Colombia	15.5	17.9	17.1	18.8	24.3	27.4	27.8	29.1	63.9	65.4	61.5	64.5
Mexico	21.6	21.9	26.6	27.7	32.0	34.7	39.0	43.0	67.4	63.2	68.1	64.3
Peru	12.0	13.1	13.7	15.5	24.7	26.7	29.5	30.9	48.5	49.3	46.3	50.2
Venezuela	16.3	17.7	16.6	17.0	23.3	24.2	25.7	26.7	69.9	73.2	64.6	63.9
LA7	19.7	21.1	22.8	23.7	30.9	32.2	34.6	36.4	63.7	65.2	65.3	64.8
China and India												
China	4.6	7.9	11.4	17.4	20.4	26.7	32.5	41.1	22.5	29.6	35.0	42.4
India	4.6	5.6	6.8	8.9	17.7	19.0	21.2	24.2	26.1	29.6	32.2	36.8

Note: The levels for group and the world are average weighted by population share.

Source: Authors' calculations.

been transferred with relative ease from industrialized economies to the developing world. Mobilization of inputs in developing economies has been remarkable, but has required far more time and effort.

Institutional barriers to accumulation of human and non-human capital must be overcome and networks among the cooperating activities must be established and enhanced. Obsolete methods for organizing production must be displaced by up-to-date techniques that employ information technology equipment and software.

The output gap between the US and the other G7 economies has widened since the US growth resurgence began in 1995. The G7 economies led the seven economic regions in output per capita, input per capita and productivity throughout the period 1989–2005. Output per capita in the G7 was, nonetheless, well below US levels. Taking US output per capita in 2000 as 100.0, G7 output per capita was 69.2 in 1989, 75.3 in 1995, 85.2 in 2000 and 91.7 in 2005. By comparison US output per capita was 79.7, 85.5, 100.0 and 109.4 in these years.

Canada was very close to the US in output per capita in 1989 (66.9 vs. 79.7), but the US–Canada gap widened over the period 1989–2005 due to lower growth rates of Canada compared with the US throughout this period.

Germany, Japan, Italy and the UK had similar levels of output per capita throughout 1989–2005, but remained considerably behind the two North American economies. Italy lagged the rest of the G7 in output per capita in 1989 and failed to gain ground during the period 1989–2005.

The US was the leader among the G7 economies in input per capita throughout the period 1989–2005. Taking the US as 100.0 in 2000, G7 input per capita was 77.6 in 1989, 82.1 in 1995, 90.2 in 2000 and 94.5 in 2005, while US input per capita was 84.5, 89.3, 100.0 and 104.0 in these years. Canada, Germany and Japan were closest to US levels of input per capita in 1989, with Japan ranking second in 1995 and 2000, and Canada ranking second in 2005. Italy lagged behind the rest of the G7 in input per capita throughout 1989–2005. The UK made substantial progress toward achieving input levels surpassing those of Germany and Japan in 2005.

Productivity in the G7 has remained close to US levels, rising from 89.2 in 1989 to 91.6 in 1995, and 94.4 in 2000, and 97.1 in 2005 with the US equal to 100.0 in 2000.

Differences among the G7 economies in output per capita can be explained by both differences in input per capita and productivity gaps. For example, in 2005, Italy's output level was 73.4 compared with 109.4 for the US, while the Italy–US gap was 69.5–104.0 on input and 95.1–105.2 on productivity.

In the economies of Developing Asia output per capita rose spectacularly from 5.7 in 1989 to 8.1 in 1995, 10.2 in 2000 and 13.8 in 2005, with the US equal to 100.0 in 2000. These vast shortfalls in output per capita, relative to the industrialized economies, are due primarily to differences in input per capita, rather than productivity gaps. Developing Asia's levels of input per capita were 20.7 in 1989, 24.8 in 1995, 28.8 in 2000 and 34.1 in 2005, while Asian productivity levels were 27.3, 32.8, 35.5 and 40.6, respectively. China started with very low levels of output, input, and productivity in 1989, which were comparable only with the poorest group of Sub-Saharan Africa. Its rapid growth in both input and productivity throughout 1989–2005, however, had driven China's output per capita to the level in 2005 far above Sub-Saharan Africa, Developing Asia and North Africa and Middle East, although still well below Latin America. India started from the same output level of output as China in 1989 and also achieved impressive growth. However, India's output level in 2005 was only half that of China.

The output level of the group of 15 non-G7 industrialized econo-mies was below the G7 economies throughout 1989–2000 but surpassed Germany and Italy in 2005. The main drivers of this group's catch-up were its substantial increase in input level and a moderate rise in productivity.

For the Latin American region output per capita rose from 18.4 to 22.2 during 1989–2005, input per capita rose from 30.0 to 35.8, but productiv-ity was essentially unchanged throughout the period at about two-thirds of the US level in 2000. The stall in productivity from 1989 to 2005 was pervasive, contrasting sharply with the rise in productivity in the G7 economies, the non-G7 industrialized economies and Developing Asia. Nonetheless, Latin America's lagging output per capita was due chiefly to insufficient input per capita, rather than a shortfall in productivity.

Brazil's economic performance has been anemic at best and has acted as a drag on the growth of Latin America and the world economy. Despite productivity levels comparable with the rest of Latin America, Brazil was unable to generate substantial growth in input per capita. Mexico lost ground in productivity between 1989 and 2005, but has made steady gains in input per capita and expanded output per capita substantially after 1995.

Argentina began the period 1989–2005 with a relatively high level of productivity and increased productivity in 1995 to a stunning 80.9, relative to US productivity of 100.0 in 2000! The shortfall in output per capita in Latin American economies was due almost entirely to low levels of input per capita, rather than productivity. By 1995 Chile had become the leader in input per capita among Latin American economies since 1995 with a level of 40.0 in 1995, 45.6 in 2000 and 51.0 in 2005.

Before the beginning of the transition from socialism in 1989, output per capita in Eastern Europe and the former Soviet Union was 27.0, well above the world economy level of 18.5, with the US equal to 100.0 in 2000. The economic collapse that accompanied the transition reduced output per capita to 19.3 by 1995, slightly below the world economy level of 20.0. A recovery between 1995 and 2005 brought the region back to 28.9 in 2005, well above the world economy average of 25.8.

Input in Eastern Europe and the former Soviet Union remained stagnant at around 34.0 during 1989–2000, and slightly rose to 35.8 in 2005. Productivity collapsed along with output per capita, declining from 80.1 in 1989 to 56.7 in 1995, before climbing back to 63.5 in 2000 and, finally, surpassing the 1989 level at 80.7 in 2005.

Output and input per capita and productivity in Sub-Saharan Africa were the lowest in the world throughout the period 1989–2005. All the economies of North Africa and the Middle East fell short of world average levels of output and input per capita. Output per capita grew slowly but steadily for the region as a whole during 1989–2005, powered by significant gains in input per capita and productivity.

5 SUMMARY AND CONCLUSIONS

World economic growth, led by the industrialized economies and Developing Asia, experienced a strong resurgence after 1995. Developing Asia accounted for almost half of world economic growth during 1989–2005 but remained well below the world average in output per capita. Sub-Saharan Africa and North Africa and the Middle East also languished below the world average. Eastern Europe and the former Soviet Union lost enormous ground during the transition from socialism but have started recovering since 1995.

Growth trends apparent in the US have counterparts throughout the world. Investment in tangible assets, including ICT equipment and software, was the most important source of growth. However, non-ICT investment predominated. The contribution of labor input was next in magnitude with hours worked outweighing labor quality. Finally, productivity was the dominant source of growth only in Eastern Europe and the former Soviet Union during the recovery from the output and productivity collapse of 1989–95 that accompanied the beginning of the transition from socialism to a market economy.

The leading role of ICT investment in the acceleration of growth in the G7 economies is especially pronounced in the US. The contribution of labor input predominated in the non-G7 industrialized economies, as well as Latin America, Eastern Europe, Sub-Saharan Africa and North

Africa and the Middle East. Productivity growth was an important source of growth in Developing Asia during the Asian Miracle before 1995, contrary to the 'Krugman thesis', but growth of capital and labor inputs rose in importance after 1995. Productivity has been stagnant or declining in Latin America, Eastern Europe, Sub-Saharan Africa and North Africa and the Middle East.

All seven regions of the world economy experienced a surge in investment in ICT equipment and software after 1995. The impact of ICT investment on economic growth was most striking in the G7 economies. The rush in ICT investment was especially conspicuous in the US, but jumps in the contribution of ICT capital input in Canada, Japan and the UK were only slightly lower. France, Germany and Italy also experienced a surge in ICT investment, but lagged considerably behind the leaders. ICT investment subsided among the G7 economies after the dot-com crash of 2000, while the contribution of non-ICT investment varied considerably and explains important differences among growth rates of the G7 economies.

The surge in investment in ICT equipment and software is a global phenomenon, but the variation in the contribution of this investment has grown considerably since 1995. The moderation in ICT investment in the industrialized countries after the dot-com crash of 2000 was accompanied by continued expansion in the contribution of ICT in the developing world, especially in Asia. The contribution of ICT investment more than doubled after 1995 in Developing Asia, Latin America, Eastern Europe, and North Africa and the Middle East and Sub-Saharan Africa.

Finally, despite spectacular growth rates in Developing Asia, levels of output per capita remain below world averages. Differences in per capita output levels are mainly due to input per capita rather than productivity. This reflects the fact that technology is relatively easy to transfer from industrialized economies to developing economies, while mobilization of capital and labor inputs requires much more time and considerably greater effort. Outmoded techniques of production must give way to newer methods that incorporate the latest technologies, especially those that utilize information and communication technologies equipment and software.

Despite stagnant productivity growth in Latin America through the period 1989–2005, Latin American productivity remained above world levels. Productivity in the leading Latin American economies, Argentina and Venezuela, had achieved North American or Western European levels by 1995. However, all Latin American economies had a substantial shortfall in GDP per capita, relative to world levels, due to large gaps in input per capita and stagnation in productivity growth. Chile and Mexico made substantial progress in reducing this gap during the period 1989–2005, largely through investment in non-ICT assets.

NOTES

* The Economic and Social Research Institute provided financial support for work on the G7 economies from its program on international collaboration through the Nomura Research Institute. Alessandra Colecchia, Mun S. Ho, Kazuyuki Motohashi, Koji Nomura, Jon Samuels, Kevin J. Stiroh, Marcel Timmer, Gerard Ypma and Bart Van Ark provided valuable data. The Bureau of Economic Analysis and the Bureau of Labor Statistics assisted with data for the US and Statistics Canada contributed the data for Canada. We are grateful to all of them but retain final responsibility for any remaining deficiencies.
1. See Jorgenson and Stiroh (2000) and Oliner and Sichel (2000). The growth accounting methodology employed in this literature is discussed by Jorgenson et al. (2005) and summarized by Jorgenson (2005).
2. Ahmad et al. (2004) have analyzed the impact of ICT investment in OECD countries. Timmer et al. (2003/2005) and Daveri (2002) have presented comparisons among European economies. Piatkowski and van Ark (2005) have compared the impact of ICT investment on the economies of Eastern Europe and the former Soviet Union.
3. This model is introduced in Jorgenson (1996, pp. 27–8).
4. http://www.ggdc.net/databases/ted_growth.htm; accessed 19 March 2010. An overview of the EU KLEMS Database is provided by Timmer et al. (2007).
5. EU KLEMS project dataset, European Commission, Research Directorate General; http://www.euklems.net/; accessed 19 March 2010.
6. The information on the report can be found on the WITSA's webpage at http://www.witsa.org/; accessed 19 March 2010.
7. The data for China may be exaggerated as pointed out by Maddison (1998) and Young (2003). For extensive references to the debate over Chinese growth rates and a review of the issues, see the critique of Maddison by Carsten Holz (2006) and Maddison's (2006) reply.
8. One may note that the labor productivity measured as Y/L, is much higher in a rich country than in a poor one because the rich country has a lot more capital per worker (K/L) in its production. The concept of productivity takes into account the quantity and quality of both L and K; and hence the variation in productivity between rich and poor countries is not as large as in labor productivity.

REFERENCES

Ahmad, Nadim, Paul Schreyer and Anita Wölfl (2004), 'ICT Investment in OECD Countries and Its Economic Impact', Chapter 4 in OECD, *The Economic Impact of ICT: Measurement, Evidence, and Implications*, Paris: Organisation for Economic Co-operation and Development.

Daveri, Francesco (2002), 'The New Economy in Europe: 1992–2001', *Oxford Review of Economic Policy*, **18**(4), 345–62.

Holz, Carsten A. (2006), 'China's Reform Period Economic Growth: How Reliable Are Angus Maddison's Estimates?', *Review of Income and Wealth*, **52**(1), March, 85–120.

Jorgenson, Dale W. (1996), 'The Embodiment Hypothesis', in *Postwar U.S. Economic Growth*, Cambridge, MA: The MIT Press.

Jorgenson, Dale W. (2001), 'Information Technology and the U.S. Economy', *American Economic Review*, **91**(1), March, 1–32.

Jorgenson, Dale W. (2003), 'Information Technology and the G7 Economies', *World Economics*, **4**(4), October–December, 139–70.

Jorgenson, Dale W. (2005), 'Accounting for Growth in the Information Age', in Philippe Aghion and Steven Durlauf, *Handbook of Economic Growth*, Amsterdam: North-Holland, pp. 743–815.

Jorgenson, Dale W. and Kevin J. Stiroh (2000), 'Raising the Speed Limit: US Economic Growth in the Information Age', *OECD Economics Department Working Papers* NO. 261, OECD Economics Department.

Jorgenson, Dale W. and Khuong Vu (2006), 'Information Technology and the World Economy', in Manual Castells and Gustavo Cardoso (eds), *The Network Society*, Washington: Johns Hopkins Center for Transatlantic Relations, pp. 71–124.

Jorgenson, Dale W., Mun S. Ho and Kevin J. Stiroh (2005), *Information Technology and the American Growth Resurgence*, Cambridge, MA: The MIT Press.

Krugman, Paul (1994), 'The Myth of Asia's Miracle', *Foreign Affairs*, **73**(6), November/December, 62–78.

Lau, Lawrence J. (1999), 'The Sources of East Asian Economic Growth', in Gustav Ranis, Sheng-Cheng Hu and Yun-Peng Chu, *The Political Economy of Comparative Development in the 21st Century*, Cheltenham, UK and Northampton, MA, USA, Edward Elgar, pp. 45–75.

Maddison, Angus (1998), *Chinese Economic Performance in the Long Run*, Development Centre of the Organisation for Economic Co-operation and Development, Paris.

Maddison, Angus (2006), 'Do Official Statistics Exaggerate China's GDP Growth? A Reply to Carsten Holz', *Review of Income and Wealth*, **52**(1), March, 121–6.

Oliner, Stephen and Daniel Sichel (2000) 'The Resurgence of Growth in the Late 1990s: Is Information Technology the Story?,' *Journal of Economic Perspectives*, **14**(4), Fall, 3–22.

Piatkowski, Marcin and Bart Van Ark (2005), 'ICT and Productivity Growth in Transition Economies: Two-phase Convergence and Structural Reforms', *TIGER Working Paper Series* No. 72, Warsaw, January 2005, available at: http://www.tiger.edu.pl/publikacje/TWPNo72.pdf; accessed 19 March 2010.

Timmer, Marcel P., Gerard Ypma and Bart Van Ark (2003, updated 2005), *IT in the European Union: Driving Productivity Divergence?*, GGDC Research Memorandum GD-67, Groningen, University of Groningen, available at: http://www.ggdc.net/publications/memoabstracthtm?id=6%; accessed 19 March 2010.

Timmer, Marcel P., Mary O' Mahony and Bart Van Ark (2007), 'EU KLEMS Growth and Productivity Accounts: An Overview', *International Productivity Monitor*, **14**, 71–85.

Young, Alwyn (1995), 'The Tyranny of Numbers: Confronting the Statistical Realities of the East Asian Growth Experience', *Quarterly Journal of Economics*, **106**(1), August, 641–80.

Young, Alwyn (2003), 'Gold into Base Metals: Productivity Growth in the People's Republic of China during the Reform Period', *Journal of Political Economy*, **111**(6), December, 1220–61.

2. Technical change and economic growth: some lessons from secular patterns and some conjectures on the current impact of ICT*

Carolina Castaldi and Giovanni Dosi

1 INTRODUCTION

This chapter evaluates the effects of the current 'revolution' in information and communication technologies (ICT) upon economic growth and development from an evolutionary perspective. Before addressing this issue, we first discuss the distinctive 'evolutionary' interpretation of the processes of innovation and technological diffusion in relation to economic growth, and look at the historical patterns of technological change and their apparent relations with economic growth.

2 OPENING UP THE 'BLACK BOX' OF TECHNOLOGICAL ACTIVITIES

Recently the evolutionary inspired literature on the economics of innovation and technical change has advanced our understanding of what is inside the 'black box of technology'.[1]

2.1 The Properties of Technological Learning

Several authors have found well-structured bodies of knowledge, referred to elsewhere by one of us as technological paradigms (Dosi, 1982, 1988; Dosi et al., 2005). Each paradigm involves knowledge bases grounded in selected physical/chemical principles and entails specific solutions to selected techno-economic problems and rules aimed at the refinement and accumulation of new knowledge. Examples of technological paradigms include the internal combustion engine, oil-based synthetic chemistry and semiconductor-based micro-electronics. In fact, a closer look at the patterns of technical change suggests the existence of 'paradigms' with different levels of generality in most industrial activities. Product and process innovations associated with each paradigm tend to proceed along relatively ordered technological trajectories.

Such trajectories have several properties. First, each paradigm shapes the rate and direction of technological change irrespective of market conditions (e.g., variations in demand and relative prices). Second, as a consequence, one observes regularities in patterns of technical change that hold under different market conditions and whose disruption is associated with radical changes in knowledge bases (that is, in paradigms). Third, technical change is partly driven by repeated attempts to cope with technological imbalances created by itself.

Learning is local and cumulative. Local means that the exploration and development of new techniques is likely to occur close to the techniques already in use. Cumulative means that current technological developments – at least at the level of individual business units – often build upon past experiences of production and innovation, and proceed via sequences of specific problem-solving junctures (Vincenti, 1990). This matches the ideas of paradigmatic knowledge and the ensuing trajectories. At any point in time, agents in a particular production process face little scope for substitution among techniques (i.e., available blueprints different from those in use), which can be put efficiently into operation according to prevailing relative input prices. On the contrary, attempts at inter-factoral substitution are in fact indistinguishable from efforts to innovate.

A paradigm-based theory of technology and production yields three predictions. First, at any point in time one or few best practice techniques dominate others irrespective of relative prices. Second, different agents are characterized by persistently diverse (better and worse) techniques and products. Third, over time the aggregate dynamics of technical coefficients in each activity is the joint outcome of the process of imitation/diffusion of existing best-practice techniques, the search for new ones and market selection among heterogeneous agents. Firms are crucial in the evolutionary view of economic change as repositories of knowledge, embedded in operational routines and organizational capabilities. Hence, technical change and organizational change are highly intertwined: technologies and organizational structures and behaviours tend to co-evolve.

The evolutionary interpretation of technological change also acknowledges that micro-processes of technological and organizational change are embedded in broader institutional frameworks at the national and/or regional level. National institutions have influenced the relative rates of technological change of different countries (Freeman, 1995). The notion of 'national systems of innovation' captures the importance of the national institutional context motivating economic actors and shaping incentives for innovation (Lundvall, 1992; Nelson, 1993). Technological learning is an 'interactive' process where relations between different participants in the innovation process (suppliers, producers, users, universities) may be affected by existing institutional structures. The related literature has also stressed the different national institutional settings and policies co-existing worldwide. The local nature of technological learning implies that the innovative performance of a region is influenced by the characteristics of local networks of production in terms of, for instance, the extent of knowledge externalities and level of mutual trust. In line with Freeman (1995), we will also argue at different points in this paper that national systems of innovation and production are even more important in a globalized world where countries wish to become attractive locations within global networks of trade and production.

2.2　The Evolutionary Path of Technological Learning in Economic Development

The evolutionary representation of technological learning has several implications for the international distribution of technological capabilities and patterns of economic development (Cimoli and Dosi, 1995). First, evolutionary interpretations account for persistent asymmetries among countries in the production processes they can master, as expressed by different inputs efficiencies (Dosi et al., 1990). One can draw two testable conjectures: (1) countries are ranked according to the efficiency of their average production techniques, and, in the product space, of the (price-weighted) performance characteristics of their outputs, irrespectively of relative prices, and (2) the absence of any significant relationship between these gaps and international differences in the capital/output ratios. Wide differences apply also to the capabilities of developing new products and to different time lags in producing them after they have been introduced into the world economy. Indeed, the international distribution of innovative capabilities regarding new products is at least as uneven as that regarding production processes.

Second, development and industrialization are strictly linked to the inter- and intra-national diffusion of 'superior' techniques. Related, there is only one or few 'best-practice' techniques of production that correspond to the technological frontier. In developing economies, industrialization is closely linked to the borrowing, imitation and adaptation of established technologies together with the adoption and diffusion of novel organizational forms from more advanced economies. These processes, in turn, are influenced by the specific capabilities of each economy. In this context, evolutionary micro-theories can account for the processes by which technological gaps and national institutional diversities jointly reproduce themselves over long time spans. Conversely, in other circumstances, this institutional and technological diversity among countries may foster catching-up (and, rarely leapfrogging) in innovative capabilities and per capita incomes. To sum up, evolutionary theories predict persistent technological gaps across firms and across countries, and persistent income gaps. The next section considers the secular evidence in this respect.

3 THE LONG-TERM DISTRIBUTION OF INNOVATIVE/IMITATIVE SEARCH FOR NEW TECHNOLOGIES AND ITS RELATION TO ECONOMIC GROWTH

After the Industrial Revolution, countries increasingly differed in innovation activities and income levels. Starting from relatively homogeneous conditions in Europe, China and the Arab World (Cipolla, 1965; Maddison, 2001), the subsequent international distribution of innovation activities has been highly skewed (Dosi et al., 1990; Castaldi et al., 2009). The innovation process has been concentrated in a small group of countries, with both restricted entry (with Japan, and more recently Korea and Taiwan, being the only entrants in the twentieth century) and few changes in relative rankings. Simultaneously, starting from similar pre-industrialization per capita income levels among countries, one observes diverging growth patterns after the Industrial Revolution. Even in the post-World War II period, considered as a period of growing uniformity, evidence does not support the hypothesis of convergence of all countries' per capita income levels (DeLong, 1988; Verspagen, 1991; Durlauf and Johnson, 1992; Easterly et al., 1992; Soete and Verspagen, 1993; Quah, 1996; and Castaldi and Dosi, 2009). On the contrary, the divergence in incomes has accelerated over time. Clark and Feenstra (2003) claim that:

> Per capita incomes across the world seemingly diverged by much more in 1910 than in 1800, and more in 1990 than 1910 – this despite the voluminous literature on exogenous growth that has stressed the convergence of economies, or, to be more precise, 'conditional' convergence. (Op. cit., p. 277)

Nevertheless, some evidence exists of *local* convergence, that is, within subsets of countries grouped according to initial characteristics such as income levels (Durlauf and Johnson, 1992) or geographical location. The patterns illustrated in Figure 2.1 from Durlauf and Quah (1998) show a

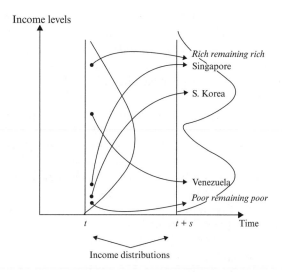

Source: Durlauf and Quah (1998).

Figure 2.1   *Evolving cross-country income distributions*

two-humped distribution of countries with low (albeit positive) transition probabilities between the 'poor' and 'rich' clubs (and vice versa).

Bimodality is a separating tendency between poor and rich countries, characterized by different income levels. Simultaneously, the same shape of a given distribution may conceal different intra-distribution dynamics (Quah, 1997). Have poor countries converged to a common low income level and rich countries to their own high income level or are the two modes the result of shifts in ranks between poor and rich countries? The answer depends on the respective weight of persistence and mobility of countries inside the distribution. The period 1960 to 1988 was character-ized by persistent relative rankings, albeit with some exceptions (ibid.). Upward mobility was demonstrated by the 'growth miracles' of countries like Hong Kong, Japan, Korea, Singapore and Taiwan, whereas 'growth disasters' include some Sub-Saharan African countries and Venezuela, which was the among the richest countries in 1960 but later on fell into the 'poor' countries' club.

Recent evidence on the world income distribution has shown that population-weighted measures of inequality decreased in the last two decades, mainly due to China and India (Bourguignon et al., 2004). This finding supports the convergence hypothesis, but does not explain the increasingly frequent 'marginalization' episodes (Melchior and Telle,

2001). There is convergence among OECD economies and within a broader group including the East Asian economies, and China and India after 1980 (Dowrick and DeLong, 2003). 'However, these episodes of successful economic growth and convergence have been counterbalanced by many economies' loss of their membership in the world's convergence club' (op. cit., p. 193).

At the same time, across-group differences in growth performances seem persistent. One observes persistently wide and in some cases growing (in some Latin American Countries) labour productivity gaps vis-à-vis the international frontier after World War II. Available evidence witnesses a persistent dispersion in productivity measures (Van Ark and McGuckin, 1999). While on average countries in the OECD area have moved closer to the US benchmark, this does not hold for the rest of the world.

A crucial issue is the relation between technical change and economic growth. Technological learning not only includes inventive discovery and patenting, but also imitation, reverse engineering and adoption of capital-embodied innovations, learning by doing and learning by using (Freeman, 1982; Dosi, 1988; Patel and Pavitt, 1994). Moreover, technological change parallels organizational innovation. Significant links exist between innovation, measured in a narrow sense by patenting and R&D activities, and GDP per capita (without suggesting causality), which, however, have changed over time.

Evidence on OECD countries suggests that the relationship between innovative activities and GDP levels grew closer over time and is highly significant after World War II (Dosi et al., 1994). Moreover, innovative dynamism, measured by the growth of patenting by different countries in the United States, seems positively correlated with per capita GDP growth, (see Table 2.1). This link is particularly robust between 1913 and 1970. In the 1970s, the relation gets weaker and loses statistical significance. The link strengthened in the 1980s, lost significance again in the 1990s and recovered in the most recent period. In our view, this circumstantial evidence shows turbulent and uncertain dynamics in the 'political economies' of different countries governing the dynamics between technological learning, demand generation and growth.

Since World War II, growth rates of GDP appear closely correlated with: (1) domestic innovative activities, (2) the rates of investment in capital equipment and (3) international technological diffusion (DeLong, 1988; Soete and Verspagen, 1993; Laursen, 2000; Meliciani, 2001). Fagerberg (1988) finds a high correlation between the level of 'economic development', in terms of per capita GDP, and the level of 'technological development', measured by R&D investment or patenting activity.[2] There is no strong evidence of convergence of innovative capabilities (PT and

Table 2.1   Correlation coefficients between innovative activity and output for OECD economies, 1890–2003

	g	y	PT	pt	Y
1890–1913					
g	1.00				
y	0.60*	1.00			
PT	0.60*	0.20	1.00		
pt	-0.22	0.05	-0.61*	1.00	
Y	-0.18	-0.66**	0.22	-0.67**	1.00
1913–1929					
g	1.00				
y	0.76**	1.00			
PT	-0.12	-1.21	1.00		
pt	0.66**	0.67**	-0.55*	1.00	
Y	-0.41	-0.62*	0.38	-0.43	1.00
1929–1950					
g	1.00				
y	0.82**	1.00			
PT	0.31	0.41	1.00		
pt	0.66**	0.58*	0.22	1.00	
Y	0.37	0.40	0.56*	0.67**	1.00

	g	y	PT	pt	Y
1970–1977					
g	1.00				
y	0.88**	1.00			
PT	-0.60**	-0.49	1.00		
pt	0.37	0.18	-0.21	1.00	
Y	-0.87**	-0.70**	0.73**	-0.14	1.00
1977–1984					
g	1.00				
y	0.88**	1.00			
PT	-0.36	-0.25	1.00		
pt	0.78**	0.82**	-0.26	1.00	
Y	-0.76**	-0.54*	0.64**	-0.63**	1.00
1984–1991					
g	1.00				
y	0.96**	1.00			
PT	-0.15	-0.13	1.00		
pt	0.94**	0.89**	-0.24	1.00	
Y	0.94**	-0.49*	0.61**	-0.58**	1.00

Table 2.1 (continued)

	g	y	PT	pt	Y
1950–1970					
g	1.00	0.75**	0.38	0.89**	−0.76**
y		1.00	0.40	0.71*	−0.76*
PT			1.00	−0.48	0.63*
pt				1.00	−0.84*
Y					1.00
1970–1977					
g	1.00	0.91**	−0.67**	0.29	−0.47
y		1.00	−0.60*	0.16	−0.48
PT			1.00	−0.28	0.66**
pt				1.00	−0.16
Y					1.00
1991–1998					
g	1.00	0.96**	−0.48*	0.37	−0.34
y		1.00	−0.46*	0.30	−0.25
PT			1.00	−0.27	0.63**
pt				1.00	−0.39
Y					1.00
1998–2003					
g	1.00	0.96**	−0.45*	0.52*	−0.44**
y		1.00	−0.40	0.51*	−0.46*
PT			1.00	−0.30	0.42*
pt				1.00	−0.17
Y					1.00

Note: g = GDP growth; y = GDP per capita growth; PT = US patents per capita at $t = 1$; pt = US patents per capita at $t = 1$. * Significance at 5% level; ** Significance at 1% level.

Sources: 1890 to 1977 for 14 OECD countries: Pavitt and Soete (1981); 1970 to 2003 for 21 OECD countries (Australia, Austria, Belgium, Canada, Denmark, Finland, France, Germany, Hungary, Ireland, Italy, Japan, Korea, Mexico, Netherlands, New Zealand, Norway, Spain, Sweden, Switzerland and United Kingdom): own elaborations on data from OECD and United States Patent and Trademark Office.

pt indicators in Table 2.1), but there is some sign of income convergence. In turn, the capability of innovating and quickly adopting new technologies is strongly correlated with successful trade performance (Dosi et al., 1990).

Moreover, despite technological diffusion taking place at high rates, at least among OECD countries, important specificities in 'national innovation systems' persist, related to the characteristics of scientific and technical infrastructures, local user–producer relationship and other institutional and policy features of countries (Lundvall, 1992; Nelson, 1993; Archibugi et al., 1999). The catch-up of countries like the UK, the United States, Japan and, most recently, the Asian Tigers, depended on their ability to build successful national innovation systems (Freeman, 2002).

To sum up, in the long run the dominant trend is the divergence in relative technological capabilities, production efficiencies and incomes. However, there are two more hopeful messages. First, notwithstanding divergent patterns, one also observed increasing average levels of technological knowledge and per capita income levels within most countries. Second, even though the 'innovators' club' has been small and sticky in its membership, some successful latecomers entered the club (with the United States, Germany and Japan in different periods being the most striking examples), whereas others fell behind and left the club (cf. Argentina over the last century). What about the long-term time-profiles of technological change and economic growth? Can one identify persistent features in the ways technologies and incomes are dynamically coupled?

4 DEVELOPMENT 'REGIMES' WITH TECHNO-ECONOMIC PARADIGMS AND COMPLEMENTARY ORGANIZATIONAL FORMS AND INSTITUTIONS

To understand the evolution of the relation between technological change and economic development, it is useful to turn to the notion of 'techno-economic paradigm' or 'regime' (Freeman and Perez, 1988).[3] One of the first definitions can be found in Perez (1985, p. 443):

> We suggest that the behavior of the relative cost structure of all inputs to production follows more or less predictable trends for relatively long periods. This predictability becomes the basis for the construction of an 'ideal type' of producing organization, which defines the contours of the most efficient and 'least cost' combinations for a given period. It thus serves as a general 'rule-of-thumb' guide for investment and technological decisions. That general guiding model is the 'techno-economic paradigm'.

Each techno-economic paradigm relies on the availability of a specific key factor that presents a set of characteristics:

> The focusing device or main organizing principle of this selective mechanism would be a particular input or set of inputs, capable of strongly influencing the behavior of the relative cost structure. Such an input, which we shall call the 'key factor', is capable of playing a steering role because it fulfills the following conditions:
> (1) clearly perceived low – and descending – relative cost,
> (2) apparently unlimited supply (for all practical purposes),
> (3) obvious potential for all-pervasive influence in the productive sphere, and
> (4) a generally recognized capacity, based on a set of interwoven technical and organizational innovations, to reduce the costs and change the quality of capital equipment, labor and products. (Op. cit. p.444)

Perez (2002) identifies five main technological revolutions in the time span from 1770 to 2000 and five corresponding techno-economic paradigms. Each has a clear 'key factor'. Table 2.2 summarizes the characteristics of the underlying industries and infrastructures of the different techno-economic regimes.

In our view one can certainly talk about a new, ICT-based, techno-economic regime. ICT share distinctive features with previous regimes. First, the new technologies are pervasive, with a range of applications spanning all industries. Second, the new regime relies on a quasi-free crucial input, which is computer power (as compared with energy/electricity yesterday). Third, the establishment of the new regime entails painstaking 'co-evolutionary' requirements between technological and organizational changes (see Sections 5 and 6, and David, 1990 for an illuminating comparison between the fates of the 'dynamo' and of the 'computer'). Fourth, the initial phase of the new regime is characterized by bubble dynamics in the 'core economies' developing them. The new economy bubble following the widespread euphoria of the 1990s bears strong similarities with the panic and euphoria dynamics of the automobile boom in the United States in the 1920s (Freeman, 2001).

The ICT-based techno-economic paradigm is occurring within a regime of globalization of international economic exchanges, but not of globalization of technological capabilities (see Section 7). The capabilities of mastering new technologies are unevenly distributed across countries, and technological leaders explore possible applications of ICT-based technologies.

Table 2.2   *The industries and infrastructures of each technological revolution*

Technological Revolution	New Technologies and New or Redefined Industries	Techno-Economic Paradigm 'Common Sense' Innovation Principles	New or Redefined Infrastructures
FIRST From 1771 *The 'Industrial Revolution'* Britain	Mechanized cotton industry Wrought iron Machinery	Factory production Mechanization Productivity/time-keeping and time-saving Fluidity of movement (as ideal for machines with water power and for transport through canals and other waterways) Local networks	Canals and waterways Turnpike roads Water power (highly improved water wheels)
SECOND From 1829 *Age of Steam and Railways* In Britain and spreading to Continent and US	Steam engines and machinery (made in iron; fuelled by coal) Iron and coal mining (now playing a central role in growth) Railway construction Rolling stock production Steam power for many industries (including textiles)	Economics of agglomeration/industrial cities/national markets Power centres with national networks Scale as progress Standard parts/machine-made machines Energy where needed (steam) Interdependent movement (of machines and transport means)	Railways (use of steam engine) Universal postal service Telegraph (mainly nationally along railway lines) Great ports, great depots and worldwide sailing ships City gas
THIRD From 1875 *Age of Steel, Electricity and Heavy Engineering* US and Germany overtaking Britain	Cheap steel (especially Bessemer) Full development of steam engine for steel ships Heavy chemistry and civil engineering Electrical equipment industry	Giant structures (steel) Economies of scale of plant/vertical integration Distributed power for industry (electricity)	Worldwide shipping in rapid steel steamships (use of Suez Canal) Worldwide railways (use of cheap steel

Table 2.2 (continued)

Technological Revolution	New Technologies and New or Redefined Industries	Techno-Economic Paradigm 'Common Sense' Innovation Principles	New or Redefined Infrastructures
	Copper and cables Canned and bottled food Paper and packaging	Science as a productive force Worldwide networks and empires (cartels) Universal standardization Cost accounting for control Great scale for world market power/'small' is successful, if local	rails and bolts in standard sizes) Great bridges and tunnels Worldwide telegraph Telephone (mainly nationally) Electrical networks (for illumination and industrial use)
FOURTH From 1908 *Age of Oil, the Automobile and Mass Production* In US and spreading to Europe	Mass-produced automobiles Cheap oil and oil fuels Petrochemicals (synthetics) Internal combustion engine for automobiles, transport, tractors, airplanes, war tanks and electricity Home electrical appliances Refrigerated and frozen foods	Mass production/mass markets Economies of scale (product & market volume)/horizontal integration Standardization of products Energy intensity Synthetic materials Functional specialization/ hierarchical pyramids Centralization/ metropolitan centres– suburbanization National powers, world agreements and confrontations	Networks of roads, highways, ports and airports Networks of oil ducts Universal electricity (industry and homes) Worldwide analogue telecommu- nications (telephone, telex and cablegrams) wire and wireless
FIFTH From 1971 *Age of Information and Telecommu- nications*	The information revolution Cheap microelectronics Computers, software Telecommunications	Information-intensity (microelectronics- based ICT) Decentralized integration/network structures	World digital telecommu- nications (cable, fibre optics, radio and satellite)

Table 2.2   (continued)

Technological Revolution	New Technologies and New or Redefined Industries	Techno-Economic Paradigm 'Common Sense' Innovation Principles	New or Redefined Infrastructures
In US and spreading to Europe and Asia	Control instruments Computer-aided biotechnology and new materials	Knowledge as capital/ intangible value-added Heterogeneity, diversity, adaptability. Segmentation of markets/proliferation of niches Economies of scope and specialization combined with scale Globalization/ interaction between global and local Inward and outward cooperation/clusters Instant contact and action/instant global communications	Internet/electronic mail and other e-services Multiple source, flexible use, electricity networks High-speed physical transport links (by land, air and water)

Source: Perez (2002).

5   THE PAINSTAKING DIFFUSION OF THE NEW REGIME

The evidence supports our view that the 'ICT revolution' is far from having expressed its full potential yet. 'Technological revolutions' display long diffusion processes, because they entail the co-evolution and co-adaptation of new technologies, new organizational forms, new institutions and new consumption patterns:

> The eventual supplanting of an entrenched techno-economic regime involves profound changes whose revolutionary nature is better revealed by their eventual breadth and depth of the clusters of innovation that emerge than by the pace at which they achieve their influence. Exactly because of the breadth and

depth of the changes entailed, successful elaboration of a new 'general purpose' technology requires the development and coordination of a vast array of complementary tangible and intangible elements: new physical plant and equipment, new kinds of workforce skills, new organizational forms, new forms of legal property, new regulatory framework, new habits of mind and patterns of taste. (David, 2001, p. 53)

The well-known claim by Robert Solow (1987) about seeing computers everywhere but in productivity statistics captured the amazement of economists for not being able to observe the gains from a new technological revolution. In fact, if one takes into account the existence of powerful retardation factors, then the paradox disappears. Productivity gains diffuse across industries through a painstaking process that needs adaptation of economic activities to the new paradigm. We are only starting to observe the real gains from the current ICT-based techno-economic paradigm (David, 2001).

An example on retardation factors refers to e-commerce and e-business, which are new forms of trade that have yet to emerge as major transaction channels (Castaldi et al., 2004). The low diffusion of e-business is associated with two bottlenecks. First, the lack of regulatory embeddedness of such transactions (e.g., enforcement of contracts) affects reputation mechanisms (i.e., ultimately, institutional retardation factors). Second, the need for reliable 'coding technologies', which guarantee that online transactions are safe and data are protected (i.e., sheer technological barriers).

These new forms of trade bring to the forefront delicate institutional issues related to the 'integrity' of the new markets. With these new technologies it becomes more difficult, for example, to check the identity of economic agents and to sanction deviant behaviours. The existing institutions that provide the 'regulatory embeddedness' for 'old' transactions are no longer sufficient to guarantee the new forms of trade. New arrangements are needed to ensure integrity and enforcement of contracts. New forms of trading demand the development of new institutional mechanisms aimed at providing trading processes within some governing institutions.

The emergence of the law merchant system protecting medieval fairs is an old example with bearings on contemporary issues (Milgrom et al., 1990). This institutional system ensured the effectiveness of reputation mechanisms even when the trade arena expanded beyond a critical level whereby traders were not meeting the same trading partners on a regular basis. The new institution successfully created incentives for merchants both to behave honestly and to sanction deviant behaviour. This was achieved using less information than would have been needed to distribute perfect information for all agents in the system, which was a condition way too costly to fulfil. The lesson for the 'new economy' is the need to develop reputation mechanisms, forms of community identification and tools for contract enforcement. This example illustrates co-evolutionary requirements linking the diffusion of new technological paradigms and the painstaking developments of new institutional arrangements governing microeconomic interactions.

Co-evolutionary requirements concern also the mutual adaptation of new technologies and corporate organizational forms crucially affecting the impact of ICT. Recent efforts aimed at understanding the role of ICT in economic growth are acknowledging these co-evolutionary require-ments. Mansell et al. (2007) review many studies where institutional and organizational changes are complementary changes that need to accom-pany technological advances in ICT. Micro-studies show that productivity gains from ICT at the firm level are closely inter-related with the ability of firms to implement complementary organizational changes. Our review of evidence on the impact of ICT starts with these studies.

6 THE EMPIRICAL EVIDENCE ON THE IMPACT OF ICT

In this section we turn to the available evidence on the economic impact of ICT. Micro-, meso- and macro-studies aim to investigate the causal link between ICT and productivity growth. We focus on the implications of stylized facts for our evolutionary interpretation. We start by discussing firm-level evidence followed by more aggregate studies.[4]

6.1 The Micro-evidence

A recent literature has relied on micro-data to estimate the impact of ICT at the level of firm or workers. Brynjolfsson and Hitt (2000) review two strands of micro-studies. First, a case-based literature provides evidence that the impact of ICT at the firm level coincides with organizational changes, such as authority relationships, decentralization of local deci-sions, shifts in task content and/or changes in reward schemes. Despite changes in organizational practice, many workers remain trapped in old work practices. Inertial forces are at work, which explain the inability of firms to instantaneously exploit the potential of new technologies (Brynjolfsson et al., 1997).

A second strand is an econometric literature using large datasets. An overview by Pilat (2004) shows that, first, most studies find a positive relation between the level of ICT and firm productivity, without implying causality. Second, different factors moderate the impact of ICT at firm level, including the co-occurrence of matching skills of the workforce, appropriate organizational practices and other forms of technological innovation. Moreover, the size and age of the firm seem to influence the effect of ICT adoption upon productivity. Third, while improvements in ICT spread quickly throughout the economy, the complementary organizational changes at the firm level rely on a process of 'co-invention' by individual firms (Bresnahan and Greenstein, 1997), suggesting co-evolutionary processes combining (1) the adoption of information and communication technologies, (2) complementary organizational changes and (3) innovation in the form of new products and services (Bresnahan et al., 2002). Conversely some evidence shows that the adoption of ICT without corresponding changes in organizational practices may be detrimental for the company. It is the combination of the three changes mentioned above that drives productivity gains. Fourth, some econometric studies (Brynjolfsson and Hitt, 1995 for the United States and Greenan et al., 2001 for France) used fixed-effects models to estimate the impact of ICT on productivity to capture firm-specific determinants. The estimates are substantially lower and indicate that the ability of firms to exploit gains from ICT relates to intrinsic organizational capabilities.

Bartelsman and Doms (2000) also discuss insights from micro-studies on the relationship between productivity and advanced technology. The use of the latest technology turns out to be highly correlated with other variables such as human capital. Doms et al. (1997) show that plants with above-average productivity levels because of ICT, also had above average performance before the introduction of this technology, as they choose consistently the most advanced technologies. In this sense, also under an ICT-centred regime of technological change asymmetries across firms are the rule. In turn, this can be interpreted as an evolutionary story of path-dependence and persistent performance differentials among firms.

6.2   The Aggregate Evidence on the Impact of ICT

A puzzling result in the empirical literature on the impact of ICT is the fact that more aggregate studies do not find the foregoing positive relation between ICT and productivity often revealed by micro-studies (Draca et al., 2007). Daveri (2002) illustrated this puzzle for Europe: labour productivity growth does not have any significant relationship with ICT investment. The Solow paradox seems to hold at a macro-level. Further insights can be gained by using an industry-level perspective. In fact, sectors display a striking variance in productivity performances: ICT-*producing* industries show strong and robust productivity gains, while the evidence is much weaker for ICT-*using* industries (Van Ark et al., 2003).

For the United States, Oliner and Sichel (2000) identify ICT investment as the main driver of the recent productivity revival. However, their results have been questioned by Gordon (2003), who argues that their growth accounting methodology over-estimates the contribution of ICT investment.[5] Most of the productivity gap between the United States and the European Union can be attributed to ICT-*using* industries (Van Ark et al., 2003), and in particular to market services. The apparent 'Solow paradox' in Europe might be due more to lower efficiency in the use of information and communication technologies than to a lower level of investment in ICT in market services (Inklaar et al., 2008).

To summarize, industry-level studies strongly point at the uneven inter-sectoral diffusion of ICT-based technologies and their equally uneven impact upon productivity growth.

Given the foregoing features of the new ICT-based regime and the evidence on its impact on productivity growth, how has this new cluster of technologies influenced the international patterns of innovation, innovation diffusion and growth?

7 THE GENERATION AND DIFFUSION OF INNOVATIONS, SKILLS AND ORGANIZATIONAL CAPABILITIES: THE INTERNATIONAL PICTURE

Innovation activities have remained concentrated within a small group of countries over time. Not surprisingly, such patterns in innovative outputs are matched by persistent international differences in the share of resources devoted to formal technological learning (as revealed by privately financed R&D). So, while Korea has overtaken 'developed' countries like Italy, most developing countries continue to display negligible levels of private investments in R&D (Figure 2.2).

Certainly, ICT technologies have facilitated the diffusion of information. However, there is little evidence of a generalized acceleration in the rates of adoption of both 'new' (e.g. ICT-related) and 'old' technologies (from telephones to tractors). This is due in part to very different levels of education and number of researchers (Table 2.3) across countries, which imply uneven national *absorptive capacities* for new technologies.

As for new technologies, the diffusion of ICT is highly asymmetric across countries, even across OECD economies. The heterogeneity observed for these advanced economies suggests even larger gaps for developing countries.

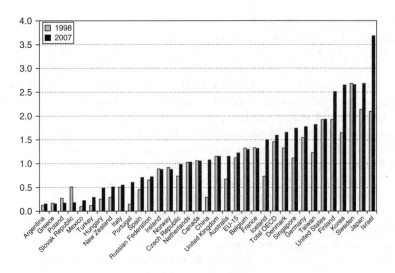

Source: Authors' calculations on the basis of Main Science and Technology Indicators, OECD (2009a).

Figure 2.2   Intensity of private sector R&D (as % of GDP), 1998–2007

Table 2.3   Number of researchers (per 1000 labour force), 1991–2006

	1991	1994	1997	2000	2003	2006
European Union (15)	4.4	4.8	5.0	5.5	5.9	6.3
US	7.6	7.7	8.4	9.0	9.7	9.4
Japan	7.5	8.1	9.2	9.6	10.1	10.7
Argentina	1.0	0.8	1.6	1.6	1.5	1.9
Brazil				0.8	0.9	1.2
Chile	0.9	1.0	1.0	1.1	1.9	
Mexico		0.4	0.6	0.6	0.8	1.1
Venezuela				0.1	0.2	0.3
Singapore		3.5	4.6	7.4	8.6	9.1
Taiwan			5.0	5.7	7.5	9.0
South Korea			4.7	4.9	6.6	8.3
China	0.7	0.8	0.8	1.0	1.1	1.6

Source: Authors' calculations on the basis of Main Science and Technology Indicators, OECD (2009a). Data for Latin America are from RICYT (2000).

Table 2.4   Operational stock of multi-purpose industrial robots, 2001–06

Country	2001	2006	2006 Density (Per 10000 Manufacturing Workers)
Japan[a]	361.232	351.658	349
Korea[a]	41.267	68.420	187[a]
Germany	99.195	132.594	186
Italy	43.911	60.049	138
United States	97.257	150.725	99

Note: a. The figures for these countries include all types of robots and are not strictly comparable to data of other countries.

Source: 2001 data from United Nations Economic Commission for Europe (UNECE) and International Federation of Robotics (IFR), *World Robotics 2003*; 2006 data from IFR.

It is useful to distinguish the relative impact of ICT on production and consumption. As for production, investment in ICT capital has increased over the last 30 years as well as investment in factory automation (from mechanical engineering to continuous cycle processes). At the same time, we are still in an initial phase of the diffusion of ICT, with an under-utilized potential, in particular in developing countries. In the United States, ICT investment represented about 28 per cent of total investment in the period 1995 to 2006, while in the European Union this share was below 18 per cent (see www.euklems.net).

Related to ICT, the degree of automation in production has greatly increased, but remained highly heterogeneous among countries. For example, the number of installed multi-purpose industrial robots was highest in Japan, followed by some European countries and Korea, and the United States in 2006 (Table 2.4). In terms of density, Japan, Korea and Germany stand out.

As for consumption, the evidence again points to highly uneven diffusion rates of ICT across countries, even within the OECD (Table 2.5). The United States is far ahead in the 'informatization' of its society and the other developed countries follow at considerable distance (except the penetration of mobile phones). Interestingly, there is evidence of a 'digital divide' within the United States (Greenstein and Prince, 2007), with non-urban areas lagging behind in terms of high-speed Internet connection as the better alternative to low-speed/dial-up connection.

At the same time communication costs still remain a barrier to ICT use in a number of OECD countries (see OECD, 2009b).

Table 2.5 Indices of ICT diffusion, per 100 population

Country	Telephone Lines and Cellular Subscribers			Internet Users			Personal Computers			
	1990	1998	2007	1990	1998	2007	1990	1998	2003	2005
OECD										
Austria	42.9	78.9	159.3	0.1	15.4	67.0	6.5	23.8	37.4	61.0
Australia	46.7	77.2	149.5	0.6	22.4	54.0	15.0	36.8	60.2	
Belgium	39.7	66.7	147.3	0	7.8	67.0	8.8	21.5	31.8	38.0
Canada	58.7	84.2	117.2	0.4	25.6	73.0	10.7	32.1	48.7	87.7
Denmark	59.6	102.4	166.4	0.1	22.6	81.0	11.5	37.7	57.7	69.5
Finland	58.6	110.2	148.2	0.2	25.4	79.0	10.0	34.9	44.2	50.0
France	50.0	77.6	146.3	0.1	6.3	51.2	7.1	23.2	34.7	57.9
Germany	44.5	73.7	182.3	0.1	9.9	72.0	9.0	27.9	48.5	60.5
Ireland	28.8	69.6	167.9	0	8.1	57.0	8.6	27.3	42.1	53.0
Italy	39.2	81.0	181.4	0	4.5	54.4	3.6	13.3	23.1	37.0
Japan	44.8	86.8	123.9	0	13.4	68.9	6.0	23.7	38.2	
Netherlands	47.0	80.5	162.1	0.3	22.2	84.0	9.4	32.4	46.7	85.5
Norway	54.8	113.4	152.9	0.7	36.0	85.0	12.1	40.5	52.8	59.4
Spain	31.7	57.7	155.0	0	4.4	52.0	2.8	10.9	19.6	27.9
Sweden	73.5	118.6	174.1	0.6	33.4	80.0	10.5	39.5	62.1	83.5
UK	46.0	80.5	173.9	0.1	13.5	72.0	10.8	26.8	40.6	76.5
US	56.9	90.7	136.9	0.8	30.8	72.5	21.8	45.2	66.0	77.3
Hungary	9.6	44.1	142.4	0	3.9	52.0	1.0	6.5	10.8	14.4
Poland	8.6	27.7	135.8	0	4.1	44.0	0.8	4.9	14.2	13.9

Latin America										
Argentina	9.3	28.1	126.2	0	0.9	25.9	0.7	5.5	8.2	9.0
Brazil	6.5	16.5	83.6	0	1.5	35.2	0.3	3.0	7.5	16.1
Chile	6.7	27.1	104.4	0	1.7	31.0	0.9	6.3	11.9	14.1
Colombia	6.9	20.0	90.7	0	1.1	26.2		3.2	4.9	4.2
Mexico	6.6	13.9	81.0	0	1.3	20.8	0.8	3.7	8.3	13.1
Peru	2.6	9.3	64.8	0	1.2	27.4		3.0	4.3	10.0
Venezuela	7.7	19.8	104.5	0	1.4	20.7	1.0	3.9	6.1	9.3
Israel	34.6	82.8	172.9	0.1	10.0	28.9	6.3	20.1	24.3	
Hong Kong	47.5	105.5	206.4	0	14.5	55.0	4.7	26.0	42.2	59.3
Singapore	36.3	73.2	175.5	0	19.1	68.0	6.6	37.0	62.2	68.4
Korea	30.8	75.1	136.6	0	6.8	76.3	3.7	18.2	55.8	53.7
India	0.6	2.3	23.4	0	0.1	6.9	0	0.3	0.7	1.5
Russ. Fed.	14.0	20.3	134.5	0	0.8	21.1	0.3	3.5	8.9	12.2
China	0.6	8.9	68.7	0	0.2	16.0	0	0.9	2.8	4.8
World average	14.9	28.2		0	3.7		3.4	8.0	12.8	

Source: Elaborations on United Nations Millennium Indicators.

63

Among developing countries, East Asian countries such as Malaysia, the Philippines and Korea have the highest share of ICT-related activities in employment and value-added. In fact, Korea is no longer a developing country and has joined the exclusive club of innovators. Conversely, most Latin American countries and few Eastern European ones remain at the bottom of the list (UNCTAD, 2006).

The OECD Information Technology Outlook (2006) reports the geographical distribution of the top 250 ICT firms. While 116 of these are US firms, followed by 39 Japanese firms, the newcomers are also represented (11 for Taiwan, six for Korea, three for Hong Kong and for India). Mexico is the only Latin American country included (with two top ICT firms).

Another trend of the last decade has been the increased outsourcing of activities by manufacturing firms in developed economies. ICT has enabled the relocation of non-core activities and services to other geographical regions (cf. Miozzo and Soete, 2001). Developing economies play an increasingly large role in ICT-enabled services, with success stories including Singapore for financial services and India for software. The spread of global production chains has made it more important for firms to decide on which activities to outsource to which countries (Cantwell and Janne, 1999). In this respect, the availability of cheap labour in a host country is only attractive for foreign firms if accompanied by good local infrastructure, high-quality labour and, also, tax advantages.

At the same time, the internationalization of innovative activities by MNCs is still incipient. Only 10–15 per cent of all patents by MNCs are originated outside their home countries, comparable to their share in the total patenting of the guest countries. Moreover, most foreign research activities occur within OECD countries (Cantwell, 1992; Patel and Pavitt, 1997; Archibugi and Pietrobelli, 2003).

Multinational companies have been reluctant to transfer key research labs to developing countries. Most firms relocate R&D activities to neighbouring countries with technological centres of excellence to enjoy agglomeration economies and spillovers of new knowledge concentrating in those areas (Dunning, 1993). Most R&D foreign affiliates are located in developed countries and only about 10 per cent in developing countries, of which 8 per cent are in Asia (Table 2.6).

Until recently R&D facilities located abroad were mostly responsible for adapting existing products to local needs and tastes, while most fundamental and strategic R&D was maintained in-house at home (Pearce, 1989). 'Support laboratories' are responsible for short-term technology transfer and facilitate the assimilation of the technologies for local affiliates (Pearce, 1999). Long-term development goals may only be achieved

Table 2.6   Geographical distribution of R&D foreign affiliates, 2004

Region/Economy		Number
Total world		2584
Developed countries		2185
of which	Western Europe	1387
	United States	552
	Japan	29
Developing countries		264
of which	Africa	4
	Latin America and the Caribbean	40
	Asia	216
	South, East and South East Asia	207
Non-attributed		135

Note: The data are based on a sample of 2284 majority-owned foreign affiliates identified in the D&B as engaged in either: commercial, physical and educational research (SIC code 8731); commercial economics and biological research (SIC code 8732); non-commercial research (SIC code 8733); testing laboratories (SIC code 8734).

Source: UNCTAD, based on the Who Owns Whom database of Dun & Bradstreet.

if multinationals move from 'support laboratories' to 'locally integrated laboratories' and even 'international independent laboratories'.

8   CONCLUDING REMARKS AND POLICY IMPLICATIONS

We have led the reader through a long tour building on an evolutionary interpretation of patterns of technological change and their links to economic development. The modes and timing of such dynamics are deeply influenced by the (rare) emergence of new techno-economic paradigms or regimes, driven by constellations of complementary, thoroughly pervasive, micro-technological paradigms.[6]

ICT are drivers of one of such changes in techno-economic regimes, but are at an early stage of diffusion, particularly in developing countries. The new techno-economic paradigm represents both an opportunity and a threat for developing countries. The pervasiveness of these new technologies makes their adoption a development necessity, independently from their patterns of 'comparative advantage'. Countries that successfully overtook technological leaders mastered the technology behind the dominant techno-economic paradigm (Freeman, 1995). Examples are Britain and the steam engine, Germany and the United States for chemicals and Fordist mass production, Japan and Korea for electronics and most recently China and India for ICT-based products and services. Thus, the catching up of technological followers depends on getting to the frontier of technological advances of the dominant techno-economic paradigm.

Given this, we offer some thoughts about a possible ICT-based development path. First, the availability of natural resources and its utilization is unrelated to the need of ICT diffusion. Natural advantages have never been a sufficient condition for a country to catch up. Instead, created advantages have been the source of sustained advantages (Freeman, 2002).

Second, catching up in ICT investment is crucial for developing countries to build their 'national absorptive capacity', also for foreign-generated knowledge (Bell and Pavitt, 1993). While latecomers have the potential to achieve the highest growth rates, this potential is only realized if local firms are able to recognize, exploit and internalize the knowledge underlying the new technologies. ICT infrastructures play a crucial role in the latter process.

Third, developing countries need to nurture their corporate organizations that can exploit the opportunities associated with ICT. The role of governmental policies for catch-up in general has been stressed already in the work of institutional economists like Amsden (1989).

The current ICT-based techno-economic regime is emerging under the 'political economy' of globalization of international economic exchanges, but not of globalization of technological capabilities so far, as shown by the evidence presented in this work. In a globalized world local and national systems of innovation come to play an even greater role. As Freeman (1995) puts it:

> national and regional systems of innovation remain an essential domain of economic analysis. Their importance derives from the networks of relationships which are necessary for any firm to innovate. Whilst external international connections are certainly of growing importance, the influence of the national education system, industrial relations, technical and scientific institutions, government policies, cultural traditions and many other national institutions is fundamental. (Op. cit. p. 5)

This point is also made by Porter (1990) in his work on the competitive advantage of nations.

There are no standard recipes for successful economic growth, yet one can identify fundamental policy ingredients and processes derived from the past, which are valid for the future (Dosi et al., 1994; Cimoli et al., 2006). First, policies aimed at increasing the opportunities for scientific and technological innovation have mostly started by ensuring a rapid expansion of the number of qualified engineers and strengthening of graduate education (Lazonick, 2007). Broader education and training policies also help to build socially distributed learning and technological capabilities. The development of technical and scientific institutions, increasingly networked with the private sector, also plays a key role. The 'congruence' between science, technology, culture and entrepreneurship as 'sub-systems' within national innovation systems has also been emphasized (Freeman, 2002).

Second, most success stories show sophisticated policy efforts fostering technological learning and penalizing rent-seeking behaviours even under regimes of partial protection of the domestic market: incentive alignment measures favouring export-oriented strategies are a major case in point. In general, targeted support measures, for instance affecting the ownership structure of firms or targeting 'national champions', are effective tools for boosting technological activities at the firm level. These have to be combined with carefully chosen selection mechanisms affecting competition, entry and bankruptcy, price regulations and allocation of finance. As a trade-off, nurturing capability-building has to be matched by mechanisms stifling inertia and rent-seeking.

Third, the patterns of information distributions and interaction across economic actors have also been subject to policy intervention. One observes diverse 'political economies' and 'social pacts', displaying nonetheless some common features of generalized consensus-building. In the case of the Far East these measures were apparently based on combinations among authoritarian politics, corporate paternalism and the ability to widely distribute the benefits from fast growth.

Fourth, at the firm level, effective ingredients for productivity growth have been high rates of physical and intangible investment and the progressive integration of production design, marketing and research activities.

Fifth, in terms of international specialization, success stories have shown a commodity composition of production and trade increasingly centred on technologies and products featuring high innovative opportunities and high income elasticities.

History shows a variety of country- and sector-specific policies with the trade-offs discussed above. A comparison between the experience of countries in East Asia and Latin America is particularly interesting. Korea – and neighbouring economies – have been able to 'twist around' absolute and relative prices and channel resources stemming from 'static' comparative advantages to the development of activities with higher learning opportunities and demand elasticities (Amsden, 1989). They penalized rent-seeking behaviours by private firms. Major actors in technological learning have been large business groups – the chaebols – which internalized skills for the selection of technologies acquired from abroad, their efficient use and their adaptation. Subsequently, they were able to develop impressive engineering capabilities (Kim, 1993).

In East Asia, this process has been further supported by policies improving human resources. This contrasts the Latin American experience, where the arrangement between the state and the private sector has often been more indulgent over inefficiencies and rent-accumulation, and less attentive to the accumulation of socially diffused technological capabilities and skills. Thus, ultimately, success or failure appears to depend on the combinations of different institutional arrangements and policies, in so far as they affect learning processes by individuals and organizations, on the one hand, and selection processes, including market competition, on the other.

A similar reasoning applies to the opportunities and threats offered by ICT. Policy-makers need to carefully balance these trade-offs and complementarities to promote a virtuous ICT-based growth path for developing countries.

NOTES

*   This chapter draws upon Cimoli and Dosi (1995) and Castaldi et al. (2004).
1.   *Inside the Black Box* is an influential book by Nathan Rosenberg (1982), who is a pioneer of the emerging discipline on the economics of innovation and technological change.
2.   His sample includes most world economies and covers the years 1960–82.
3.   'Techno-economic paradigm' is a *macro* notion, while the 'paradigms' discussed in Section 2 address the features of individual technologies. In fact, the two notions are complementary, with the former being composed of interrelated constellations of the latter.
4.   We will not discuss here the difficulties of measuring ICT and its contribution to productivity growth (Van Ark, 2002). Productivity growth measures are sensitive to the methods used to account for price declines and quality changes, and the definition of ICT.
5.   First, their methodology assumes that instantaneous productivity gains from ICT capital. Retardation factors imply a necessary time lag for economic actors to enjoy the benefits of a new technology. Second, most aggregate productivity growth comes from the productivity revival in the retail sector, which in turn can be attributed solely to the displacement of less productive establishments with more productive ones (Foster et al., 2002).
6.   In the predominant US literature following Freeman and Perez (1988), these have become known under the heading of 'general-purpose technologies' (Bresnahan and Trajtenberg, 1995).

REFERENCES

Amsden, A.H. (1989), *Asia's Next Giant: South Korea and Late Industrialization*, Oxford: Oxford University Press.

Archibugi, D. and Pietrobelli, C. (2003), 'The globalisation of technology and its implications for developing countries. Windows of opportunity or further burden?', *Technological Forecasting and Social Change*, **70**(9), 861–83.

Archibugi, D., Howells, J. and Michie, J. (1999), *Innovation Policy in a Global Economy*, Cambridge, UK: Cambridge University Press.

Bartelsman, E.J. and Doms, M. (2000), 'Understanding productivity: lessons from longitudinal microdata', *Journal of Economic Literature*, **38**(3), 569–94.

Bell, M. and Pavitt, K. (1993), 'Technological accumulation and industrial growth: contrasts between developed and developing countries', *Industrial and Corporate Change*, **2**(2), 157–210.

Bourguignon, F., Levin, V. and Rosenblatt, D. (2004), 'Declining international inequality and economic divergence: reviewing the evidence through different lenses', *Economie Internationale*, **100**(4), 13–15.

Bresnahan, T. and Greenstein, S. (1997), 'Technical progress and co-invention in computing and in the use of computers', *Brookings Papers on Economics Activity: Microeconomics*, **1996**, 1–83.

Bresnahan, T. and Trajtenberg, M. (1995), 'General purpose technologies: "Engines of Growth"', *Journal of Econometrics*, **65**(1), 83–108.

Bresnahan, T.F., Brynjolfsson, E. and Hitt, L.M. (2002), 'Information technology, workplace organization and the demand for skilled labor: firm-level evidence', *Quarterly Journal of Economics*, February, **117**(1), 339–76.

Brynjolfsson, E. and Hitt, L.M. (1995), 'Information technology as a factor of production: the role of differences among firms', *Economics of Innovation and New Technology*, **3**(4), 183–200.

Brynjolfsson, E. and Hitt, L.M. (2000), 'Beyond computation: information technology, organizational transformation and business performance', *The Journal of Economic Perspectives*, **14**(4), 23–48.

Brynjolfsson, E., Renshaw, A. and Van Alstyne, M. (1997), 'The matrix of change', *Sloan Management Review*, **38**(2), 37–54.

Cantwell, J. (1992), 'The internationalization of technological activity and its implications for competitiveness', in O. Granstrand, L. Hakanson and S. Sjolander (eds), *Technology, Management and International Business*, Chichester and New York: Wiley.

Cantwell, J. and Janne, O. (1999), 'Technological globalization and innovative centres: the role of corporate technological leadership and locational hierarchy', *Research Policy*, **28**(2–3), 119–44.

Castaldi, C. and Dosi, G. (2009), 'The patterns of output growth of firms and countries: new evidence on scale invariances and specificities', *Empirical Economics*, **37**(3), 475–95.

Castaldi, C., Cimoli, M., Correa, N. and Dosi, G. (2004), 'Technological learning, policy regimes and growth in a "Globalized Economy": general patterns and the Latin American experience', LEM Working Paper 2004/01, Sant'Anna School of Advanced Studies, Pisa, Italy.

Castaldi, C., Cimoli, M., Correa, N. and Dosi, G. (2009), 'Technological learning, policy regimes and growth: the long term patterns and some specificities of a "Globalized" economy', in Cimoli, Dosi and Stiglitz (2009).

Cimoli, M. and Dosi, G. (1995), 'Technological paradigms, patterns of learning and development: an introductory roadmap', *Journal of Evolutionary Economics*, **5**(3), 243–68.

Cimoli, M., Dosi, G. and Stiglitz, J. (eds) (2009), *Industrial Policy and Development:*

The Political Economy of Capabilities Accumulation, Oxford/New York: Oxford University Press.

Cimoli, M., Dosi, G., Nelson, R. and Stiglitz, J. (2006), 'Institutions and policies shaping industrial development: an introductory note', *LEM Working Paper* No. 2006/02, forthcoming in Cimoli, Dosi and Stiglitz (2009).

Cipolla, C.M. (1965), *Guns and Sails in the Early Phase of European Expansion, 1400–1700*, London: Collins.

Clark, G. and Feenstra, R. (2003), 'Technology in the great divergence', in M.D. Bordo, A.M. Taylor and J.G. Williamson (eds), *Globalization in Historical Perspective*, Chicago and London: University of Chicago Press.

Daveri, F. (2002), 'The New Economy in Europe, 1992–2001', *Oxford Review of Economic Policy*, **18**(3), 345–62.

David, P.A. (1990), 'The dynamo and the computer: an historical perspective of the modern productivity paradox', *American Economic Review Papers and Proceedings*, **80**(2), 355–61.

David, P.A. (2001), 'Understanding digital technology's evolution and the path of measured productivity growth: present and future in the mirror of the past', in E. Brynjolfsson and B. Kahin (eds), *Understanding the Digital Economy*, Cambridge, MA: MIT Press.

DeLong, B.J. (1988), 'Productivity growth, convergence and welfare', *American Economic Review*, **78**(5), 1138–54.

Doms, M.E., Dunne, T. and Troske, K. (1997), 'Workers, wages and technology', *Quarterly Journal of Economics*, **112**(1), 253–90.

Dosi, G. (1982), 'Technological paradigms and technological trajectories: a suggested interpretation of the determinants and directions of technical change', *Research Policy*, **11**(3), 147–62.

Dosi, G. (1988), 'Sources, procedures and microeconomic effects of innovation', *Journal of Economic Literature*, **26**(3), 1120–71.

Dosi, G., Freeman, C. and Fabiani, S. (1994), 'The process of economic development: introducing some stylized facts and theories on technologies, firms and institutions', *Industrial and Corporate Change*, **3**(1), 1–45.

Dosi, G., Orsenigo, L. and Sylos Labini, M. (2005), 'Technology and the Economy', in N.J. Smelser and R. Swedberg (eds), *Handbook of Economic Sociology*, 2nd edition, Princeton, NJ: Princeton University Press.

Dosi, G., Pavitt, K. and Soete, L. (1990), *The Economics of Technical Change and International Trade*, London: Harvester Wheatsheaf.

Dowrick, S. and DeLong, B. (2003), 'Globalization and convergence', in M. Bordo, A.M. Taylor and J.G. Williamson (eds), *Globalization in Historical Perspective*, Chicago and London: University of Chicago Press.

Draca, M., Sadun, R. and Van Reenen, J. (2007), 'Productivity and ICT: a review of the evidence', in Mansell et al. (eds).

Dunning, J.H. (1993), *Multinational Enterprises and the Global Economy*, Wokingham, UK and Rending, MA, USA: Addison-Wesley.

Durlauf, S.N. and Johnson, P.A. (1992), 'Local versus global convergence across national economies', *NBER Working Paper No. 3996*.

Durlauf, S.N. and Quah, D. (1998), 'The new empirics of economic growth', London School of Economics, Centre for Economic Performance, Discussion Paper No. 384.

Easterly, W., King, R., Levine, R. and Rebelo, S. (1992), 'How do national policies affect long-run growth? A research agenda', World Bank, Discussion Paper.

Fagerberg, J. (1988), 'Why growth rates differ', in G. Dosi, C. Freeman, R. Nelson, G. Silverberg and L. Soete, *Technical Change and Economic Theory*, London: Pinter.

Foster, L., Haltiwanger, J. and Krizan, C.J. (2002), 'The link between aggregate and micro productivity growth: evidence from retail trade', *NBER Working Paper* No. 9120.

Freeman, C. (1982), *The Economics of Industrial Innovation*, London: Francis Pinter.

Freeman, C. (1995), 'The "national system of innovation" in historical perspective', *Cambridge Journal of Economics*, **19**(1), 5–24.

Freeman, C. (2001), 'A hard landing for the "New Economy"? Information technology and the US national system of innovation', *Structural Change and Economic Dynamics*, **12**(2), 115–39.

Freeman, C. (2002), 'Continental, national and sub-national innovation systems – complementarity and economic growth', *Research Policy*, **31**(2), 191–211.

Freeman, C. and Perez, C. (1988), 'Structural crises of adjustment: business cycles and investment behaviour', in G. Dosi, C. Freeman, R. Nelson, G. Silverberg and L. Soete (eds), *Technical Change and Economic Theory*, London: Pinter.

Gordon, R.J. (2003), 'Hi-tech innovation and productivity growth: does supply create its own demand?', *NBER Working Paper* No. 9437.

Greenan, N., Mairesse, J. and Topiol-Bensaid, A. (2001) 'Information technology and research and development impact on productivity and skills: looking for correlations on French firm level data', in M. Pohjola (ed.), *Information Technology Productivity and Economic Growth*, Oxford: Oxford University Press, pp. 119–48.

Greenstein, S. and Prince, J. (2007), 'Internet diffusion and the geography of the digital divide in the United States', in Mansell et al. (eds).

Inklaar, R., Timmer, M.P. and Van Ark, B. (2008), 'Market services productivity across Europe and the US', *Economic Policy*, **23**(53), 139–94.

Kim, L. (1993), 'National system of industrial innovation: dynamics of capability building in Korea', in R. Nelson (ed.), *National Innovation Systems*, Oxford: Oxford University Press.

Laursen, K. (2000), *Trade Specialization, Technology and Economic Growth: Theory and Evidence from Advanced Countries*, Cheltenham, UK and Northampton, MA, USA: Edward Elgar.

Lazonick, W. (2007), 'Globalization of the ICT force', in Mansell et al. (eds).

Lundvall, B.A. (1992), *National Systems of Innovation: Towards a Theory of Innovation and Interactive Learning*, London: Pinter.

Maddison, A. (2001), *The World Economy: A Millennial Perspective*, Paris: OECD.

Mansell, R., Avgerou, C., Quah, D. and Silverstone, R. (2007), *The Oxford Handbook of Information and Communication Technologies*, Oxford: Oxford University Press.

Melchior, A. and Telle, K. (2001), 'Convergence and marginalisation', *Forum for Development Studies*, **28**(1), 75–98.

Meliciani, V. (2001), *Technology, Trade and Growth in OECD Countries*, London, New York: Routledge.

Milgrom, P.R., North, D.C. and Weingast, B.R. (1990), 'The role of institutions in the revival of trade: the law merchant, private judges, and the champagne fairs', *Economics and Politics*, **2**(19), 1–23.

Miozzo, M. and Soete, L. (2001), 'Internationalization of services: a technological perspective', *Technological Forecasting and Social Change*, **67**(2&3),
159–85.

Nelson, R.R. (1993), *National Innovation Systems*, Oxford: Oxford University
Press.

OECD (2006), *Information Technology Outlook*, Paris: OECD.

OECD (2009a), *Main Science and Technology Indicators 2009-2*, Paris: OECD.

OECD (2009b), *Communications Outlook*, Paris: OECD.

Oliner and Sichel (2000), 'The resurgence of growth in the late 1990s: is information technology the story?', *Journal of Economic Perspectives*, **14**(4), 3–22.

Patel, P. and Pavitt, K. (1994), 'Uneven (and divergent) technological accumulation among advanced countries: evidence and a framework of explanation',
Industrial and Corporate Change, **3**(3), 759–87.

Patel, P. and Pavitt, K. (1997), 'The technological competencies of world's largest
firms: complex and path-dependent, but not much variety', *Research Policy*,
26(2), 141–56.

Pavitt, K. and Soete, L. (1981), 'International differences in economic growth
and the international location of innovation', in H. Giersch (ed.), *Emerging
Technologies: Consequences for Economic Growth, Structural Change and
Unemployment*, Tubingen: JCB Mohr.

Pearce, R.D. (1989), *The Internationalisation of Research and Development by
Multinational Enterprises*, London: Macmillan.

Pearce, R.D. (1999), 'Decentralized R&D and strategic competitiveness: globalised
approaches to generation and use of technology in multinational enterprises',
Research Policy, **28**(2–3), 157–78.

Perez, C. (1985), 'Micro-electronics, long waves and world structural change: new
perspectives for developing countries', *World Development*, **133**, 441–63.

Perez, C. (2002), *Technological Revolutions and Financial Capital*, Cheltenham,
UK and Northampton, MA, USA: Edward Elgar.

Pilat, D. (2004), 'The ICT productivity paradox: insights from micro-data', *OECD
Economic Studies*, **38**(2004/1).

Porter, M. (1990), *The Competitive Advantage of Nations*, New York: Free Press,
Macmillan.

Quah, D. (1996), 'Twin peaks: growth and convergence in models of distribution
dynamics', *Economic Journal*, **106**(437), 1045–55.

Quah, D. (1997), 'Empirics for growth and distribution: stratification, polarization
and convergence clubs', *Journal of Economic Growth*, **2**(1), 27–59.

RICYT (2000), *El Estado de la Ciencia: Principales Indicadores de Ciencia y
Tecnologia Iberoamericanos/Interamericanos 2000*, Buenos Aires.

Rosenberg, N. (1982), *Inside the Black Box: Technology and Economics*, Cambridge,
MA: Cambridge University Press.

Soete, L. and Verspagen, B. (1993), 'Technology and growth: the complex dynamics of catching up, falling behind and taking over', in A. Szirmai, B. Van Ark
and D. Pilat (eds), *Explaining Economic Growth*, Amsterdam: Elsevier Science
Publishers.

Solow, R. (1987), 'We'd better watch out', *New York Times Book Review*, 12 July.

UNCTAD (2006), *Information Economy Report 2006: The Development Perspective*,
United Nations.

Van Ark (2002), 'Measuring the New Economy: an international comparison',
Review of Income and Wealth, **48**(1), 1–14.

Van Ark, B. and McGuckin, R.H. (1999), 'International comparisons of labor productivity and per capita income', *Monthly Labor Review*, July, 33–41.

Van Ark, B., Inklaar, R. and McGuckin, R.H. (2003), '"Changing gear": productivity, ICT and service industries: Europe and the United States', in J.F. Christensen and P. Maskell (eds), *The Industrial Dynamics of the New Digital Economy*, Cheltenham, UK and Northampton, MA, USA: Edward Elgar.

Verspagen, B. (1991), 'A new empirical approach to catching up or falling behind', *Structural Change and Economic Dynamics*, **2**(2), 359–80.

Vincenti, W.G. (1990), *What Engineers Know and How They Know It*, Baltimore, MD: Johns Hopkins University Press.

3. ICT and productivity growth in Europe: an update and comparison with the US

Mary O'Mahony, Marcel Timmer and Bart Van Ark

1 INTRODUCTION

During the second half of the 1990s the comparative growth performance of Europe vis-à-vis the United States has undergone a marked change. For the first time since World War II labour productivity growth in most countries that have been part of the European Union (EU) fell behind the US for a considerable length of time.[1] Until the beginning of the 1970s, rapid labour productivity growth in the EU was commensurate with a catching-up in terms of GDP per capita levels on the US. A first break in this pattern occurred in the mid-1970s. While catching-up of labour productivity continued, the gap in GDP per capita levels between the EU and the US has not narrowed any further since the mid-1970s (see Figure 3.1). This reflects the slowdown in the growth of labour input in Europe, which was related to increased unemployment, a decline in the labour force participation rates and a fall in average working hours. The second break, which is the focus of this paper, occurred in the mid-1990s when the catching-up of labour productivity also came to a halt. Whereas average annual labour productivity growth in the US accelerated from 1.3 per cent during the period 1980–95 to 2.3 per cent during 1995–2005, EU growth declined from 2.4 per cent to 1.5 per cent.[2] Despite a largely cyclical growth acceleration in EU GDP during 2006 and 2007, productivity growth has not shown any significant improvement.

The striking acceleration in output and productivity growth in the US in the mid-1990s has been much discussed in the literature. A consensus has emerged that faster growth can be traced at least in part to the effects of the ICT revolution. These effects have occurred through rapid technological progress in the production of ICT goods, a large uptake in ICT investment in particular during the second half of the 1990s and productivity growth

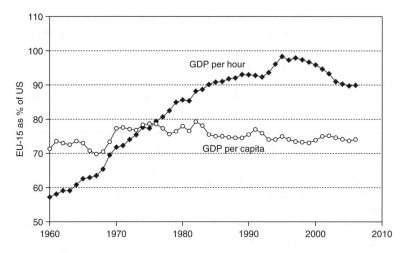

Note: EU-15 refers to the 15 countries constituting the European Union before 2004 and includes Austria, Belgium, Denmark, Finland, France, Germany, Greece, Ireland, Italy, Luxembourg, the Netherlands, Portugal, Spain, Sweden and the United Kingdom. The EU has expanded to include ten new member states mainly in Central and Eastern Europe in 2004 and another two in 2007, which are not included here. Relative levels are based on purchasing power parities for GDP for 2002 from the OECD.

Source: The Conference Board and Groningen Growth and Development Centre, Total Economy Database, January 2007, http://www.conference-board.org/economics/ database.htm; accessed 21 March 2010.

Figure 3.1   Total economy GDP, GDP per hour worked and GDP per capita in EU-15 (US = 100), 1955–2005

as a result of more intensive ICT use, in particular in the service sector of the economy, such as finance and distributive trades sectors (Triplett and Bosworth, 2004; Jorgenson et al., 2005; Oliner et al., 2007).

While the impact of ICT on growth has not been studied as intensively as for the US, evidence has been piling up that the EU as a whole has been lagging behind the US in terms of ICT investment since 1980. As a result the labour productivity growth advantage of the US over the EU in the market sector during the period 1995–2005 is in part due to higher contributions from ICT capital input (0.2 percentage points). Second, the difference in the size of the ICT-goods-producing sector, especially semi-conductors, accounts for another 0.2 percentage points of the EU–US productivity growth differential. Together, these two effects account for about half of the US productivity lead in labour productivity growth since 1995.

What has been missing so far in the analysis of the ICT impact on productivity growth in Europe has been a sector- and industry-specific approach. Van Ark et al. (2003) show that there was little acceleration in labour productivity growth in ICT-using sectors in Europe during the second half of the 1990s, but until recently the data for a full-scale industry-level growth accounting approach have not been available. This has changed recently, with the publication of the EU KLEMS Growth and Productivity Accounts (see Timmer et al., 2007 and http://www.euklems. net). The EU KLEMS Growth and Productivity Accounts include measures of output growth, employment and skill creation, capital formation and multi-factor productivity (MFP) at the industry level for European Union member states from 1970 onwards. The input measures include various categories of capital (K), labour (L), energy (E), material (M) and service inputs (S).

In this paper we first briefly introduce the growth accounting methodology, including the measurement of labour and capital services (Section 2). We then provide a discussion of the key characteristics of the EU KLEMS database and the variables, country and industry coverage (Section 3). In Section 4 we provide an analysis of how ICT have impacted on growth and productivity by sector, and we look at the differences between the EU and the US as well as differences between EU member states.

2   GROWTH ACCOUNTING METHODOLOGY

The EU KLEMS growth accounts are based on the growth accounting methodology as theoretically motivated by the seminal contribution of Jorgenson and Griliches (1967) and put in a more general input–output framework by Jorgenson et al. (1987, 2005). Growth accounting allows one to assess the relative importance of labour, capital and intermediate inputs to growth, and to derive measures of MFP growth. MFP indicates the efficiency with which inputs are being used in the production process and is an important indicator of technological change.[3] Under the assumptions of competitive factor markets, full input utilization and constant returns to scale, the growth of output in industry j can be expressed as the (compensation share) weighted growth of inputs and multi-factor productivity (denoted by A^Y):

$$\Delta \ln Y_{jt} = \overline{v}_{jt}^X \Delta \ln X_{jt} + \overline{v}_{jt}^K \Delta \ln K_{jt} + \overline{v}_{jt}^L \Delta \ln L_{jt} + \Delta \ln A_{jt}^Y \quad (3.1)$$

where $\overline{v}^i$ denotes the two-period average share of input i in nominal output and $\overline{v}^L + \overline{v}^K + \overline{v}^X = 1$. Each element on the right-hand side indicates the proportion of output growth accounted for by growth in intermediate inputs, capital services, labour services and MFP, respectively. Accurate measures of labour and capital input are based on a breakdown of aggregate hours worked and aggregate capital stock into various components. Hours worked are cross-classified by various categories to account for differences in the productivity of various labour types, such as high- versus low-skilled labour. Similarly, capital stock measures are broken down into stocks of different asset types. Short-lived assets like computers have a much higher productivity than long-lived assets like buildings, and this should be reflected in the capital input measures. The contribution of intermediate inputs is broken down into the contribution of energy goods, intermediate materials and services.

2.1 Measurement of Capital Services

The availability of investment series by asset type and by industry is one of the unique characteristics of the EU KLEMS database. They are based on series obtained from national statistical institutes, allowing for a detailed industry-by-asset analysis. Importantly, we make a distinction between three ICT assets (office and computing equipment, communication equipment and software) and four non-ICT assets (transport equipment, other machinery and equipment, residential buildings and non-residential structures). ICT assets are deflated using a quality-adjusted investment deflator, except for those countries that have not yet implemented adequate quality adjustment where we used the harmonization procedure suggested by Schreyer (2002). The real investment series are used to derive capital stocks through the accumulation of investment into stock estimates using the Perpetual Inventory Method (PIM) and the application of geometric depreciation rates. Then capital service flows are derived by weighting the growth of stocks by the share of each asset's compensation in total capital compensation as follows:

$$\Delta \ln K_t = \sum_k \bar{v}_{k,t} \Delta \ln S_{k,t} \qquad (3.2)$$

where $\Delta \ln S_{k,t}$ indicates the growth of the stock of asset k and weights are given by the average shares of each asset in the value of total capital compensation. In this way, aggregation takes into account the widely different marginal products from the heterogeneous stock of assets. The weights are related to the user cost of each asset.

The user cost approach is crucial for the analysis of the contribution of capital to output growth. This approach is based on the assumption that marginal costs reflect marginal productivity. If the cost of leasing one euro of, say, computer assets is higher than leasing one euro of buildings, computers have a higher marginal productivity, and this should be taken into account. There are various reasons why the costs of computers are higher than for buildings. While computers may typically be scrapped after five or six years, buildings may provide services for several decades. Besides, prices of new computers are rapidly declining and those of buildings are normally not. Hence the user cost of ICT machinery is typically 50 to 60 per cent of the investment price, while that of buildings is less than 10 per cent. Therefore one euro of computer capital stock should get a heavier weight in the growth of capital services than one euro of building stock. This is ensured by using the rental price of capital services as weights.

2.2 Measurement of Labour Services

The productivity of various types of labour input, such as low- versus high-skilled, will also differ. Standard measures of labour input, such as numbers employed or hours worked, will not account for such differences. Hence one needs measures of labour input that take the heterogeneity of the labour force into account in analysing productivity and the contribution of labour to output growth. These measures are called labour services, as they allow for differences in the amount of services delivered per unit of labour in the growth accounting approach. It is assumed that the flow of labour services for each labour type is proportional to hours worked, and workers are paid their marginal productivities. Then the corresponding index of labour services input L is given by:

$$\Delta \ln L_t = \sum_l \overline{v}_{l,t} \Delta \ln H_{l,t} \tag{3.3}$$

where $\Delta \ln H_{l,t}$ indicates the growth of hours worked by labour type l and weights are given by the average shares of each type in the value of labour compensation. In this way, aggregation takes into account the changing composition of the labour force. We cross-classify labour input by educational attainment, gender and age with the aim to proxy for differences in work experience, which provides 18 labour categories (3*2*3 types). Typically, a shift in the share of hours worked by low-skilled workers to high-skilled workers will lead to a growth of labour services that is larger than the growth in total hours worked. We refer to this difference as the labour composition effect.

Series on hours worked by labour types are not part of the standard statistics reported by National Statistical Institutes (NSIs), not even at the aggregate economy level. Also, there is no single international database on skills that can be used for this purpose. For each country covered in EU

KLEMS, a choice has been made to use survey data that provide the best sources for consistent wage and employment data at the industry level. In most cases this was a labour force survey (LFS), sometimes together with an earnings survey when wages were not included in the LFS. In other cases, use has been made of establishment surveys or a social-security database, or a mix of sources. Care has been taken to arrive at series that are consistent over time, which was important as most employment surveys are not designed to track developments over time, and breaks in methodology or coverage frequently occur.

3 THE EU KLEMS DATABASE

The EU KLEMS Growth and Productivity Accounts are the result of a research project, financed by the European Commission, to analyse productivity in the European Union at the industry level. This database is meant to support empirical research in the area of economic growth, such as study of the relationship between skill formation, investment, technological progress and innovation on the one hand and productivity on the other. In addition, the database may facilitate the conduct of policies aimed at supporting a revival of productivity and competitiveness in the European Union. These policies require comprehensive measurement tools to monitor and evaluate progress. The construction of the database should also support the systematic production of high-quality statistics on growth and productivity using the methodologies of national accounts and input–output analysis.

The first public release of the EU KLEMS database in March 2007 covered 25 EU countries (EU-25),[4] as well as Japan and the United States. The subsequent release in November 2007 and March 2008 updated the estimates for most countries to 2005. A key strength of the EU KLEMS database is that it moves beneath the aggregate economy level to examine the productivity performance of individual industries and their contribution to aggregate growth. The OECD and the Groningen Growth and Development Centre maintain MFP series for aggregate OECD economies, but not at the industry level with the exception of a single study by Inklaar et al. (2005) including four European countries (France, Germany, the Netherlands and the United Kingdom).[5] The latter study showed that there is enormous heterogeneity in output and productivity growth across industries, so analysts should focus on the industry-level detail to understand the origins of the European growth process. The number of industries covered include 62 (for labour productivity post-1995), 48 (for labour productivity pre-1995) and 31 industries (for growth accounts).

Appendix Table 3A.2 provides a listing of industries for which growth accounting variables are available (Appendix Table 3A.1). This list also includes higher-level aggregates provided in the EU KLEMS database. The data series are publicly available from the EU KLEMS website (http://www.euklems.net). More information on the methodology used in EU KLEMS can be found in the document *EU KLEMS Growth and Productivity Accounts, Version 1.0, PART I Methodology*. Detailed source descriptions are given in *PART II Sources*, which are also downloadable from the EU KLEMS website. O'Mahony and Timmer (2009) provide a summary of the main issues.

4   ICT, GROWTH AND PRODUCTIVITY[6]

The results from the EU KLEMS database confirm earlier observations suggesting that the growth performance of the European Union has undergone a marked change during the second half of the 1990s (O'Mahony and Van Ark, 2003; Van Ark et al., 2008). Even though average GDP growth of the EU-15 remained constant at 2.2 per cent, labour productivity growth slowed dramatically from 2.6 per cent from 1970–1995 to 1.3 per cent from 1995–2005 (see Table 3.1a). This structural slowdown in productivity for the European Union as a whole is striking in the light of a comparison with the United States, where productivity growth significantly accelerated from 1.2 per cent averaged over 1970–95 to 2.3 per cent from 1995–2005 (Table 3.1b). When looking at the market economy only, the forging ahead of the US becomes even more pronounced.[7]

However, the EU KLEMS database documents a wide variation in productivity growth rates across EU member states. Among the 'old' member states the fastest productivity growth rates were recorded in Finland and Sweden.[8] Among the larger countries in the 'old' EU, the UK has shown the fastest productivity growth since 1995, ahead of France and Germany. At the lower end of the productivity ranks are the two large countries in the southern part of the EU, that is, Italy and Spain. The dismal productivity performance of the latter two countries impacts significantly on the average growth rate in the Union. However, whereas slow productivity growth in Spain was related to rapid improvement in labour input growth, the Italian economy experienced no compensating effect from an acceleration in employment growth. In general, the productivity growth rates from 1995–2005 were by far the highest for the new member states, reflecting the restructuring of the economies in Central and Eastern Europe. However, labour input growth in the new member states has generally been negative, in particular in manufacturing (Timmer et al., 2007).

Table 3.1   Gross value-added, labour input and labour productivity, 1970–95 and 1995–2005, European Union-15 (old EU-15)

3.1a   European Union-15

	Annual Average Volume Growth Rates, in %				Average Share in Total Hours Worked (%)	Contribution to LP Growth in Total Industries
	Gross value-added	Total persons engaged	Total hours worked	GVA per hour worked		
1970–95						
TOTAL INDUSTRIES	2.4	0.4	−0.2	2.6	100.0	2.6
Electrical machinery, post and communication	4.1	−0.4	−0.9	5.0	4.3	0.2
Manufacturing, excluding electrical	1.6	−1.3	−1.8	3.4	21.9	0.9
Other goods-producing industries	1.2	−2.1	−2.5	3.7	19.5	0.9
Distribution services	2.7	0.8	0.3	2.5	19.8	0.4
Finance and business services	3.8	3.4	2.9	0.9	8.4	0.0
Personal and social services	2.0	2.1	1.7	0.3	8.1	0.0
Non-market services	2.8	2.1	1.5	1.2	18.2	0.2
Reallocation of labour effect						−0.1
1995–2005						
TOTAL INDUSTRIES	2.0	1.2	0.8	1.3	100.0	1.3
Electrical machinery, post and communication	5.5	−0.6	−1.0	6.5	3.4	0.2
Manufacturing, excluding electrical	0.8	−0.7	−1.1	2.0	16.2	0.3

Innovation and economic development

Table 3.1   (continued)

	Annual Average Volume Growth Rates, in %				Average Share in Total Hours Worked (%)	Contribution to LP Growth in Total Industries
	Gross value-added	Total persons engaged	Total hours worked	GVA per hour worked		
Other goods-producing industries	1.1	−0.2	−0.4	1.6	13.4	0.2
Distribution services	2.3	1.1	0.6	1.7	20.4	0.4
Finance and business services	3.6	3.5	3.3	0.3	14.0	0.0
Personal and social services	1.7	2.6	2.1	−0.4	11.1	0.0
Non-market services	1.6	1.3	1.0	0.6	21.4	0.1
Reallocation of labour effect						0.0

3.1b   United States

	Annual Average Volume Growth Rates, in %				Average Share in Total Hours Worked (%)	Contribution to LP Growth in Total Industries
	Gross value-added	Total persons engaged	Total hours worked	GVA per hour worked		
1970–95						
TOTAL INDUSTRIES	2.8	1.7	1.5	1.3	100.0	1.3
Electrical machinery, post and communication	8.1	0.5	0.6	7.5	4.1	0.3
Manufacturing, excluding electrical	1.7	−0.2	−0.1	1.8	16.6	0.4
Other goods-producing industries	0.7	0.9	0.6	0.1	11.7	0.0
Distribution services	4.0	1.8	1.4	2.6	21.0	0.6

Table 3.1 (continued)

	Annual Average Volume Growth Rates, in %				Average Share in Total Hours Worked (%)	Contribution to LP Growth in Total Industries
	Gross value-added	Total persons engaged	Total hours worked	GVA per hour worked		
Finance and business services	4.2	4.2	4.0	0.2	11.7	0.0
Personal and social services	2.4	2.6	2.5	−0.1	11.2	0.0
Non-market services	2.5	1.9	1.8	0.7	23.7	0.2
Reallocation of labour effect						−0.1
1995–2005						
TOTAL INDUSTRIES	3.3	1.1	0.8	2.4	100.0	2.4
Electrical machinery, post and communication	10.5	−1.2	−1.4	11.9	3.2	0.4
Manufacturing, excluding electrical	1.8	−2.0	−2.2	4.0	11.9	0.6
Other goods-producing industries	1.6	1.5	1.6	0.0	10.9	0.0
Distribution services	4.1	0.8	0.4	3.6	20.5	0.8
Finance and business services	4.3	2.4	2.2	2.0	16.1	0.3
Personal and social services	2.6	1.6	1.6	1.0	13.2	0.1
Non-market services	2.4	1.6	1.3	1.2	24.2	0.3
Reallocation of labour effect						0.0

Source: EU KLEMS Database, March 2008, http://www.euklems.net; accessed 22 March 2010.

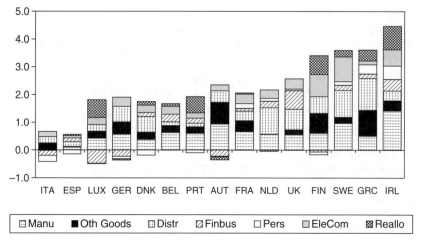

Note: Industry legend, see Table 3.1.

Source: EU KLEMS Database, March 2008, http://www.euklems.net; accessed 22 March 2010.

Figure 3.2   Contributions of industries to market economy labour productivity growth 1995–2005 (in %)

The underlying analysis of the industry contributions to labour productivity since 1995 shows that the manufacturing sector continues to contribute significantly to European growth, partly through high labour productivity growth in the electrical machinery sector (0.2 percentage points, primarily from ICT production industries), and partly from the rest of the manufacturing sector (0.3 percentage points) (Table 3.1a). Also, growth in distribution services and in other goods-producing industries contributed each 0.4 percentage points to post-1995 growth in the EU-25. Nevertheless, compared with the United States, the striking differences in labour productivity growth originate from the much smaller contribution of market services, notably the distribution sector as well as finance and business services, which together contributed 1.1 percentage points in the US since 1995 (Table 3.1b).

EU aggregates hide considerable country variation in industries driving growth. For example, some European countries (Finland, Sweden and Ireland as well as Estonia, Hungary and Latvia) showed a major contribution from ICT production (see Figure 3.2). Some have major contributions from other manufacturing, such as some fast-growing new EU countries, Austria, Ireland and Sweden, while in other countries other goods production (which includes agriculture, mining, utilities and construction) is an important source of growth. Also, differences in the productivity contribution of market services appear to be a major driver of divergence within Europe.

The growth accounting analysis from the EU Growth and Productivity Accounts is the most innovative and hitherto unavailable component of the database. It concentrates on a sub-sample of 11 'old' EU countries and four new member states for which full labour and capital accounts could be constructed.[9] In Table 3.2a, a decomposition of value-added growth in the market economy of the old EU countries is given. GDP growth in the market economy remained stable at 2.1–2.2 per cent before and after 1995. But underlying the stable GDP trend, there was a strong improvement in the contribution of labour input, increasing from a zero contribution to a 0.6 percentage point contribution. Almost all of this faster growth in labour input arose from an increase in total hours worked, whereas the increase in labour composition, reflecting the improvement in the overall skill level of the workforce, remained stable.

The contribution of capital input to value-added growth has not changed much at the aggregate level, but the distribution has shifted somewhat from non-ICT capital to ICT capital. However, compared with the United States the shift towards intensive use of ICT capital has generally not been as pronounced. Notably, when comparing the ratio of capital to labour contributions to growth in the EU, there are signs of a declining capital intensity in the EU. This development is in sharp contrast to the US trend in capital intensity since 1995 (see Table 3.2b).

The factor contributing most to the diverging trends in Europe and the US is the trend in MFP growth. In the US, MFP growth in the market economy accelerated by a full percentage point from 0.7 per cent from 1980–95 to 1.7 per cent from 1995–2007 (Table 3.2b). In contrast, MPF in the market economy of the European Union slowed from 1 per cent from 1980–95 to 0.4 per cent since 1995 (Table 3.2a). This slowdown in MFP growth is recorded almost everywhere across the Union, with the exception of Finland and the Netherlands where it improved since 1995. In France, MFP growth in the market economy has remained stable at 0.7 per cent, but it slowed sharply in Germany and in the United Kingdom. In Italy and Spain, MFP growth was even negative reflecting the lack of technology and innovation spillovers and market rigidities, in particular in services industries (Figure 3.3).

When decomposing growth to both industry as well as the sources of growth, it appears that market services play a major role of the divergent performance of European economies since 1995, both among themselves as well as relative to the United States. Table 3.2a shows causes of the

Table 3.2 Gross value-added growth and contributions, 1980–95 and 1995–2005 (annual average volume growth rates, in %)

3.2a European Union-15 (excluding Greece, Ireland, Luxembourg, Portugal and Sweden)

	VA	L	H	LC	K	KIT	KNIT	MFP
	(1) = (2) + (5) + (8)	(2) = (3) + (4)	(3)	(4)	(5) = (6) + (7)	(6)	(7)	(8)
1980–95								
MARKET ECONOMY	2.1	0.0	−0.3	0.3	1.1	0.4	0.7	1.0
Electrical machinery, post and communication	3.6	−0.6	−0.9	0.3	1.6	0.9	0.7	2.6
Manufacturing, excluding electrical	1.1	−1.2	−1.5	0.3	0.7	0.2	0.5	1.7
Other goods-producing industries	1.1	−1.1	−1.4	0.2	0.7	0.1	0.6	1.6
Distribution services	2.6	0.3	0.1	0.2	0.8	0.3	0.5	1.5
Finance and business services	3.5	2.4	1.9	0.4	2.1	0.9	1.2	−1.0
Personal and social services	1.7	1.8	1.5	0.3	0.9	0.2	0.6	−1.1
1995–2005								
MARKET ECONOMY	2.2	0.6	0.4	0.2	1.2	0.6	0.6	0.4
Electrical machinery, post and communication	5.5	−0.4	−0.6	0.2	1.7	1.2	0.5	4.1

Manufacturing, excluding electrical	0.8	-0.4	-0.7	0.3	0.6	0.3	0.3	0.7
Other goods-producing industries	1.1	0.0	-0.1	0.2	0.7	0.1	0.6	0.4
Distribution services	2.3	0.6	0.5	0.1	1.1	0.4	0.7	0.6
Finance and business services	3.6	2.2	1.9	0.3	2.2	1.3	0.9	-0.8
Personal and social services	1.7	1.5	1.4	0.1	1.0	0.3	0.7	-0.8

3.2b United States

1980–95								
MARKET ECONOMY	3.0	1.2	1.0	0.2	1.1	0.5	0.6	0.7
Electrical machinery, post and communication	6.6	0.1	-0.3	0.4	1.9	1.0	0.9	4.6
Manufacturing, excluding electrical	1.7	0.1	-0.2	0.3	0.6	0.3	0.3	0.9
Other goods-producing industries	0.7	0.7	0.4	0.3	0.7	0.2	0.5	-0.7
Distribution services	3.9	1.3	1.2	0.2	1.2	0.6	0.6	1.3
Finance and business services	4.4	2.9	2.7	0.2	1.8	1.0	0.9	-0.3
Personal and social services	2.9	2.5	2.5	0.1	0.5	0.2	0.3	-0.2

Table 3.2 (continued)

	VA	L	H	LC	K	KIT	KNIT	MFP
	(1) = (2) + (5) + (8)	(2) = (3) + (4)	(3)	(4)	(5) = (6) + (7)	(6)	(7)	(8)
1995–2005								
MARKET ECONOMY	3.7	0.7	0.4	0.3	1.3	0.8	0.6	1.7
Electrical machinery, post and communication	10.5	−0.4	−0.8	0.5	2.2	1.4	0.8	8.7
Manufacturing, excluding electrical	1.8	−1.0	−1.4	0.3	0.6	0.4	0.2	2.2
Other goods-producing industries	1.6	1.1	1.0	0.1	0.8	0.2	0.6	−0.3
Distribution services	4.1	0.6	0.3	0.3	1.5	1.0	0.5	2.1
Finance and business services	4.3	1.9	1.5	0.4	1.9	1.2	0.7	0.4
Personal and social services	2.6	1.7	1.4	0.3	0.9	0.4	0.6	0.0

Notes: The EU-15 in Table 3.2a consists of Austria, Belgium, Denmark, Finland, France, Germany, Italy, Netherlands, Spain and the United Kingdom. It excludes Greece, Ireland, Luxembourg, Portugal and Sweden.
VA = Gross value-added growth
L = Contribution of labour input growth
H = Contribution of total hours worked
LC = Contribution of labour composition
K = Contribution of capital input growth
KIT = Contribution of ICT capital
KNIT = Contribution of non-ICT capital
MFP = Contribution of multi-factor productivity growth.

Source: EU KLEMS Database, March 2008, http://www.euklems.net; accessed 22 March 2010.

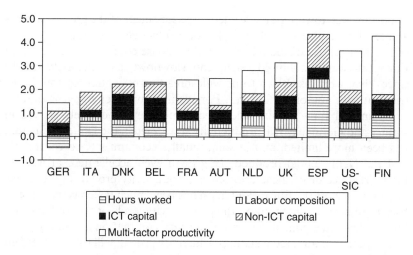

Source: EU KLEMS Database, March 2008, http://www.euklems.net; accessed 22 March 2010.

Figure 3.3 *Contributions to market economy GDP growth 1995–2005 (in %)*

slowing or stagnation of output growth in various market services. While the contribution of factor inputs to growth has generally stayed up, multi-factor productivity growth in the market services stagnated or even turned negative in many European countries. The reasons for the slowdown in multi-factor productivity growth in market services are an important avenue for further research (see, for example, Inklaar et al., 2008).

5 CONCLUDING REMARKS

The EU KLEMS Growth and Productivity Accounts represent a new set of data that provide researchers, policy-makers, media and others with a rich source of information on the sources of growth by industry and country in the European Union. Using national accounts and supplementary official statistics in combination with state-of-the-art growth accounting techniques, this database allows one to detect the key areas of growth and slowdown for individual countries, as well as convergence and divergence across economies. More precise measurement of the sources of growth at industry level is important for the analysis of the causes of the growth slowdown. In particular the breakdown of capital and labour inputs into asset types and labour categories (skill, gender and age) is an important step towards a more adequate assessment of the growth sources and less biased measures of multi-factor productivity growth.

The first release of the EU KLEMS database confirmed the view that European countries showed a significant slowdown in productivity growth since 1995, which is shown to be widespread across countries and industries but with notable differences. For example, productivity growth rates in Spain and Italy seriously declined, while they moderately slowed in France and Germany. The productivity slowdown in the United Kingdom has been more limited, and in some smaller economies (Greece, Ireland and the Netherlands) productivity growth even accelerated, at least in the market sector of those economies. Productivity growth in most new member states of the European Union has been much faster as these countries have been catching up on the productivity levels of the 'old' EU-15, but this has often gone together with a sharp contraction in employment.

The potential for a recovery in productivity growth will to a large extent depend on the EU's capability to transform the economy towards one that makes more productive use of its resources. Much will depend on the capacity of markets to facilitate the reallocation of resources to industries that show rapid productivity growth. However, it is difficult to predict which industries will be the most productive in the future, as technology and innovation trends are inherently difficult to forecast. For now, a productive use of a larger input from skilled employment and the exploitation of ICT investments in service industries appear the most successful policy avenues for a European productivity revival. The EU KLEMS database will be a useful policy tool to track the progress made.

NOTES

1. This refers to the 15 European Union countries that constituted the Union up to 2004.
2. Business cycles in the US and the EU are not completely synchronized. However, the divergent trend growth rates are clear.
3. Under strict neoclassical assumptions, MFP growth measures disembodied technological change. In practice, MFP is derived as a residual and includes a host of effects such as improvements in allocative and technical efficiency, changes in returns to scale and mark-ups and technological change proper. All these effects can be broadly summarized as 'improvements in efficiency', as they improve the productivity with which inputs are being used in the production process. In addition, being a residual measure MFP growth also includes measurement errors and the effects from unmeasured output and inputs.
4. All member states of the EU as of 1 May 2004.
5. For OECD series, see www.oecd.org/dataoecd/27/39/36396940.xls; accessed 21 March 2010. For GGDC series, see http://www.ggdc.net/database/ted_growth.htm; accessed 31 March 2010, described in Timmer and Van Ark (2005).
6. For a country-specific analysis of results from the first release in March 2007, see Van Ark et al. (2007).
7. Market economy excludes health (ISIC industry N), education (ISIC M) and government

sectors (ISIC L). We also exclude real estate (ISIC 70), because output in this industry mostly reflects imputed housing rents rather than sales of firms.
8. Greece and Ireland also showed rapid productivity growth but, just as in the new member states, this largely reflects 'catching-up' growth.
9. The 11 'old' EU countries in the growth accounts analysis refer to Austria, Belgium, Denmark, Finland, France, Germany, Italy, the Netherlands, Spain, Sweden and the United Kingdom. The four new member states refer to Czech Republic, Hungary, Poland and Slovenia.

REFERENCES

EU KLEMS Database, March 2008, http://www.euklems.net.
Inklaar, R., M. O'Mahony and M.P. Timmer (2005), 'ICT and Europe's Productivity Performance; Industry-level Growth Account Comparisons with the United States', *Review of Income and Wealth*, **51**(4), 505–36.
Inklaar, R, M.P. Timmer and B. Van Ark (2008), 'Market Services Across Europe and the U.S.', *Economic Policy*, **23**(53), January, 139–94.
Jorgenson, D.W. and Z. Griliches (1967), 'The Explanation of Productivity Change', *Review of Economic Studies*, **34**(3), 249–83.
Jorgenson, D.W., F.M. Gollop and B.M. Fraumeni (1987), *Productivity and U.S. Economic Growth*, Cambridge, MA: Harvard University Press.
Jorgenson, Dale W., Mun Ho and Kevin J. Stiroh (2005), *Information Technology and the American Growth Resurgence*, Cambridge, MA: MIT.
O'Mahony, M. and M.P. Timmer (2009), 'Output, Input and Productivity Measures at the Industry Level: the EU KLEMS Database', *Economic Journal*, **119**(538), F374–F403.
O'Mahony, M. and B. Van Ark (eds) (2003), *EU Productivity and Competitiveness: An Industry Perspective – Can Europe Resume the Catching-up Process?*, Luxembourg: Office for Official Publications of the European Communities.
Oliner, S.D., D.E. Sichel and K.J. Stiroh (2007), 'Explaining a Productive Decade', *Brookings Papers on Economic Activity*, No. 1, pp. 81–137.
Schreyer, P. (2002), 'Computer Price Indices and International Growth and Productivity Comparisons', *Review of Income and Wealth*, **48**(1), 15–31.
Timmer, Marcel P. and Bart Van Ark (2005), 'IT in the European Union: A Driver of Productivity Divergence?', *Oxford Economic Papers*, **57**(4), 693–716.
Timmer, M.P., Mary O'Mahony and Bart Van Ark (2007), *The EU KLEMS Growth and Productivity Accounts: An Overview*, University of Groningen & University of Birmingham.
Triplett, J.E. and B.P. Bosworth (2004), *Productivity in the U.S. Services Sector; New Sources of Economic Growth*, Washington DC: Brookings Institution.
Van Ark, B., R. Inklaar and R.H. McGuckin (2003), 'ICT and Productivity in Europe and the United States. Where do the Differences Come From?', *CESifo Economic Studies*, **49**(3), 295–318.
Van Ark, B., Mary O'Mahony and Gerard Ypma (eds.) (2007), *The EU KLEMS Productivity Report*, Issue 1, University of Groningen & University of Birmingham, March.
Van Ark, B., M. O'Mahony and M.P. Timmer (2008), 'European Growth: the End of Convergence', *Journal of Economic Perspectives*, **22**(1), 25–44.

APPENDIX 3A.1   SUPPLEMENTAL TABLES

Table 3A.1   Variables in EU KLEMS database

Basic Variables	
Values	
GO	Gross output at current basic prices (in millions of local currency)
II	Intermediate inputs at current purchasers' prices (in millions of local currency)
IIE	Intermediate energy inputs at current purchasers' prices (in millions of local currency)
IIM	Intermediate material inputs at current purchasers' prices (in millions of local currency)
IIS	Intermediate service inputs at current purchasers' prices (in millions of local currency)
VA	Gross value-added at current basic prices (in millions of local currency)
COMP	Compensation of employees (in millions of local currency)
GOS	Gross operating surplus (in millions of local currency)
TXSP	Taxes minus subsidies on production (in millions of local currency)
EMP	Number of persons engaged (thousands)
EMPE	Number of employees (thousands)
H_EMP	Total hours worked by persons engaged (millions)
H_EMPE	Total hours worked by employees (millions)
Prices	
GO_P	Gross output, price indices, 1995 = 100
II_P	Intermediate inputs, price indices, 1995 = 100
VA_P	Gross value-added, price indices, 1995 = 100
Volumes	
GO_QI	Gross output, volume indices, 1995 = 100
II_QI	Intermediate inputs, volume indices, 1995 = 100
IIE_QI	Intermediate energy inputs, volume indices, 1995 = 100
IIM_QI	Intermediate material inputs, volume indices, 1995 = 100
IIS_QI	Intermediate service inputs, volume indices, 1995 = 100
VA_QI	Gross value-added, volume indices, 1995 = 100
LP_I	Gross value-added per hours worked, volume indices, 1995 = 100

Growth Accounting Variables	
LAB	Labour compensation (in millions of local currency)
CAP	Capital compensation (in millions of local currency)

Table 3A.1   (continued)

LAB_QI	Labour services, volume indices, 1995 = 100
CAP_QI	Capital services, volume indices, 1995 = 100
VA_Q	Growth rate of value-added volume (% per year)
VAConL	Contribution of labour services to value-added growth (percentage points)
VAConH	Contribution of hours worked to value-added growth (percentage points)
VAConLC	Contribution of labour composition change to value-added growth (percentage points)
VAConKIT	Contribution of ICT capital services to output growth (percentage points)
VAConKNIT	Contribution of non-ICT capital services to output growth (percentage points)
VAConTFP	Contribution of TFP to value-added growth (percentage points)
TFPva_I	TFP (value-added based) growth, 1995 = 100
GO_Q	Growth rate of gross output volume (% per year)
GOConII	Contribution of intermediate inputs to output growth (percentage points)
GOConIIM	Contribution of intermediate energy inputs to output growth (percentage points)
GOConIIE	Contribution of intermediate material inputs to output growth (percentage points)
GOConIIS	Contribution of intermediate services inputs to output growth (percentage points)
GOConL	Contribution of labour services to output growth (percentage points)
GOConK	Contribution of capital services to output growth (percentage points)
GOConTFP	Contribution of TFP to output growth (percentage points)
TFPgo_I	TFP (gross output-based) growth, 1995 = 100

Additional Variables

CAPIT	ICT capital compensation (share in total capital compensation)
CAPNIT	Non-ICT capital compensation (share in total capital compensation)
CAPIT_QI	ICT capital services, volume indices, 1995 = 100
CAPNIT_QI	Non-ICT capital services, volume indices, 1995 = 100
CAPIT_QPH	ICT capital services per hours worked, 1995 reference
CAPNIT_QPH	Non-ICT capital services per hours worked, 1995 reference
LABHS	High-skilled labour compensation (share in total labour compensation)

Table 3A.1   (continued)

LABMS	Medium-skilled labour compensation (share in total labour compensation)
LABLS	Low-skilled labour compensation (share in total labour compensation)
LAB_QPH	Labour services per hours worked, 1995 reference
H_HS	Hours worked by high-skilled persons engaged (share in total hours)
H_MS	Hours worked by medium-skilled persons engaged (share in total hours)
H_LS	Hours worked by low-skilled persons engaged (share in total hours)
H_M	Hours worked by male persons engaged (share in total hours)
H_F	Hours worked by female persons engaged (share in total hours)
H_29	Hours worked by persons engaged aged 15–29 (share in total hours)
H_49	Hours worked by persons engaged aged 30–49 (share in total hours)
H_50+	Hours worked by persons engaged aged 50 and over (share in total hours)

Source: EU KLEMS Database, March 2008, http://www.euklems.net; accessed 22 March 2010.

Table 3A.2   *Industry lists for growth accounting variables*

Description	Code
TOTAL INDUSTRIES	TOT
MARKET ECONOMY	MARKT
ELECTRICAL MACHINERY, POST AND COMMUNICATION SERVICES	ELECOM
Electrical and optical equipment	30t33
Post and telecommunications	64
GOODS PRODUCING, EXCLUDING ELECTRICAL MACHINERY	GOODS
TOTAL MANUFACTURING, EXCLUDING ELECTRICAL	MexElec
Consumer manufacturing	Mcons
Food products, beverages and tobacco	*15t16*
Textiles, textile products, leather and footwear	*17t19*
Manufacturing nec*; recycling	*36t37*
Intermediate manufacturing	Minter
Wood and products of wood and cork	*20*
Pulp, paper, paper products, printing and publishing	*21t22*

Table 3A.2 (continued)

Description	Code
Coke, refined petroleum products and nuclear fuel	*23*
Chemicals and chemical products	*24*
Rubber and plastics products	*25*
Other non-metallic mineral products	*26*
Basic metals and fabricated metal products	*27t28*
Investment goods, excluding high-tech	Minves
Machinery, nec	*29*
Transport equipment	*34t35*
OTHER PRODUCTION	OtherG
Mining and quarrying	C
Electricity, gas and water supply	E
Construction	F
Agriculture, hunting, forestry and fishing	AtB
MARKET SERVICES, EXCLUDING POST AND TELECOMMUNICATIONS	MSERV
DISTRIBUTION	DISTR
Trade	50t52
Sale, maintenance and repair of motor vehicles and motorcycles; retail sale of fuel	*50*
Wholesale trade and commission trade, except motor vehicles and motorcycles	*51*
Retail trade, except motor vehicles and motorcycles; repair of household goods	*52*
Transport and storage	60t63
FINANCE AND BUSINESS, EXCEPT REAL ESTATE	FINBU
Financial intermediation	J
Renting of m&eq and other business activities	71t74
PERSONAL SERVICES	PERS
Hotels and restaurants	H
Other community, social and personal services	O
Private households with employed persons	P
NON-MARKET SERVICES	NONMAR
Public admin, education and health	LtN
Public admin and defence; compulsory social security	*L*
Education	*M*
Health and social work	*N*
Real estate activities	70

Note: * nec = not elsewhere classified.

Source: EU KLEMS Database, March 2007, http://www.euklems.net; accessed 22 March 2010.

4. ICT investment in Latin America: does it matter for economic growth?

Gaaitzen J. De Vries, Nanno Mulder, Mariela Dal Borgo and André A. Hofman*

1 INTRODUCTION

Information and communication technologies (ICT), as a general-purpose technology, have contributed substantially to economic and productivity growth in member countries of the Organisation for Economic Cooperation and Development (OECD) in the past decade. Evidence on the growth impact of ICT in the United States is paramount. The acceleration of growth in the United States after 1995 is largely attributed to the intensive use of ICT in the production process (Oliner and Sichel, 2000; Jorgenson, 2001). Studies for the European Union and Japan also find that ICT investment contributed substantially to growth and productivity in the past decade (Schreyer, 2000; Jorgenson and Motohashi, 2003; Van Ark and Piatkowski, 2004; Timmer and Van Ark, 2005; Piatkowski, 2006). For Latin America, official ICT investment series are not available, and their importance and growth impact is uncertain. Scarce evidence for Latin America, based on imputing ICT investment from expenditure data drawn from private data sources, suggests that the contribution of ICT investment to economic growth has been relatively modest over the past decade (Pohjola, 2003; Jorgenson and Vu, 2005 and Chapter 1 this volume).

This paper breaks new ground in the estimation of ICT investment and the contribution of ICT capital services to economic growth for Latin America. In the first part of this paper, we estimate ICT investment for five Latin American countries (namely, Argentina, Brazil, Chile, Costa Rica and Uruguay) using national accounts data from statistical offices.[1] We estimate investment in hardware and communication equipment by applying investment ratios in ICT from input–output tables to time series of domestic production and imports and exports of ICT goods. This procedure follows Van Ark et al. (2002) and earlier practices in European national statistical offices. To estimate software investment in

Latin America, we use elasticities of a fixed-effects panel data model for 20 OECD countries. We find that only in Chile is the ICT investment share in GDP converging to the average investment level in Europe. The second part of the paper examines the contribution of ICT investment to output growth using a growth accounting framework. We adopt recent advances in the growth accounting methodology (OECD, 2001a). This includes measuring the capital contribution to growth by means of a flow in capital services and weighting assets by their respective user costs. We find that ICT capital services, as a factor of production in the productive process, contributed between 0.21 percentage points (for Brazil) and 0.62 percentage points (for Chile) to economic growth from 1990 to 2004.

ICT contributes to economic growth via three transmission channels. First, as a result of rapid price declines in ICT goods (Triplett, 1996), investors substitute traditional capital investment for ICT. Capital services flowing from investment in ICT, which clearly embody technology, contribute to economic growth. That contribution of ICT capital to economic growth is central in this paper. Second, new technologies are a potential source for reducing inefficiency, creating spillovers and stimulating technological change in the production process by streamlining productive activities or inducing business reorganizations. The contribution of ICT investment in reducing inefficiency and increasing multi-factor productivity gains in Latin America is the main focus of a paper by Aravena et al. (2007). A third growth impact originates from high productivity growth in ICT-producing sectors. That impact is not examined for Latin America, but we know from other indicators that the ICT-producing sector in Latin America is relatively small, except for Costa Rica, Mexico and possibly Brazil.

The rest of this paper is structured as follows. First, we explain the so-called commodity-flow method of ICT investment series and use it to estimate investment in computer and communication equipment in current prices for five Latin American countries. We also describe the framework and estimation of software investment. In the subsequent section, we deflate the nominal ICT investment series using harmonized ICT deflators. Section 4 discusses the construction of an ICT capital stock from real investment series and the resulting ICT capital service flows. Section 5 incorporates ICT capital service flows in a growth accounting decomposition, and Section 6 concludes.

2 ESTIMATION OF ICT INVESTMENT

Official ICT investment series from statistical offices in Latin America are not yet available.[2] As noted above, other studies that examine the adoption and growth impact of ICT in the region derived investment from ICT expenditure data from private data sources whose quality is highly questionable. Instead, we estimate ICT investment in Latin American countries directly using official data. After defining ICT goods, we explain how we use a commodity-flow method to estimate investment in computer and communication equipment across Latin America. Software investment cannot be imputed using this method because of missing information. We therefore employ elasticities of a fixed-effects panel data regression for 20 OECD countries to approximate software investment in Latin America.

2.1 Definition of ICT Assets

This paper defines ICT assets according to several industry categories of the International Standard Industrial Classification (ISIC Rev. 3), following OECD's Working Party on Indicators for the Information Society (see Table 4.1). This broad definition includes various traditional assets, but it facilitates the use of national accounts, international trade data and input–output tables to estimate investment series.

Hardware and communication equipment are produced by two manufacturing industries (ISIC Rev. 3): Industry 30 (office and computer equipment, including computers, printers, photocopiers and other peripheral equipment), and Industry 32 (radio, TV and communication equipment). Software originates from software producers; it includes prepackaged, own account and customized software.[3]

Table 4.1   Definition of ICT equipment according to ISIC Rev. 3

Industry	Description
3000	Office, accounting and computing machinery
3130	Insulated wire and cable
3210	Electronic valves and tubes and other electronic components
3220	Television and radio transmitters and apparatus for line telephony and line telegraphy
3230	Television and radio receivers, sound or video recording or reproducing apparatus, and associated goods
3312	Instruments and appliances for measuring, checking, testing, navigating and other purposes except industrial process control equipment
3313	Industrial process control equipment

Source: Core ICT Indicators (Partnership on Measuring ICT for Development, 2006).

2.2 Estimation of Computer and Communication Equipment Investment

Investment in computer hardware and communication equipment is estimated using the commodity-flow method. This supply-side method, which was pioneered by Van Ark et al. (2002) and adapted to the case of Latin America, traces domestically produced and imported ICT goods to their final destination: exports, consumption and investment.

The commodity-flow method involves two steps. The first step consists of estimating the investment ratio of domestically available ICT goods using input–output (IO) or supply-and-use (SU) tables by:

$$\text{Investment ratio} = \frac{I_{i,t}^{IO}}{(Q_{i,t}^{IO} + M_{i,t}^{IO} - E_{i,t}^{IO})}, \quad (4.1)$$

where I refers to investment, Q to domestic production, M to imports, E to exports, superscript IO to input–output tables, and the subscripts t and i to time and type of investment (that is, computer equipment or communication equipment), respectively. Input–output tables and supply and use tables are available for five Latin American countries for several years (see Table 4A.1 in the Appendix for investment ratios obtained using equation (4.1)). These data suggest that investment ratios are higher for computer equipment than for communication equipment. For years without such tables, we assumed that the investment ratios equalled those of the closest year available.

The second step involves estimating the investment series using longitudinal production and trade data. We apply obtained investment ratios to time series of domestic production plus imports and minus exports:

$$I_{i,t} = \frac{I_{i,t}^{IO}}{(Q_{i,t}^{IO} + M_{i,t}^{IO} - E_{i,t}^{IO})} * (Q_{i,t} + M_{i,t} - E_{i,t}). \quad (4.2)$$

Data on trade in computer and communication equipment are directly available, but this is not the case for production. Data on exports and imports (excluding re-exports) of computer and communication equipment are directly obtained from a United Nations COMTRADE trade database. In contrast, data on production (ISIC Rev. 3 Industries 30 and 32) are usually not available separately, apart from for years when industrial surveys are conducted, but rather are contained within broader production categories (ISIC Rev. 2 classification). We assume that ICT production within this broader production category equals the ICT share in exports in the same broader category.[4]

2.3 Estimation of Software Investment

As no official data for software investment are available and the use of indirect estimates based on private data from the World Information Technology and Services Alliance (WITSA) yielded unsatisfactory results, we impute software investment using elasticities of a fixed-effects regression model for OECD countries.[5] We implicitly assume that the elasticity of hardware to software investment in OECD countries, and several control variables, may be representative for Latin America. Since we have estimated hardware investment in Latin America, we can impute software investment by applying the resulting elasticity for OECD countries to time series of hardware investment for Latin America.

We explored several control variables of software investment in addition to hardware investment, mainly because we expect that the proportionate investment in customized and own-account software is lower in Latin America than in the OECD area. We include key factors suggested by the literature (see Kraemer et al., 2000; Caselli and Coleman, 2001; Guerrieri et al., 2004), such as wealth, the structure of the economy, Internet use and the long-term interest rate. Countries with more national wealth should have more capital. The structure of the economy affects software demand, because some industries, such as finance and business services, are more information technology-intensive than others. Finally, investment is influenced by long-term interest rates.

We estimated the following equation:

$$\log\left(\frac{SI_{it}}{GDP_{it}}\right) = \alpha + \beta \log X_{it} + \eta_i + \mu_{it}, \qquad (4.3)$$

where SI_{it} is software investment in country i and year t, X_{it} is a set of explanatory variables, η_i is a country effect and μ_{it} is the measurement error, which is assumed to be independent and identically distributed among countries and years. The determinants X_{it} for 20 OECD countries are hardware investment (normalized by GDP), GDP per capita, the size of financial services in the total economy, the number of Internet users per 100 inhabitants and the long-term interest rate.

Full regression results are shown in Table 4A.2 in the Appendix. Here we focus on the regression results of equation (4.3).[6] The elasticity of hardware investment with respect to software investment is positive and significant. Also, a larger financial sector and an increase in the number of Internet users increase the demand for software. The interest rate, a cost measure of investment, is negatively related to software investment, as expected.

The coefficient of GDP per capita is negative, but it is not significant in our preferred equation (4.3).

We use the elasticities to make an out-of-sample prediction of software investment in Latin America. The implicit assumption underlying this approach is that the average elasticity from OECD countries is similar to that for Latin America.[7] Table 4A.3 in the Appendix presents the resulting investment series (normalized by GDP). The share of software investment in GDP for Latin America is clearly below that of OECD countries. Furthermore, the region displays substantial variation across countries, with Chile having the highest investment share and Brazil the lowest.

2.4 ICT Investment Series

We added up the investment in computers, communication equipment and software. Total ICT investment series, as a share of GDP in current national prices, are shown in Figure 4.1. Chile has the highest investment share, whereas Argentina, Brazil, Costa Rica and Uruguay invested less. ICT investment shares increased in the 1990s; they bounced back temporarily after 2000, except in Costa Rica. Similar patterns are observed in the European Union and the United States, but here investments in new technologies are much higher.

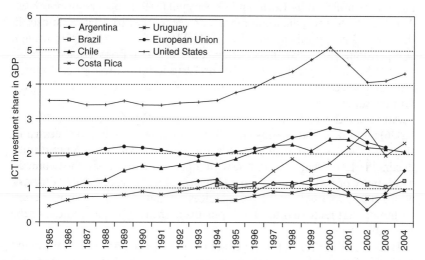

Sources: Latin American countries from own calculations; European Union and United States from updated tables by Van Ark et al. (2002), available at www.ggdc.net; accessed 22 March 2010.

Figure 4.1 ICT investment share as a percentage of GDP

3   ICT DEFLATORS

The estimated ICT investment series in current prices should be deflated to obtain real values. However, few statistical offices in the world, and none in Latin America, take into account the enormous quality improvements and subsequent price declines for similar models of ICT goods. Moreover, these series, if available, should be made comparable among countries, which would require the adoption of some kind of harmonization procedure. Here we apply ICT deflators from the United States to the context of Latin America using the harmonization method proposed by Schreyer (2002).

Two case studies examine price declines in ICT goods in Latin America. Guerrero de Lizardi (2006) considers price developments for desktop PCs and laptops in 1990–2004 in Mexico. His findings are questionable, as they suggest similar price developments for ICT goods in Mexico and the United States. Similar price developments imply that the prices of ICT goods in Mexico fell faster than in the United States, as overall inflation was much higher in the former country. This result overstates price declines by hedonic regressions, which occur more often in these types of regressions. A preferable approach would be to compare (or even average) these findings with a matched pairs index. A study on microcomputers in Brazil by Luzio and Greenstein (1995) appears more robust. These authors apply hedonic regression techniques to a large dataset in the 1980s. During this period, Brazil shielded off its market from foreign competition. Protected infant Brazilian computer firms copied models from IBM and Apple. Findings for the 1980s indicate rapid price declines, although prices fell with a lag relative to similar computer goods in the United States.

Although the hedonic deflators constructed by Guerrero de Lizardi (2006) and Luzio and Greenstein (1995) cannot be used directly because of their limited coverage of ICT goods, they seem to confirm the rapid price declines in Latin America. In line with other studies that also faced limited availability of ICT price deflators (Daveri, 2001; Schreyer, 2002; Van Ark et al., 2002), we use hedonic price indices estimated for the United States, assuming that relative price developments in the region match those of the United States.[8]

Hedonic price indices for the United States can be applied to the context of Latin America in at least three ways (Schreyer, 2002; Van Ark and Piatkowski, 2004). First, the United States deflator can be applied directly, without adjusting for domestic inflation, assuming similar overall inflation rates across countries. Second, the United States deflator can be adjusted for domestic inflation. This can be written as follows:

$$\Delta \ln (P_{ICT}^{other}) = \Delta \ln (P_{N}^{other}) + \Delta \ln (P_{ICT}^{US}) - \Delta \ln (P_{N}^{US}), \qquad (4.4)$$

where P is the deflator for the national economy (N) or the ICT goods (ICT) in the United States (US) or Latin American countries (*other*). The third method adjusts the United States ICT deflators using the official exchange rate of each country (Daveri, 2001):

$$\Delta \ln (P_{ICT}^{other}) = \Delta \ln (P_{ICT}^{US}) + \Delta \ln (e_{US}^{other}). \qquad (4.5)$$

Like Schreyer (2002), we used a Törnqvist volume index to examine the ICT deflators from these different methods. The second and third methods yield similar results, whereas the estimates of the first alternative are very different. We opted for the second alternative (that is, the United States ICT deflator adjusted for domestic inflation) because the inflation history and production structure in Latin America differ strongly from those of the United States and because exchange rates were distorted in Latin America at several points in time.[9] Table 4A.4 in the Appendix shows the percentage share of capital assets in total gross fixed capital formation.

4 CAPITAL SERVICES

Time series of investment in the three major traditional asset categories (namely, residential buildings, non-residential buildings and machinery and equipment) were taken from updated time series in Hofman (2000). We thus have long time series for three non-ICT capital assets from 1950 to 2004 and for three ICT assets from 1980 to 2004. The capital stock is constructed using the perpetual inventory method. Following Jorgenson and Griliches (1967), we assumed geometric depreciation, with the depreciation rates for capital assets from Timmer and Van Ark (2005).[10]

The quantity of capital input is measured by capital services.[11] Following Jorgenson and Griliches (1967), we can express the growth of capital services as follows:

$$\dot{K} = K_t - K_{t-1} = \sum_i \bar{\tau}_{i,t}(K_{i,t} - K_{i,t-1}), \qquad (4.6)$$

where K is the capital stock and weights τ are the average shares of asset types in the value of capital compensation. Specifically,

$$\bar{\tau}_{i,t} = (1/2)(\tau_{i,t} + \tau_{i,t-1}); \qquad (4.7)$$

$$\tau_{i,t} = \frac{p_{i,t}K_{i,t}}{\sum_i p_{i,t}K_{i,t}}. \tag{4.8}$$

We then define $p_{i,t}$ as the rental price of capital services from asset type i:

$$p_{i,t} = p^I_{i,t}(r_t + \delta_i - \pi_{i,t}), \tag{4.9}$$

where $p^I_{i,t}$ is the investment price, r the nominal rate of return, δ the depreciation rate and $\pi_{i,t}$ the rate of inflation.[12] The aggregation of capital services is based on user weights and a Törnqvist quantity index.

The nominal rate of return, r, can be estimated ex post (as an internal rate of return) or ex ante (external rate of return) (Oulton, 2005). The ex post approach uses capital revenue, CR, as derived from the gross operating surplus (excluding the income of self-employed persons).[13] The estimated internal rate of return is thus:

$$r_T = \frac{CR^T - \sum (\delta_i - \pi_{i,T})K_{i,T}}{\sum K_{i,T}}. \tag{4.10}$$

The ex post approach assumes constant returns to scale in the production process, perfect competition (and thus zero profits) and an expected (ex ante) rate of return equal to the realized (ex post) rate of return.

We adopted an ex ante approach and used market interest rates to calculate the rate of return. The rationale for using interest rates to estimate rates of return is based on two channels: interest rates represent both the opportunity costs investors face (who compare alternative expected earnings) and the cost of a loan eventually used to finance investment (that is, the expected rate of return from the investment is compared with the interest on the loan). A disadvantage of the ex ante approach is the difference between estimated capital revenues and those presented in national accounts. This difference might arise from the less-than-perfect competition in Latin American markets that allows firms to generate profits, but it could also reflect an incorrect aggregation of capital stemming from intermediate capital consumption. Given the more stringent underlying assumptions of the ex post approach and the widespread availability of external rates of return, we opted for the ex ante approach.

The next section presents our results calculated using the external rate of return (ex ante approach). Real interest rates for each country were obtained from the World Bank database, Global Development Finance. We therefore measure the rental price using the real interest rate, the depreciation rate and the relative price change of each capital asset.

5 GROWTH ACCOUNTING DECOMPOSITION

We use a standard growth accounting framework to estimate the contribution of ICT investment to economic growth. Consider for this decomposition of output growth the aggregate production function:

$$Y = A*F(L, K_n, K_{it}), \qquad (4.11)$$

where Y is output,[14] A represents Hicks-neutral technological change, L is labour input in hours and K_n and K_{it} are services from non-ICT and ICT capital, respectively. In our decomposition, output includes dwellings, and non-ICT capital includes investments in residential buildings. To accurately measure productivity, dwellings and residential investment should preferably be excluded, since these are not considered producer activities (OECD, 2001b). Unfortunately, we were unable to do so, although it is likely that excluding dwellings and residential investment would result in a higher ICT investment contribution to growth. By rewriting equation (4.11), we estimate multi-factor productivity as the residual:

$$\Delta \ln A = \Delta \ln Y - \overline{v_L}\Delta \ln L - \overline{v_{Kn}}\Delta \ln K_n - \overline{v_{Kit}}\Delta \ln K_{it}. \qquad (4.12)$$

This output decomposition assumes that factor markets are perfectly competitive. Consequently, each input is remunerated by its marginal product, and prices correspond to their rate of substitution. We also assume constant returns to scale (that is, $v_L + v_{Kn} + v_{Kit} = 1$).

We use equation (4.12) to decompose economic growth into its main determinants. Table 4.2 shows the results for Latin America from 1990 to 2004. In the table, GDP growth is expressed as the average annual logarithmic growth rate (last column); other columns show the components of GDP growth. In 1990–2004, GDP growth varied strongly across Latin American countries. Chile and Costa Rica rapidly increased output, whereas Argentina, Brazil and Uruguay grew moderately. On average, technological change is positive throughout the period except in Argentina.[15] Our decomposition of output growth suggests that non-ICT capital is the main driver of growth for all countries in Latin America.

The contribution of ICT capital services to economic growth is substantial. The average annual contribution of ICT capital to growth ranges from 0.21 percentage points in Brazil to 0.62 percentage points in Chile. This finding indicates that Latin America has not been excluded from the ICT revolution, but the differences across countries are huge. ICT adopters can be divided into two clusters. The first cluster includes Chile and Costa Rica, which invested substantially in computers, communication

Table 4.2   Components of economic growth, 1990–2004 (in percentage points)

Country	ICT Capital	Non-ICT Capital	Total Capital	Labour Hours	Multi-factor Productivity	GDP Growth
Argentina[a]	0.24	1.05	1.29	0.84	(0.28)	1.84
Brazil[b]	0.21	0.72	0.93	0.74	0.51	2.18
Chile	0.62	2.74	3.37	1.31	0.84	5.52
Costa Rica	0.51	1.99	2.50	1.93	0.20	4.63
Uruguay[c]	0.23	1.33	1.56	(0.99)	0.39	0.96

Notes:
a. 1992–2004.
b. 1995–2004.
c. 1995–2004.

Sources: Time series data on output, non-ICT investment series, employment and hours worked are from updated series in Hofman (2000). Depreciation rates of ICT and non-ICT capital are taken from Timmer and Van Ark (2005). The external rate of return, real interest rates for each country, were obtained from the World Bank database, Global Development Finance.

equipment and software. In the second cluster are Argentina, Brazil and Uruguay, which invested relatively little in new technologies.

Table 4A.5 in the Appendix shows the growth contribution of production factors during various sub-periods. The table gives insight into ICT investment patterns across time. The simple average for Latin America reveals an apparent trend that is in line with the ICT history of developed economies. In the period from 1995 to 2000, the ICT contribution increased relative to 1990–95. This trend is the opposite of the other production factors (namely, non-ICT capital and labour) and technological change. ICT investment declined slightly from 2000 to 2004.

Two other growth accounting approaches are common in the literature, and we explored these approaches as well. First, the contribution of capital services to growth can be measured ex post by using an internal rate of return (see Section 4 for a discussion). Table 4A.6 in the Appendix presents the results from the ex post approach. The ICT capital services contribution to growth is lower than our previous estimates in ten out of 13 country periods. Hence, using an internal rate of return results in lower weights on the rental prices of ICT assets.

Second, the contribution of capital investment to output growth can be studied through the growth rate of the capital stock. This approach is still standard in the growth accounting literature. However, it does not take into account the higher user costs of ICT goods, but rather weights capital assets by their share in total capital. Table 4A.7 in the Appendix presents our results based on measuring the ICT capital contribution through the change in the ICT capital stock. The contribution of ICT capital is much lower with this approach. That finding indicates that measuring capital goods by their respective user costs, and not by their capital share, is particularly important for assessing the contribution of ICT capital services to economic growth.

6 CONCLUDING REMARKS

This paper has estimated ICT investment series for five Latin American countries and examined its impact on economic growth. Our findings indicate that ICT investment in Latin America has been substantially below the levels of the United States and the European Union, but results differ substantially among countries in the region. Chile is proportionally the largest investor in ICT, converging to European levels of ICT investment. The other countries do not show any convergence. We examined the contribution of ICT capital services to economic growth within a growth accounting framework from 1990 to 2004. ICT capital services, as a factor of production, contributed between 0.21 percentage points (in Brazil) and 0.62 percentage points (in Chile) to economic growth from 1990 to 2004.

Our results on ICT investment and ICT contributions to growth in Latin America differ from those found by Pohjola (2003) and Jorgenson and Vu (2005 and Chapter 1 this volume). Pohjola (2003) finds a convergence of ICT investment to United States levels, based on WITSA data. In contrast, we find that ICT investment is still well below the level found in the United States (see figure 4.1) and that no clear convergence is apparent. Jorgenson and Vu (2005 and Chapter 1 this volume) suggest similar contributions to economic growth for 1995–2000, but their results indicate that the contribution of ICT to growth slightly increased during 2000–05. We find that their contribution fell.[16] These two studies used WITSA data, which most likely overestimate investment in Latin America. Jorgenson and Vu (2005 and Chapter 1 this volume) aim to estimate ICT capital contributions to growth across several regions in the world. In this chapter, out goal was to estimate ICT investment for a small group of Latin American countries directly, using official data sources.

By estimating genuine ICT investment series for Latin America, this paper represents a major step forward towards official ICT investment series. Several issues should be carefully addressed in future research, however. These issues relate foremost to measurement errors. Gross output in the computer and communications industry should be measured accurately. So far, output data are incomplete or missing. Another issue is the limited availability and level of detail of input–output tables. Various Latin American countries (including Colombia and Mexico) still use the ISIC Rev. 2 classification in constructing input–output tables. That classification complicates the use of the commodity-flow method in constructing investment series.

ICT contributes to growth via three channels: (1) ICT is a capital input in the production process; (2) ICT-goods-producing industries contribute to multi-factor productivity growth; and (3) ICT generates spillovers to ICT-using services industries. This paper studies the first transmission channel, and it provides some indication on the third by means of multi-factor productivity growth estimates. Future research should aim at expanding our understanding of the transmission channels from this new technology. Aravena et al. (2007) develop a possible approach for examining the relation between ICT adoption and technological change in Latin America. Externalities, the third transmission channel, can be incorporated into a production framework such as ours by extending the Cobb-Douglas framework towards a dynamic flexible cost function (Morrison and Siegel, 1997).

NOTES

*   At the time of writing this chapter, Mariela Dal Borgo was working as a researcher of the Division of Production, Productivity and Management at the Economic Commission for Latin America and the Caribbean (ECLAC) in Santiago, Chile. We are grateful for help, comments and suggestions by Claudio Aravena, Bart Van Ark, Alvaro Diaz, Christian Hurtado, Mathilde Mas, Paul Schrever, Marcel Timmer and participants at two seminars at ECLAC in Santiago on 30 November–1 December 2006 and 29–30 March 2007. The opinions expressed here are those of the authors and do not necessarily reflect those of ECLAC.
1. Pohjola (2003) and Jorgenson and Vu (2005 and Chapter 1 this volume) use ICT expenditure data from private sources such as the World Information Technology and Services Alliance (WITSA).
2. Argentina and Chile are exceptions. The statistical office of Argentina (INDEC) estimated a capital stock of computer hardware and communication equipment for 1993. In Chile, the statistical office (INE) produced an ICT satellite account for 2004, including investment data for that year. Neither country, however, offers publicly available ICT investment time series.
3. Measurement instruments, wire and cable are excluded here because they cannot be separated from investment in other industries.
4. Export data are taken from UN's COMTRADE database, which follows the SITC Rev. 3 classification starting from the early 1990s. Data were extrapolated backwards with matched trade data at the four-digit level of ISIC Rev. 2. Production data were taken from industrial surveys, industrial statistics from the United Nations Industrial Development Organization (UNIDO), and ECLAC's PADI database. The share of computer goods and communication goods in trade data was estimated using detailed product qualifications at the four-digit level.

5. WITSA data for Latin America seem highly implausible for two reasons. First, in many cases they seem to be based on simple extrapolation. For example, WITSA data for Chile show a constant ratio of software to hardware spending for Chile for 2000–04. Second, these data show unjustifiable differences among Latin American countries in the relationship between hardware and software expenditure. Notably, in Chile, spending on software seems unreasonably low compared with hardware spending, while in Costa Rica the opposite was found. In Chile, official data for 2004 suggest that software spending was three times the amount indicated by WITSA. For Brazil, we suspect that both hardware and software spending are upwardly biased compared with hardware investment estimated through the commodity-flow method.

6. The Hausman test for this regression indicates that the fixed-effects estimator is preferable to the random-effects estimator.

7. We checked this assumption by running fixed-effects regressions for determinants of hardware investment in OECD countries and Latin American countries. A comparison of resulting coefficients indicates that for rather simple model specifications, the sign and significance of determinants are similar.

8. These price indices are constructed using a hedonic regression function, in which the price of an ICT good is regressed on several of its characteristics. Estimated coefficients are used to translate changes in the characteristics into price changes.

9. This method is not applicable to periods of very high inflation (such as the late 1980s in Argentina and Brazil). We therefore extrapolated series backwards by starting with the growth rate in machinery and equipment and then adding the difference between the average growth rate of ICT assets and machinery and equipment for the 1990s. This biases the results, but rapid depreciation of ICT assets eliminates the bias for results in the 1990s.

10. Common alternative depreciation patterns include straight-line depreciation, sum-of-the-digits depreciation and a geometric depreciation pattern. With straight-line depreciation, a capital asset (in constant prices) declines by the same amount each time period. With sum-of-the-digits depreciation, the capital asset declines linearly over the lifetime of the asset. Geometric depreciation assumes a constant rate of depreciation in each time period. This constant rate of depreciation is defined by R/T, where R is the declining balance rate and T is the service life of the asset. While there is no agreement on the depreciation pattern that should be used in constructing the capital stock, it has become common in recent years to use a geometric depreciation rate.

11. The contribution of capital (including ICT capital) to output growth has traditionally been estimated using the capital stock. The use of gross or net capital stock presents several problems for productivity studies, however, and the current general consensus is that capital services better reflect the contribution of capital in the production process (OECD, 2001a). The first problem with using capital stocks is its inconsistency with respect to the other variables in a growth accounting exercise, all of which are flows. A second problem is related to the productive efficiency of capital assets. The gross capital stock values all assets according to their historic price and therefore assumes that all assets are equally productive, independent of age. The net capital stock uses market price to value older assets, but this generally overstates the productive efficiency profile of capital assets. Finally, each asset in the capital stock is weighted by its market value. This weighting scheme implies that assets with the same market value contribute equally to the production process. If, however, capital assets with the same market value have different service lives, the capital assets with a shorter service life should contribute to the production process at a faster rate. Capital assets with a shorter service life are thus understated, whereas those capital assets with a longer service life are overstated.

12. Expression (4.9) represents investment equilibrium, in which an investor is indifferent between earning a nominal rate of return on an investment, q, or buying capital and collecting a rental price, p, and then selling the depreciated asset in the next period $(1 - \delta)q$. This can be defined formally by $(1 + r_T)q_{i,T-1} = p_{i,T} + (1 - \delta_i)q_{i,T}$, where

      rearranging terms and dividing by the previous-period price of investment results in expression (4.9).
13. The compensation of self-employed workers is assumed to be equal to the wages of salaried workers. Estimates for the number of self-employed workers are taken from censuses.
14. Time series data on output, employment and hours worked are from updated series in Hofman (2000).
15. The contribution of labour quality to growth is included in multi-factor productivity.
16. An underlying reason for this divergence might be some mistakes in the secondary sources that Jorgenson and Vu (2005) used. For example, they find that the GDP growth rate in Argentina in 2000–04 was 2.64 per cent. (These data are taken from updated growth accounting results by Jorgenson and Vu, available at http://www.economics.harvard.edu/faculty/jorgenson; accessed 31 March 2010.) Using national accounts data, we find a 2000–04 GDP growth rate for Argentina of 0.27 per cent. This lower growth rate is largely due to the severe crisis in 2002.

REFERENCES

Aravena, C., C. Hurtado and A.A. Hofman (2007), 'Crecimiento, productividad y tecnologías de la información y las comunicaciones en Latinoamérica, 1950–2005', Working Paper, United Nations Economic Commission for Latin America and the Caribbean (ECLAC).

Caselli, F. and W.J. Coleman (2001), 'Cross-country technology diffusion: the case of computers', *American Economic Review*, **91**(2), 328–35.

Daveri, F. (2001), 'Information technology and growth in Europe', Working Paper.

Guerrero de Lizardi, C. (2006), 'Una aproximación al sesgo de medición del precio de las computadoras personales en México', *Economía Mexicana*, **15**, 97–124.

Guerrieri, P., C. Jona-Lasinio and S. Manzocchi (2004), 'Searching for the determinants of IT investment: panel data evidence on European countries', *LLEE Working Document*, No. 4, Rome: Luiss Lab on European Economics.

Hofman, A.A. (2000), *The Economic Development of Latin America in the Twentieth Century*, Cheltenham, UK and Northampton, MA, USA: Edward Elgar.

Jorgenson, D.W. (2001), 'Information technology and the U.S. economy', *American Economic Review*, **91**(1), 1–32.

Jorgenson, D.W. and Z. Griliches (1967), 'The explanation of productivity change', *Review of Economic Studies*, **34**(99), 249–83.

Jorgenson, D.W. and K. Motohashi (2003), 'Economic growth of Japan and the United States in the information age', *RIETI Discussion Paper*, No. 03-E-015, Tokyo: Research Institute of Economy, Trade and Industry.

Jorgenson, D.W. and K. Vu (2005), 'Information technology and the world economy', *Scandinavian Journal of Economics*, **107**(4), 631–50.

Kraemer, K.L., J. Dedrick and E. Shih (2000), 'Determinants of IT investment at the country level', University of California, Irvine, unpublished, available at: http://www.escholarship.org/uc/item/3jh7n9jp; accessed 22 March 2010.

Lizardi, G. de (2006), 'Una aproximación al sesgo de medición del precio de las computadoras personales en México', *Economía Mexicana Nueva Época*, **15**(1), 97–124.

Luzio, E. and S. Greenstein (1995), 'Measuring the performance of a protected infant industry: the case of Brazilian microcomputers', *Review of Economics and Statistics*, **77**(4), 622–33.

Morrison, C.J. and D. Siegel (1997), 'External capital factors and increasing returns in US manufacturing', *Review of Economics and Statistics*, **79**(4), 647–54.

OECD (2001a), *Measuring Capital: A Manual on the Measurement of Capital Stocks, Consumption of Fixed Capital and Capital Services*, Paris: OECD Publishing.

OECD (2001b), *Measuring Productivity: Manual on Measurement of Aggregate and Industry-Level Productivity Growth*, Paris: OECD Publishing.

Oliner, S.D. and D.E. Sichel (2000), 'The resurgence of growth in the late 1990s: is information technology the story?', *Journal of Economic Perspectives*, **14**(4), 3–22.

Oulton, N. (2005), 'Ex post versus ex ante measures of the user cost of capital', *EU KLEMS Working Paper*, No. 5, Groningen.

Partnership on Measuring ICT for Development (2006), *Core ICT Indicators*, New York: United Nations.

Piatkowski, M. (2006), 'Can information and communication technologies make a difference in the development of transition economies?', *Information Technologies and International Development*, **3**(1), 39–53.

Pohjola, M. (2003), 'The adoption and diffusion of ICT across countries: patterns and determinants', in Derek Jones (ed.), *The New Economy Handbook*, San Diego, CA: Academic Press.

Schreyer, P. (2000), 'The contribution of information and communication technology to output growth: a study of the G7 countries', *OECD Science, Technology and Industry Working Paper*, No. 2000/2, Paris: OECD Publishing.

Schreyer, P. (2002), 'Computer price indices and international growth and productivity comparisons', *Review of Income and Wealth*, **48**(1).

Timmer, M. and B. Van Ark (2005), 'Does information and communication technology drive EU–US productivity growth differentials?', *Oxford Economic Papers*, **57**(4), 693–716.

Triplett, J. (1996), 'High tech industry productivity and hedonic price indices', *Industry Productivity. International Comparison and Measurement Issues*, OECD Proceedings, 119–42, Paris: OECD.

Van Ark, B. and M. Piatkowski (2004), 'Productivity, innovation and ICT in old and new Europe', *International Economics and Economic Policy*, **1**(2), 215–46.

Van Ark, B., J. Melka, N. Mulder, M. Timmer and G. Ypma (2002), 'ICT investments and growth accounts for the European Union, 1980–2000', *GGDC Research Memorandum*, No. 56, Groningen Growth and Development Centre.

APPENDIX 4A.1   SUPPLEMENTAL TABLES

Table 4A.1   Ratios of investment to domestic supply[a]

Country	Year	Type of Table	Computer Equipment	Communication Equipment
Argentina	1997	I/O	0.585	0.588
Brazil	1996	I/O	0.336	Na
	2000	I/O	0.299	0.331
Costa Rica	1991	S/U	0.698	0.276
	1992	S/U	0.659	0.281
	1993	S/U	0.657	0.273
	1994	S/U	0.706	0.275
	1995	S/U	0.606	0.272
	1996	S/U	0.537	0.276
	1997	S/U	0.692	0.284
	1998	S/U	Na	0.268
	1999	S/U	Na	0.298
	2000	S/U	Na	0.325
	2001	S/U	Na	0.294
	2002	S/U	Na	0.292
	2003	S/U	Na	0.299
Chile	2004	S/U	0.697	0.693
Uruguay	1997	S/U	0.559	0.385

Note: a. See equation (4.1).

Sources: Argentina, Brazil, Costa Rica and Uruguay input–output or supply-and-use tables from national statistical offices; Chile from Cuenta Satélite de Tecnologías de Información y Comunicación en Chile, March 2006.

Table 4A.2   Determinants of software investment (SI) in OECD countries: fixed-effects regressions[a]

Explanatory Variable	(1)	(2)	(3)	(4)	(5)
	Log of *SI*	Log of *SI*	Log of *SI*	Log of *SI*	Log of *SI*
Log of hardware investment/GDP	1.161 (28.06)**	0.99 (26.04)**	0.89 (26.36)**	0.919 (26.84)**	0.573 (10.75)**
Log of GDP per capita		1.276 (12.93)**	−0.877 (5.13)**	−0.279 −1.47	−0.489 −1.63
Log of size business employment			2.062 (14.48)**	1.645 (10.88)**	1.235 (4.22)**

Table 4A.2 (continued)

Explanatory Variable	(1)	(2)	(3)	(4)	(5)
	Log of *SI*	Log of *SI*	Log of *SI*	Log of *SI*	Log of *SI*
Log of interest rate				−0.024	−0.057
				−1.04	−1.81
Log of Internet users (per 100 inhabitants)					0.063
					(4.29)**
Constant	−0.287	−12.869	3.258	−1.516	1.481
	(11.45)**	(13.22)**	(2.34)*	−0.97	−0.53
No. observations	495	495	470	416	246
No. countries	20	20	20	20	20
R-squared	0.62	0.72	0.82	0.81	0.8

Notes:
* Statistically significant at the 5% level.
** Statistically significant at the 1% level.
a. Absolute value of *t* statistics are in parentheses.

Table 4A.3 *Software investment as a share of GDP*[a]

Year	Argentina	Brazil	Chile	Costa Rica	Uruguay	Latin American Average	OECD Average
1980			0.05			0.05	0.17
1981			0.08			0.08	0.21
1982			0.08			0.08	0.27
1983			0.09			0.09	0.38
1984			0.11	0.02		0.06	0.51
1985			0.14	0.03		0.09	0.59
1986			0.15	0.05		0.10	0.50
1987			0.19	0.07		0.13	0.46
1988			0.19	0.06		0.12	0.49
1989			0.22	0.07		0.15	0.56
1990			0.25	0.09		0.17	0.50
1991			0.29	0.10		0.19	0.52
1992			0.31	0.13		0.22	0.53
1993			0.41	0.18		0.30	0.61
1994		0.26	0.40	0.28		0.31	0.63
1995	0.29	0.27	0.47	0.29	0.24	0.31	0.62
1996	0.26	0.29	0.55	0.30	0.29	0.34	0.64
1997	0.30	0.27	0.58	0.35	0.34	0.37	0.78

Table 4A.3   (continued)

Year	Argentina	Brazil	Chile	Costa Rica	Uruguay	Latin American Average	OECD Average
1998	0.23	0.29	0.63	0.41	0.36	0.38	0.91
1999	0.40	0.35	0.58	0.41	0.42	0.43	1.01
2000	0.41	0.37	0.75	0.44	0.41	0.48	1.21
2001	0.38	0.38	0.74	0.63	0.46	0.52	1.27
2002	0.28	0.37	0.72	0.70	0.52	0.52	1.14
2003	0.47	0.38	0.77	0.55	0.49	0.53	1.17
2004	0.46	0.35	0.72	0.68	0.52	0.54	0.85

Notes: a. Latin American countries are calculated using equation (4.3) from Table 4A.2; OECD average is from OECD Productivity Database and GGDC Growth Accounting Database.

Table 4A.4   Gross fixed capital formation by category[a]

Category and Country	1990	1995	2000	2004
Office and computer equipment				
Argentina	0.13	0.30	1.51	3.23
Brazil	0.04	0.24	1.27	1.99
Chile	0.41	0.73	3.25	4.57
Costa Rica	0.29	0.66	4.34	9.83
Uruguay	0.05	0.40	2.07	5.27
Communication equipment				
Argentina	2.03	2.53	4.00	6.13
Brazil	1.32	2.64	4.41	5.38
Chile	2.38	2.20	4.59	4.50
Costa Rica	0.55	0.80	1.33	1.77
Uruguay	1.11	1.39	2.23	3.58
Software				
Argentina	0.61	1.57	2.52	3.06
Brazil	0.19	1.10	1.91	2.22
Chile	0.94	1.82	3.64	3.65
Costa Rica	0.31	1.41	2.51	4.01
Uruguay	0.58	1.58	3.10	5.70
Total ICT				
Argentina	2.77	4.40	8.03	12.42
Brazil	1.56	3.98	7.59	9.59
Chile	3.73	4.75	11.48	12.72

Table 4A.4 (continued)

Category and Country	1990	1995	2000	2004
Costa Rica	1.15	2.88	8.17	15.62
Uruguay	1.74	3.37	7.39	14.55
Non-ICT machinery and equipment				
Argentina	22.49	30.99	29.71	26.14
Brazil	20.21	26.01	20.29	29.98
Chile	22.26	30.26	25.78	28.09
Costa Rica	54.34	50.18	50.00	44.46
Uruguay	32.30	31.67	27.47	26.93
Construction				
Argentina	74.74	64.61	62.26	61.44
Brazil	78.23	70.01	72.11	60.44
Chile	74.01	65.00	62.74	59.19
Costa Rica	44.51	46.94	41.82	39.92
Uruguay	65.96	64.96	65.14	58.52

Note: a. As a percentage share of total gross fixed capital formation; in constant 2000 prices.

Table 4A.5 *Components of economic growth, by sub-period (percentage points)*

Sub-period and Country	ICT Capital	Non-ICT Capital	Total Capital	Labour Hours	Multi-factor Productivity	GDP Growth
1990–95						
Argentina[a]	0.25	1.90	2.15	(0.57)	1.21	2.78
Chile	0.45	3.46	3.91	1.58	2.84	8.33
Costa Rica	0.22	2.25	2.47	2.02	0.84	5.32
Average LA	0.31	2.54	2.84	1.8	1.63	5.48
1995–2000						
Argentina	0.28	1.42	1.71	1.46	(0.62)	2.54
Brazil	0.21	0.77	0.98	1.05	0.17	2.20
Chile	0.86	2.97	3.82	0.98	(0.73)	4.07
Costa Rica	0.60	2.00	2.60	2.08	0.13	4.81
Uruguay	0.31	2.06	2.37	(1.47)	1.20	2.09
Average LA	0.45	1.84	2.3	0.82	0.67	3.14
2000–04						
Argentina	0.17	(0.06)	0.11	1.13	(0.98)	0.27
Brazil	0.21	0.66	0.88	0.34	0.93	2.14

Table 4A.5   (continued)

Sub-period and Country	ICT Capital	Non-ICT Capital	Total Capital	Labour Hours	Multi-factor Productivity	GDP Growth
2000–04						
Chile	0.56	1.57	2.12	1.38	0.32	3.83
Costa Rica	0.76	1.67	2.43	1.63	(0.51)	3.55
Uruguay	0.13	0.41	0.54	(0.37)	(0.62)	(0.45)
Average LA	0.37	1.08	1.22	0.82	0.03	1.87

Note: a. Argentina 1992–95.

Table 4A.6   *Components of economic growth, ex post approach (percentage points)*

Sub-period and Country	ICT Capital	Non-ICT Capital	Total Capital	Labour Hours	Multi-factor Productivity	GDP Growth
1990–2004						
Argentina[a]	0.18	0.92	1.09	0.84	(0.09)	1.84
Brazil[b]	0.24	0.71	0.95	0.74	0.49	2.18
Chile	0.42	2.67	3.10	1.31	1.12	5.52
Costa Rica	0.42	1.94	2.36	1.93	0.34	4.63
Uruguay[b]	0.27	1.13	1.40	(0.99)	0.54	0.96
1990–95						
Argentina[c]	0.20	1.68	1.88	(0.57)	1.47	2.78
Chile	0.35	3.30	3.64	1.58	3.11	8.33
Costa Rica	0.16	2.14	2.30	2.02	1.00	5.32
1995–2000						
Argentina	0.20	1.35	1.54	1.46	(0.46)	2.54
Brazil	0.30	0.79	1.09	1.05	0.06	2.20
Chile	0.53	2.87	3.40	0.98	(0.31)	4.07
Costa Rica	0.45	1.96	2.42	2.08	0.32	4.81
Uruguay	0.33	2.10	2.42	(1.47)	1.14	2.09
2000–04						
Argentina	0.14	(0.19)	(0.05)	1.13	(0.81)	0.27
Brazil	0.17	0.61	0.77	0.34	1.03	2.14
Chile	0.39	1.64	2.03	1.38	0.41	3.83

Table 4A.6 (continued)

Sub-period and Country	ICT Capital	Non-ICT Capital	Total Capital	Labour Hours	Multi-factor Productivity	GDP Growth
Costa Rica	0.71	1.67	2.38	1.63	(0.46)	3.55
Uruguay	0.20	(0.07)	0.13	(0.37)	(0.20)	(0.45)

Notes:
a. 1992–2004.
b. 1995–2004.
c. 1991–95.

Table 4A.7 Components of economic growth, standard approach (%)

Sub-period and Country	ICT Capital	Non-ICT Capital	Total Capital	Labour Hours	Multi-factor Productivity	GDP Growth
1990–2004						
Argentina[a]	0.07	0.88	0.94	0.84	0.06	1.84
Brazil[b]	0.06	0.69	0.74	0.74	0.70	2.18
Chile	0.14	2.54	2.68	1.31	1.53	5.52
Costa Rica	0.14	1.92	2.06	1.93	0.64	4.63
Uruguay[b]	0.05	1.42	1.47	(0.99)	0.48	0.96
1990–95						
Argentina[c]	0.08	1.21	1.29	(0.57)	2.06	2.78
Chile	0.10	2.95	3.05	1.58	3.70	8.33
Costa Rica	0.04	2.01	2.06	2.02	1.25	5.32
1995–2000						
Argentina	0.07	1.25	1.32	1.46	(0.23)	2.54
Brazil	0.06	0.77	0.83	1.05	0.32	2.20
Chile	0.16	2.78	2.94	0.98	0.14	4.07
Costa Rica	0.12	1.93	2.05	2.08	0.68	4.81
Uruguay	0.06	2.10	2.16	(1.47)	1.40	2.09
2000–04						
Argentina	0.04	0.17	0.22	1.13	(1.08)	0.27
Brazil	0.06	0.58	0.64	0.34	1.17	2.14
Chile	0.17	1.73	1.91	1.38	0.54	3.83
Costa Rica	0.28	1.79	2.07	1.63	(0.16)	3.55
Uruguay	0.04	0.56	0.60	(0.37)	(0.68)	(0.45)

Notes:
a. 1992–2004.
b. 1995–2004.
c. 1991–1995.

5. Growth, productivity and information and communications technologies in Latin America, 1950–2005

**Claudio Aravena, Marc Badia-Miró,
André A. Hofman, Christian Hurtado and
José Jofré González***

1 INTRODUCTION

Half a century has passed since Solow (1957) developed his model for analysing economic growth, which he used to demonstrate that growth was attributable to a number of sources, with capital and labour being the main factors of production. One of the main results is the role of technological progress in growth, calculated from the residual of the aggregate function for GDP and the aforementioned factors of production. Solow estimated that 87.5 per cent of the total increase in output per person-hour in the United States could be attributed to technological progress and the remaining 12.5 per cent to increased use of capital. Since the mid-1950s, numerous articles based on Solow's concepts have sought to produce new measures of productivity, which is seen as the component that can enable countries to achieve high and sustained growth rates.

The concept of multi-factor productivity (MFP) represented a major step forwards in growth analysis. Much remained to be explained, however, and many papers have attempted to reduce the residual growth component, increasing the explanatory power of factors of production.

A residual estimate of the contribution of efficiency or MFP can be calculated based on an aggregate production function for GDP and using independent measurements for output and each of the factors of production. Like other residuals, MFP reflects the difficulty of specifying the function used and measuring the observed variables. Despite these and other limitations, the accounting approach to sources of growth provides a powerful empirical approximation of the contribution of the main growth factors, and it remains an essential tool in studying countries' economic growth.

In the past 50 years, Latin America has seen very strong fluctuations in its growth pattern and in the contribution of the various factors. Possible causes include capital disinvestment and fluctuations in productivity. In particular, MFP growth has shown sharp variations since the 1980s, when it appears to have fallen and then stagnated.

The purpose of this paper is to determine the causes of those changes. We start by analysing economic growth in ten countries of the region: Argentina, Bolivia, Brazil, Chile, Colombia, Costa Rica, Ecuador, Mexico, Peru and Venezuela. We then draw inferences for the region as a whole based on those country results.

The paper is structured as follows: the second section presents the stylized facts on per capita GDP growth in the region. Section 3 explains the methodology of the traditional accounting approach to growth, with an emphasis on variations in MFP in the region, and notes quality-based improvements in factors of production. Section 4 presents an econometric analysis of panel data to explain the behaviour of MFP, and the final section concludes.

2   STYLIZED FACTS ON THE ECONOMIC GROWTH OF TEN LATIN AMERICAN COUNTRIES (1950–2005)

The growth of economic activity (measured by per capita GDP) in Latin America during the period 1950–2005 includes two notable characteristics: (1) the presence of breaks in the long-term trend, as illustrated by comparing country growth with a constant growth trend,[1] and (2) the heterogeneity of per capita GDP, which translates into disparities in their respective levels and in the growth rates from the second half of the twentieth century on.

We use per capita GDP to analyse long-term trends in the selected Latin American economies. It reflects the growth of each economy and takes into account the correction of the total GDP figure according to population.

From the perspective of long-term growth, the history of the Latin American economies is traditionally divided into five periods (Figure 5.1), marked by economic, political and international events that affected the behaviour of their growth.[2] Those periods, and the identifying events and characteristics, are as follows:

Latin America

Source: Authors' elaboration, on the basis of Hofman (1999).

Figure 5.1   Per capita GDP in Latin America, 1950–2005 (1950 = 100)

1   The period of strong and sustained growth following World War II, through the end of the low oil prices (1950–73). Most of the countries adopted state-run industrialization policies and promoted import substitution in this period.

2   The period of structural problems and reform (1973–80), characterized by the first oil shock and, at the domestic level, the appearance of authoritarian regimes that implemented aggressive structural reforms. Surprisingly, the region's positive growth trend continued despite those developments.

3   The lost decade (1980–90), characterized by a weakening of the growth rates of per capita economic activity, external debt servicing problems, inflation, balance-of-payments deficits and strong deindustrialization processes.

4   The recovery period (1990–98) for most of the Latin American economies, with annual per capita GDP growth rates of 1.6 per cent. This was still well below the figure for industrialized countries.

5   The post-Asian-crisis period (1998 to present). External shocks and increased volatility of fuel prices forced the countries' economic policy-makers to take steps to prevent the worsening of negative external shocks, with varied results.

As for variations among countries, a comparison of per capita GDP levels in 1950 and 2005 shows no drastic differences in ranking, with a

Table 5.1 Per capita GDP, selected countries and years (in 1980 international dollars)

1950		2005	
Country	Per Capita GDP	Country	Per Capita GDP
Argentina	2727	Chile	6957
Venezuela	2483	Mexico	5750
Chile	2179	Argentina	5407
Mexico	1826	Costa Rica	4256
Peru	1436	Venezuela	3885
Costa Rica	1252	Brazil	3433
Colombia	1227	Colombia	3208
Ecuador	1025	Ecuador	3046
Brazil	1012	Peru	2678
Bolivia	926	Bolivia	1182

Source: Authors' elaboration, on the basis of Hofman (1999).

few exceptions. Argentina and Chile rank the highest, with Bolivia and Ecuador at the bottom of the table. The most significant changes were the downward slip suffered by the Bolivarian Republic of Venezuela, the rise of Mexico and Brazil and Peru's decline. This shows that the initial levels of per capita GDP do not predict the long-term trend, although they influence it considerably. Thus, the highest placed of the countries of the region continue to occupy strong positions; those near the bottom of the table remain the same, with fairly poor performances throughout the period (Table 5.1).

With regard to per capita GDP growth rates, the highest value during the period 1950–2005 was 2.3 per cent per year. This rate was achieved by Costa Rica, which ranked sixth in the table for 1950. Brazil reached 2.2 per cent per year (Brazil began in ninth place, but gradually rose to sixth place), followed by Chile and Mexico with 2.1 per cent.[3]

Next we compare actual performance with projections assuming a long-run annual rate of 2 per cent and taking the initial levels of per capita GDP in 1950 as our starting point. Brazil, Costa Rica and Mexico are the only countries where growth rates exceeded the projected trends, although the changes were slight and gradual. The other countries did not always see positive movements in their growth rates, and their performances were much more irregular (see Figure 5.2).

Bolivia, Peru and Venezuela recorded sluggish growth in the long term, mostly owing to the stagnation that began in the 1970s. This outcome is especially dramatic considering that two of the three countries (Bolivia

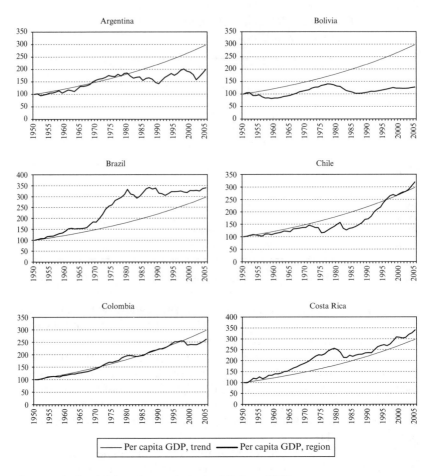

Source: Authors' elaboration, on the basis of Hofman (1999).

Figure 5.2   GDP per capita in selected countries of Latin America, 1950–
2005 (1950 = 100)

and Peru) began with the lowest levels of per capita GDP. In contrast, Argentina posted a performance similar to that of Peru; it had one of the highest rates of per capita GDP in 1950. The Bolivarian Republic of Venezuela registered a similar performance, although its strongest growth was in the initial period and its subsequent fall was steeper (its dependence on oil and fluctuations in oil prices are the major factors in its economic performance).

From 1950 to 1973, most of the countries showed positive trends, with

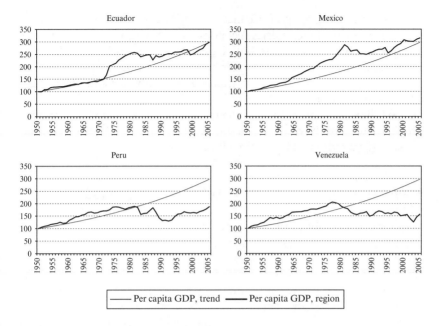

Figure 5.2 (continued)

growth rates exceeding 2 per cent per year, except for Bolivia. This is partly due to the effects of state-run industrialization based on a process of import substitution.

Per capita GDP growth rates were uneven in Latin America in the period 1973–80. It was a very favourable period for Brazil, Costa Rica, Ecuador and Mexico (Ecuador and Mexico are significant oil producers, although their output is less than Brazil's). Argentina, Colombia and, to a lesser extent, Peru also enjoyed periods of growth close to 2 per cent per year. Chile, however, saw a considerable downturn caused by the impact of across-the-board liberalization measures.

In the past 55 years of economic history, crisis periods have affected the Latin American economies in different ways and to different extents: (1) the lost decade of the 1980s[4] affected all the countries, but the impact was greater for oil producers such as Ecuador, Mexico and Venezuela, which suffered acute shocks resulting from falling world oil prices; (2) external trade imbalances were widespread, but most severe for Chile and Peru; (3) the 1990s were characterized by signs of recovery in some cases (such as Brazil, Chile and Costa Rica), but other countries continued to be affected by the debt crisis; and (4) the subsequent period of recovery was abruptly interrupted by the Asian crisis in the late 1990s and the Argentine crisis of 2000.

These differences in performance within Latin America were caused by differences in the countries' economic policies (and in the degree of success in terms of achieving policy goals), differences in the allocation of resources and in countries' integration into international markets, the impact of internal and external shocks and, generally speaking, each country's institutional structure.[5]

The following sections analyse the factors that contributed to economic growth in each of the historical periods between 1950 and 2005, as well as those that caused the differences mentioned above.

3   ACCOUNTING APPROACH TO GROWTH

Economic theory states that an economy's output results from the combination of two factors of production (labour and capital) and the available technology. Economic growth is therefore the result of an increase in the quantity of one or both factors of production or an increase in MFP. Thus, one way of examining growth is to separate the contributions of increases in labour, capital and MFP, as proposed by Solow (1957).

One of the major questions to be answered in growth accounting is whether the dynamics of economic growth are attributable to the accumulation of factors or to technological advances and the organization of production.

Growth accounting exercises can be used for different purposes, such as explaining cross-country differences in growth rates and shedding light on the processes of convergence and divergence by assessing the role of technological progress and gauging losses in potential output. Growth accounting cannot, however, provide a complete causal explanation. It furnishes us with a proximate, rather than an ultimate, causality based on changes in the components of growth. In other words, it does not explain the underlying national or international policy considerations or circumstances, but it does identify what phenomena or events require further explanation.

Ultimate causes are economic growth factors that are difficult to quantify in models, such as the role of institutions, pressure from interest groups, historical accidents and economic policy at the national level. They also involve considerations related to the international economic order and exogenous shocks.

The proximate causes of growth are not independent of the ultimate causes. Indeed, proximate causes represent a dimension through which ultimate causes operate. The interaction and interdependency of the different sources of growth should be underscored. An example of interdependency at the proximate level is the interaction between capital accumulation and technological progress.

The basic framework of growth accounting makes it possible to measure how much increases in inputs and technological progress contribute to economic growth. The starting point for such an analysis is a Cobb-Douglas production function with constant returns to scale, in which GDP (Y) is defined as a function of multi-factor productivity (A) and factor inputs (capital, K, and labour, L):

$$Y_t = A_t K_t^{\alpha} L_t^{1-\alpha}, \tag{5.1}$$

where α is the ratio of income to capital.

Taking logs and differentiating with respect to time, and assuming perfect competition, Solow (1957) shows how estimates of the share of capital inputs can be used to weight the contribution of the rate of increase in inputs to arrive at simple estimates of MFP growth as a residual. Nonetheless, Solow's estimated residuals are quite sensitive to modifications in factor inputs, in respect of both their level of utilization and their quality.

We assume zero adjustment costs for capital accumulation and perfect competition in factor markets, so that the payment received by each of them is equal to their social marginal product.

By applying logarithms and derivatives with respect to time to equation (5.1), we obtain the standard estimate for MFP growth:

$$a_t = y_t - \alpha k_t - (1 - \alpha)l_t. \tag{5.2}$$

In this initial breakdown, the capital stock is simply the sum of its machinery equipment, non-residential and residential construction. Labour is incorporated without adjusting for hours worked or level of education.

To improve the MFP estimates, we first eliminate the residential construction component of capital stock, leaving an estimate of capital stock that we denote productive capital. We also correct the labour factor for the number of hours worked. In this paper, we look at possible changes in the quality of factor inputs based on the use of indices that reflect changes in the composition of capital stock and the labour force that make the additional inputs more productive. Hence, the production function (equation (5.1)) can be redefined as:

$$Y_t = A_t (K_t Z_t)^{\alpha} (L_t H_t^{1-\alpha}). \tag{5.3}$$

If equation (5.3) is differentiated with respect to time, we obtain equation (5.4), which is the one used in the growth accounting exercise:

$$y_t = a_t + \alpha k_t + \alpha z_t + (1 - \alpha)l_t + (1 - \alpha)h_t, \qquad (5.4)$$

where Z and H are the quality indices for capital and labour, respectively. H is an index for the quality of the labour force based on education level. Using Hofman's (2000) methodology, we then construct the quality index (H_i) for each country i[6] as a weighted average of the proportions of the population possessing education levels j (Eij):

$$H_t = \sum_{ij} \phi_j E_{ij}. \qquad (5.5)$$

The data on education levels are constructed on the basis of national census information published by ECLAC.[7] The proportions Φ_j are based on the returns to schooling by educational level, with values of 1.0, 1.4 and 2.0 for primary, secondary and tertiary schooling, respectively. We then compare the results obtained from applying the educational quality factors described above with the results from applying the coefficients used by Psacharopoulos (1994a, 1994b) and Psacharopoulos and Patrinos (2004) and those from applying the factors of returns to education calculated by Contreras and Gallegos (2006). We find no significant differences with the coefficients used by Hofman (1999) in his estimation of education's impact on growth.

In the case of capital, failing to adjust for the utilization rate, Z_t, can lead to errors in the measurement of MFP, because growth variations are then attributed to MFP when they actually reflect changes in capital stock utilization rather than improvements in efficiency. If we assume that capital and labour have similar utilization rates, then we can use the unemployment rate as a proxy for the rate of capital utilization. The drawback is that this assumes a strong capital–labour complementarity throughout the cycle.

Another way to correct the capital stock for utilization has been proposed by Costello (1993), who employs a country's aggregate energy consumption as a proxy for the capital used in its economy. This approximation has the advantage of being based on an independent measurement as a proxy for capital, adjusted for its use, but it has the disadvantage of assuming a high degree of complementarity between capital and energy. In our exercise, we use the deviation of the consumption series for modern primary energy sources[8] from its long-term trend, calculated on the basis of a signal extraction model.[9]

The results of this exercise are shown in Table 5.2 and Figure 5.3, divided by historiographic period and by decade, respectively. We find positive growth rates for individual factors of production for all the periods in the Latin American countries as a group, but at the aggregate level, MFP is negative in 1980–90 and 1998–2005.

In the years before the crisis of the 1980s, the Latin American countries

Table 5.2   *Factor contributions to growth in Latin America, by period (%)*

		GDP	Labour	Capital	MFP
1950–73	Argentina	4.1	1.4	1.9	0.8
	Bolivia	3.3	1.2	0.9	1.2
	Brazil	6.7	2.5	3.7	0.4
	Chile	3.9	0.9	1.6	1.4
	Colombia	5.1	1.9	1.5	1.7
	Costa Rica	7.1	2.1	2.6	2.4
	Ecuador	5.3	1.3	2.2	1.8
	Mexico	6.4	2.2	3.0	1.2
	Peru	5.3	1.3	2.0	2.0
	Venezuela	6.5	2.7	2.5	1.3
	Latin America	5.7	2.0	2.6	1.2
1973–80	Argentina	3.3	1.0	2.1	0.2
	Bolivia	3.3	2.6	1.8	−1.1
	Brazil	8.0	2.9	4.5	0.6
	Chile	2.5	1.7	0.8	0.0
	Colombia	5.2	3.4	2.1	−0.3
	Costa Rica	5.2	3.3	3.4	−1.5
	Ecuador	8.7	1.6	3.0	4.1
	Mexico	6.7	4.0	3.1	−0.4
	Peru	3.9	3.7	2.5	−2.3
	Venezuela	4.4	4.5	3.0	−3.1
	Latin America	6.1	2.9	3.2	0.0
1980–90	Argentina	−1.0	0.3	1.0	−2.3
	Bolivia	0.2	2.6	0.7	−3.0
	Brazil	1.7	2.8	2.1	−3.2
	Chile	3.3	2.6	1.3	−0.6
	Colombia	3.4	2.4	1.9	−0.8
	Costa Rica	2.5	2.9	1.7	−2.1
	Ecuador	2.2	3.3	2.0	−3.1
	Mexico	1.9	3.1	1.7	−2.8
	Peru	−0.9	2.7	1.2	−4.7
	Venezuela	0.7	2.4	1.1	−2.8
	Latin America	1.4	2.5	1.7	−2.8
1990–98	Argentina	6.1	1.3	0.7	4.1
	Bolivia	4.3	4.4	1.2	−1.3
	Brazil	2.0	1.7	1.0	−0.6
	Chile	8.2	2.2	2.7	3.3
	Colombia	4.0	2.2	1.6	0.2
	Costa Rica	4.8	2.5	1.8	0.6
	Ecuador	3.4	2.2	1.0	0.2
	Mexico	2.9	0.8	1.1	0.9

Table 5.2 (continued)

		GDP	Labour	Capital	MFP
	Peru	5.4	4.5	1.0	0.0
	Venezuela	3.4	3.7	0.1	−0.3
	Latin America	3.3	1.8	1.0	0.5
1998–2005	Argentina	1.4	1.6	0.6	−0.8
	Bolivia	2.9	2.8	1.5	−1.4
	Brazil	2.0	2.0	1.1	−1.1
	Chile	3.6	1.7	2.7	−0.8
	Colombia	2.1	2.0	1.0	−1.0
	Costa Rica	4.9	1.7	2.2	0.9
	Ecuador	2.9	1.7	0.9	0.3
	Mexico	3.1	2.5	1.9	−1.3
	Peru	3.0	2.6	1.2	−0.8
	Venezuela	1.5	1.4	0.4	−0.3
	Latin America	2.4	2.0	1.3	−1.0

Source: Authors' calculations.

made a positive effort in terms of accumulating production factors, with capital being the factor that made the greatest contribution to economic growth. This began to change, however, as a lower level of factor accumulation was coupled with a decrease in the relative contribution and labour became the leading contributor to GDP growth. This difference in performance is even more striking in the case of MFP.

During the debt crisis, MFP was negative for all the countries. This is quite similar to the pattern after 1998, when all the countries except Costa Rica and Ecuador again witnessed losses in productivity. These two situations were both directly related to slackening GDP growth rates. In the other periods, factor productivity was positive, especially between 1950 and 1973, when the regional economy's growth rates showed a 1.2 percentage point increase (twice the rate of the years immediately following the crisis of the 1980s). This is explained by the greater contribution of the capital that was accumulated as a consequence of state-led industrialization policies and import substitution.

Latin America's development strategy underwent significant changes in the 1980s. One of the major components of its new strategy was the orientation of production structures towards international markets, which marked the end of the region's long-standing import-substitution industrialization (ISI) effort. In many cases, this new outward-looking orientation was accompanied by the dismantling of national industries.

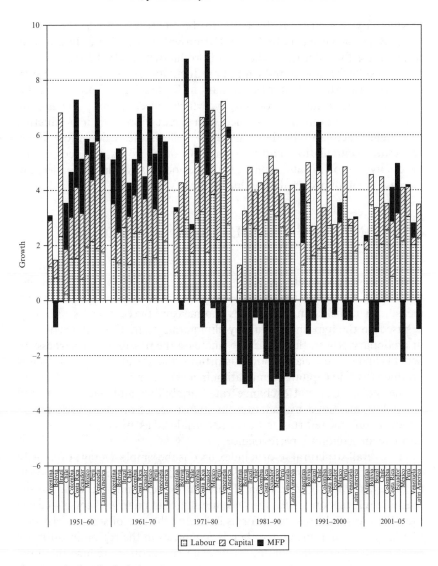

Figure 5.3   Latin America: factor contributions to growth

The picture becomes quite heterogeneous when we take into account the countries' individual performances as well as the regional results. For example, Bolivia has consistently registered negative factor productivity with the exception of the 1960s, while in Brazil, the contribution of productivity was nil from the 1950s to the 1970s, which was the period when Brazil achieved its highest GDP growth rates. The only uniform result across the countries is the loss of productivity in the 1980s.

The results for labour and capital productivity represent the other side of the coin in terms of factor accumulation. Table 5.2 and Figure 5.3 show a relative drop in factor productivity, which reflects a sharp increase in labour and capital inputs combined with a reduction in their productivity. Higher factor productivity, however, reflects the region's low levels of capital accumulation, and vice versa. In other words, the decrease in productivity growth rates seen over the period as a whole may reflect an increase in factor accumulation during those years.

4 ESTIMATING THE DETERMINANTS OF PRODUCTIVITY

Given the wide variance in MFP, as computed in the previous section, we developed an equation to assess the effect of selected variables on this measure. The inclusion of variables that measure the economy's efficiency is based on the hypothesis that, by eliminating restrictions and reducing discretionary power, these variables increase the possibility of harnessing benefits and reduce relative price distortions, thereby affecting both factor productivity and capital accumulation in an economy.

The model uses real exchange rate variability[10] and macroeconomic instability, measured by inflation, as indicators of an economy's inefficiency. Economic reforms, in turn, are considered as measures that tend to improve an economy's performance.

The overall structural reform index used is the simple average of indices constructed by Morley et al. (1999) for trade, national and international finance, taxes and privatization. These authors examine the various far-reaching reforms on tariffs, tax and international finance. They also consider, to a lesser degree, the reforms involving the role of state enterprises and labour regulations undertaken by countries in the region in order to open up the domestic economy to foreign competition, reduce the government's role in resource allocation and production management, and diminish the distortionary effects of the tax system on private decision-making.

MFP is clearly procyclical, so it is also necessary to incorporate variables relating to the economic cycle, such as the terms of trade[11] and currency undervaluation.

The impact of the dissemination of ICT on productivity may be used as a proxy for technological progress. It is therefore important to measure

Table 5.3 Reference values for ICT, 1960–2004[a]

Variable	Reference Value, 1960–64	Reference Value, 1965–79	Reference Value, 1980–99	Reference Value, 1999–2004
No. fixed-line telephones (NFT)	60	60	60	60
No. mobile telephones (NMT)	–	–	85	100
No. Internet users (IU)	–	–	85	85
No. televisions (NT)	–	85	100	100
No. computers (NC)	–	–	85	100

Note: a. For a methodological note on reference values, see www.itu.int/ITU-D/ict/dai/; accessed 24 March 2010.

Source: Authors' elaboration, on the basis of the International Telecommunication Union's Digital Access Index.

this impact and incorporate it into these estimates. For this purpose, we prepared an index to measure the degree of ICT penetration in a country's economic structure.

The index is the result of the unweighted averages of the rates of each of the countries in the different groups. These are based on similarity criteria. To obtain them, we combined five representative ICT variables (see equation (5.6) below): number of fixed-line telephones, number of mobile telephones, number of personal computers, number of television sets and number of Internet users.[12] Since the variables are not homogeneous owing to existing differences between the potential values of degrees of penetration and their different levels of maturity (that is, technologies that appear in different periods), they have been weighted on the basis of the reference values used for preparing the Digital Access Index (see Table 5.3).

The rates referred to above result from the non-homogeneity in the variables used in constructing the index. The use of fixed-line telephones corresponds to a distribution based on the family or business unit, with two or more individuals per unit in both cases; for these reasons, the reference value is approximately 60. In contrast, mobile telephones have a single user, so the chosen reference value is 100. The dissemination of entertainment devices and the use of information tools are such that both televisions and computers have a pattern of use similar to that observed for mobile telephones; we therefore again chose a reference value of 100.

Since several of the variables used to construct the index involve technologies incorporated during the period under review, the reference value used for the first three periods is 85, which is considered tantamount to total installation of the new technology. The choice of variables for constructing the index was based on three criteria: representativeness of the variables within ICT; the need for widespread ICT coverage combining new and more traditional technologies (notwithstanding the need for certain adjustments); and the availability of data for the countries included in the sample (Argentina, Bolivia, Brazil, Chile, Colombia, Costa Rica, Ecuador, Mexico, Peru and Venezuela).

The first criterion is undoubtedly the most difficult to meet. It is based on the different variables combined in preparing the Digital Access Index, with reference to the comparative study conducted by Minges (2005). Of all the data used in constructing the indices, the focus is on those components that refer to the infrastructure endowment, since the rest refer to qualitative variables.[13]

The second criterion is covered by the combination of more traditional ICT variables (such as the number of fixed-line telephones, the number of television sets and the number of computers) and other more modern items (such as mobile telephones and Internet users) that appear in the 1980s and 1990s. According to Minges (2005), one of the problems that arises is precisely the non-existence of more traditional ICT; hence the interest in incorporating them.

The third criterion prevents us from incorporating price variables such as the cost of Internet connection or the cost of communications by type of technology used.

We use NFT to denote the number of fixed-line telephones per 100 inhabitants, NMT the number of mobile telephones per 100 inhabitants, IU the number of Internet users per 100 inhabitants, NT the number of television sets per 100 inhabitants and NC the number of computers per 100 inhabitants. ICT is the ICT index to be measured, and it is calculated as follows:

$$ICT = \frac{NFT}{a} + \frac{NMT}{b} + \frac{IU}{c} + \frac{NT}{d} + \frac{NC}{e}, \qquad (5.6)$$

where a, b, c, d and e are the coefficients incorporated to make the adjustments to each of the variables. The values chosen in each case are those presented in Table 5.3.

Figure 5.4 presents the result for the ten countries of the sample, grouped by geographical area, for the period 1960 to 2004. The values obtained for the different countries are consistent with what we initially expected given the ICT dissemination indices for the region. Likewise, the variation over time of the series of indices clearly incorporates the significant change that the massive use of new technologies implies for ICT trends.

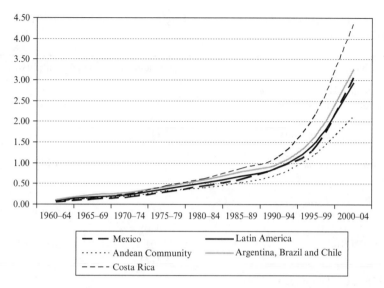

Source: Authors' elaboration.

Figure 5.4 *ICT index for Latin America and the Caribbean, 1960–2004*

The next step is to estimate the following equation with panel data for the ten countries:

$$y_{i,t} = \beta x_{i,t} + U_{i,t}, \tag{5.7}$$

where $y_{i,t}$ is the MFP growth rate adjusted for the average education level and use of installed capacity, $x_{i,t}$ is the set of variables that account for its behaviour and $U_{i,t}$ is the error term (where i is the country and t is time). For the estimation of this equation, the error term, U, is broken down into three components: the individual effect, μ_i, which allows us to control for unobservable heterogeneity across countries; the time effect, δ_t; and a random innovation ε_{it}. Thus, analytically, the growth equation to be tested is given by:

$$y_{i,t} = \beta x_{i,t} + \mu_i + \delta_t + \varepsilon_{it}. \tag{5.8}$$

On the basis of the fixed-effects panel estimation,[14] μ_i is considered to be an individual-specific constant term. In the formulation of this model, we assume that the differences between units may be measured through the differences in this constant term, so that in equation (5.8)

Table 5.4   Estimate of the determinants of multi-factor productivity in Latin America[a]

Variable	Coefficient	Probability
Economic efficiency variables		
Macroeconomic instability	−0.975	0.089
	(0.493)	
Exchange rate volatility	−0.940	0.000
	(0.111)	
Economic reforms	2.312	0.147
	(1.418)	
Economic cycle variables		
Currency overvaluation	0.128	0.012
	(0.040)	
Terms of trade	−4.101	0.773
	(3.773)	
Technological progress variable		
ICT penetration index	0.014	0.059
	(0.006)	
Constant	2.398	0.016
	(0.762)	
R-squared	0.84	

Note: a. The estimation methodology uses a least squares panel data model with fixed effects. The dependent variable is multi-factor productivity. The sample period is 1960 to 2005. Standard errors are in parentheses.

Source: Authors' calculations.

each μ_i is an unknown parameter, which is to be estimated. The estimate is then carried out in terms of deviations from the averages of the group, that is, through a regression of $y_{it} - \bar{y}_t$ over $x_{it} - \bar{x}_t$ in the model $y_{it} - \bar{y}_t = (x_{it} - \bar{x}_t)'\beta + (\varepsilon_{it} - \bar{\varepsilon}_t)$.

The results obtained from the estimate of the explanatory variables of multi-factor productivity suggest that the economy's efficiency variables, exchange rate variability, macroeconomic instability and especially the reform index are the most important group for explaining the productivity dynamics in the countries of the region (see Table 5.4).

The signs obtained for all the variables are consistent with our expectations. The macroeconomic instability indicators and exchange rate variability have a negative impact, while the structural reforms variable has a positive sign. The two cycle indicators (namely, currency undervaluation and the terms of trade) relate positively and negatively, respectively, to

MFP, although the coefficient on the terms of trade is not statistically significant. Lastly, the technological advance variable, ICT, generates increases in productivity.

These results suggest that the volatility of Latin American economies in the 1980s is the principal cause of the negative performance of productivity. Although there appears to be a significant positive relationship between technology penetration and productivity, the coefficient is too small to account for the variations of productivity.

5 CONCLUSIONS

This study has considered the factors that determine economic growth at the individual and regional level, in terms of both factor accumulation and total productivity. If we look at the pattern of economic activity (measured in terms of per capita GDP) in Latin America during the period 1950–2005, two important facts emerge: (1) when growth for the period is compared with a rate of 2 per cent per year breaks emerge in the long-term trend; and (2) the per capita GDP trend displays heterogeneity, which reflects a disparity in its levels and in growth rates starting in the second half of the twentieth century.

The results from the growth accounting exercise, which corrects for the quality of the labour input and capacity utilization, show positive growth in individual productive factors for all periods in the group of Latin American countries, but the periods 1981–90 and 1998–2005 show negative multi-factor productivity (MFP).

In the period leading up to the crisis of the 1980s, the Latin American countries made a positive effort to accumulate productive factors, with capital being the factor that contributed most to the increase in activity. The trend changed after that date, and it has since reflected weaker factor accumulation and a modification in its relative contribution, with labour being the main contributor to GDP growth today. In the case of MFP, this difference in performance is even more marked after that date.

During the debt crisis, MFP was negative for all countries. A very similar context occurred after 1998, when all the countries, except Costa Rica and Ecuador, again recorded productivity losses. Both situations were directly related to the fall in GDP growth rates. MFP was positive in the other periods, especially between 1951 and 1972, when the growth rate of the regional economy increased by 1.2 percentage points. While modest, this is double the rate recorded in the years immediately following the crisis of the 1980s.

To quantify the role of efficiency and the economic cycle, together with the impact of ICT dissemination (as a proxy for technological progress) on MFP performance, we estimated a fixed-effects panel data model considering the following explanatory variables:

1. real exchange rate variability, macroeconomic instability (measured by inflation) and an index of economic reforms, which represent the efficiency variables;
2. sources of procyclical behaviour, estimated through currency undervaluation and the terms of trade;
3. an ICT index, which measures ICT adoption in the country's economic structure on the basis of five representative variables: number of fixed-line telephones, number of mobile telephones, number of personal computers, number of television sets and number of Internet users.

The results obtained suggest that the economy's efficiency variables (namely, exchange rate variability, macroeconomic instability and especially the reform index) are the most important group for explaining the productivity dynamics in the countries of the region in the period 1960–2005. The results thus suggest that the volatility of Latin American economies recorded in the 1980s was the main cause of the negative performance of productivity.

Finally, although it was possible to significantly relate the evolution of factor productivity to a set of ICT variables, these variables proved to play only a limited role in its determination. In the future, more light must be shed on this factor's contribution to economic growth. One approach would be to incorporate capital services and, with it, investment in ICT, as demonstrated by de Vries et al. (2007) for five countries in the region, where their contribution has been more favourable than stock utilization.

NOTES

*   When doing the research for this chapter, Marc Badia-Miró, Christian Hurtado and José Jofré González were working at the Division of Statistics and Economic Projects of the Economic Commission for Latin America and the Caribbean (ECLAC), Santiago, Chile. We are grateful for help, comments and suggestions by Ariel Coremberg, Nanno Mulder, Francisco Villarreal and participants at the seminar 'ICT, Growth and Productivity in Latin America', organized by ECLAC in Santiago on 30 November–1 December 2006. The opinions expressed here are those of the authors and do not necessarily reflect those of ECLAC.
1.   The annual growth rate trend is 2 per cent, which corresponds to a constant growth rate similar to that observed for the United States in the twentieth century.

2. See Hofman (1999); Bethell (2000); Cárdenas et al. (2000a, 2000b); Bulmer-Thomas (2003).
3. Economic diversification was crucial in Costa Rica; in Brazil and Mexico, the key factor was increased industrialization; and in Chile, it was specialization in semi-manufacturing based on the processing of natural resources.
4. The lost decade was characterized by the end of high oil prices, severe indebtedness for some countries, rising interest rates and trade imbalances. This explains the situation in most of the countries.
5. For a more detailed and extensive analysis, see Hofman (1999).
6. Argentina, Bolivia, Brazil, Chile, Colombia, Costa Rica, Ecuador, Mexico, Peru and the Bolivarian Republic of Venezuela.
7. ECLAC, *Social Panorama of Latin America*, Santiago, Chile, various years.
8. Coal, oil, hydroelectric power, gas and nuclear energy.
9. Based on Villarreal (2006).
10. ECLAC, *Economic Survey of Latin America*, various issues.
11. ECLAC database, available online at http://websie.eclac.cl/sisgen/ConsultaIntegrada. asp; accessed 24 March 2010.
12. In each case, the variables have been measured per 100 inhabitants.
13. We chose these variables because they are included among the core indicators in various ICT indices, in particular the Digital Access Index (DAI) (see Partnership on Measuring ICT for Development, *Core ICT Indicators*, p. 3, New York, United Nations, available online at www.itu.int/ITU-D/ict/partnership/material/CoreICTIndicators.pdf; accessed 24 March 2010). They are the same variables found in the section on infrastructure in the E-government Readiness Index, prepared by the United Nations Online Public Administration Network (UNPAN). Furthermore, a considerable number of the variables used are considered in the construction of some of the 12 indices considered in the Minges (2005) study. Most indices include the number of fixed-line telephones and mobile telephones per inhabitant, together with the number of Internet users (or, failing this, the number of servers). The number of television sets and the number of computers only appear in some indices.
14. Corroborated by the Hausman test.

REFERENCES

Bethell, L. (2000), 'Economía y sociedad desde 1930', *Historia de América Latina*, vol. 11, Barcelona: Cambridge University Press.
Bulmer-Thomas, V. (2003), *The Economic History of Latin America Since Independence*, Cambridge, UK: Cambridge University Press.
Cárdenas, E., J.A. Ocampo and R. Thorp (2000a), *An Economic History of Twentieth-century Latin America*, vol. 2, *Latin America in the 1930s: The Role of the Periphery in World Crisis*, New York: Palgrave.
Cárdenas, E., J.A. Ocampo and R. Thorp (2000b), *An Economic History of Twentieth-century Latin America*, vol. 3, *Industrialization and the State in Latin America: The Postwar Years*, New York: Palgrave.
Contreras, D. and S. Gallegos (2006), 'Descomponiendo la desigualdad salarial en América Latina. Una década de cambios', Santiago: University of Chile.
Costello, D.M. (1993), 'A cross-country, cross-industry comparison of productivity growth', *Journal of Political Economy*, 101(2), 207–22.
De Vries, G., N. Mulder, M. Dal Borgo and A.A. Hofman (2007), 'ICT investment in Latin America: does it matter for economic growth?', Santiago, Chile: Economic Commission for Latin America and the Caribbean (ECLAC).

Hofman, A.A. (1999), *Latin American Economic Development: A Causal Analysis in Historical Perspective*, Monograph Series, No. 3, Groningen Growth and Development Centre.

Hofman, A.A. (2000), *The Economic Development of Latin America in the Twentieth Century*, Cheltenham, UK and Northampton, MA, USA: Edward Elgar.

Minges, M. (2005), 'Evaluation of e-readiness indices in Latin America and the Caribbean', Project Document, No. 73 (LC/W.73), Santiago, Chile: Economic Commission for Latin America and the Caribbean (ECLAC).

Morley, S.A., R. Machado and S. Pettinato (1999), 'Indexes of structural reform in Latin America', *Reformas económicas series* (LC/L1166), Santiago, Chile: Economic Commission for Latin America and the Caribbean (ECLAC).

Psacharopoulos, G. (1994a), 'Returns to investment in education', *World Bank Research Observer*, vol. 10.

Psacharopoulos, G. (1994b), 'Returns to investment in education: a global update', *World Development*, **22**(9), 1325–43.

Psacharopoulos, G. and H. Patrinos (2004), 'Returns to investment in education: a further update', *Education Economics*, **12**(2), 111–34.

Solow, R. (1957), 'Technical change and the aggregate production function', *Review of Economics and Statistics*, **39**(3), August, 312–20.

Villarreal, F. (2006), 'Extracción de señales de series de tiempo económicas', Santiago, Chile: Economic Commission for Latin America and the Caribbean (ECLAC), unpublished.

6. The impact of information and communication technologies on economic growth in Latin America in comparative perspective

Nauro F. Campos*

1 INTRODUCTION

For the last 20 years or so, the world economy has witnessed spectacular rates of technological change. These rates seem to have been driven by a powerful new 'general-purpose technology', namely information and communication technologies (hereafter ICT). The impressive cost reduction in computing power has driven these innovations to spill over from manufacturing and services (where they made their first strides in the 1970s and early 1980s) to consumer goods more generally after that. The advent and fast diffusion of personal computers and mobile phones (which are also personal in a similar sense) have made these technologies ubiquitous and have dramatically changed day-to-day life even in the poorest economies of the world. Many examples have been provided about how useful mobile phones can be in developing countries as the lowering of the cost of information transmission and exchange can help integrate (or enlarge) markets and thus foster economic growth. Traditional (mid-1990s) examples tend to be, for instance, of fishing boats calling different ports to check on current catch prices. Five years or so ago, the strongest examples on the economic importance of mobile phones were of customers using prepaid airtime as a way of transferring money. But now we have 'cellular banking': *The Economist* (28 October 2006, p. 109) reports that 'about half a million South Africans now use their mobile phones as a bank. Besides sending money to relatives and paying for goods, they can check balances, buy airtime and settle utility bills'. From a way of exchanging information with minimum infrastructure costs to a way of directly generating wealth, mobile phones came a long way: ICT no longer just mediate the process of wealth accumulation, they now seem to create wealth themselves.

All these developments have not, of course, escaped economists' attention and a large literature has developed trying to understand the micro- and macroeconomic drivers and consequences of these changes. However, it would not be fair to characterize this (economics) literature as showing an *overwhelming* consensus in favour of the view that ICT have had a positive and statistically significant impact on economic growth around the world. Indeed, economists are so far sceptical of such long-term impacts and (arguably) nowhere is this scepticism stronger than in the vast empirical literature on the determinants of economic growth. Levine and Renelt (1992) search econometrically for 'the' robust set of growth determinants and conclude that ICT-related variables should not to be included in this set. More recently, but equally influentially, Doppelhofer et al. (2004) apply a less restrictive statistical test to the same question but using a broader set of potentially important explanatory variables and conclude, again, that ICT variables should not be included in the set of robust growth determinants. Durlauf et al. (2005) also review this literature and reach similar conclusions with respect to the relative importance of ICT investment. Last, but not least, this view is not limited to growth economists: Stiroh reviews the evidence of ICT on growth and argues that it 'suggests that IT does matter, although the specific point estimate of the IT-elasticity is fragile' (2004, p. 2). We argue that the time is ripe to try to identify how fragile (or, how robust) this relationship actually is.

Despite the lack of consensus regarding the ICT growth payoffs, economists' interest on the issue is far from restricted to its long-term growth implications. There is a large body of econometric evidence from labour economics trying to assess the labour market effects of the fast diffusion of computers as well as the impact of computer use on workers' earnings (e.g., Dolton and Makepeace, 2004). Still at the micro-level, an impressive body of evidence has emerged using rich firm-level datasets to gather evidence on the effects of ICT investment, adoption and use on various aspects of firm performance (e.g., Brynjolfsson and Hitt, 2003). At the more macro-level, the long-standing tradition of growth accounting exercises has been extensively put to use to try to grasp the contribution of ICT to economic growth (e.g., Jorgenson, 2005).[1]

The objective of this paper is to try to contribute to the econometric literature on the macroeconomic impacts of the diffusion of ICT with emphasis on the experience of Latin America, in international comparative perspective. Our central question is therefore: how econometrically robust is the effect of ICT diffusion in terms of long-term per capita economic growth rates? And more specifically, we are interested in providing answers to the following questions: how significant is the impact of ICT on growth in Latin America? If significant, is this impact smaller in Latin

America than in other regions of the world (OECD, Asia, Eastern Europe and Africa)? Has the impact of ICT on Latin American growth changed since 1960?

The econometric analysis of the effect of ICT on growth has a long history (and this is true even disregarding the literature on the impacts of infrastructure, in which ICT are clearly included, on economic growth). Its starting point is, arguably, Jipp's famous 1963 paper in the *Telecommunications Journal* in which the author establishes the existence of a strong relation between telecommunications infrastructure and the relative wealth of nations, which become known afterwards simply as the 'Jipp Curve'. Another important reference in the evolution of this literature is the 1980 paper by Hardy in *Telecommunications Policy* in which this relationship is studied in a relatively large sample of 15 developed and 45 developing countries. Two important conclusions this paper puts forward are that although the impact of telephones on economic growth is important, the same can not be said of, for instance, radios. This is a result that elegantly encapsulates the notion that the exchange of information matters more (at least economically) than its diffusion, as it underpins the reduction of transaction costs (which are one main reason for the deepening of markets). A second important finding from Hardy's work is that this important statistical effect vanishes in split samples. In other words, these results obtain only when the model is fitted to the whole sample of countries, but they do not hold when the model is fitted only to developed countries or when it is fitted only to developing countries. A third particularly interesting piece in this literature, for our specific purposes, is the 1991 contribution by Cronin et al. in *Telecommunications Policy* in which the issue of endogeneity bias arising from the possibility of reverse causality is first (to the best of our knowledge) treated econometrically in some depth. The cause for concern is the possibility that countries that experience fast per capita GDP growth rates will invest more heavily in telecommunications technologies, while countries that invest large amounts in ICT are likely to reap the returns of these investments in terms of fast overall per capita GDP growth rates. Cronin et al. (1991) use annual data across countries and find that such dual causation (feedback system) is likely to be at work, thus casting doubts on the existing econometric findings.

A number of important papers have appeared in the last five years or so (see Qiang et al., 2004 and Indjikian and Siegel, 2005, for authoritative surveys of this literature); chiefly among them is the influential work of Röller and Waverman (2001), which carefully tackles the reverse causality bias by presenting system estimates for a sample of OECD countries and puts forward the notion that ICT investment is a major determinant of long-run economic growth (at least in the developed world). Sridhar and Sridhar (2004) extend the Röller-Waverman model to developing countries and, interestingly, find that the impact of ICT on growth is substantially smaller in less developed than in more developed (richer) economies. We call attention also to the important paper by Teltscher and Korka (2005) in which cross-section estimates are provided annually for a set of 147 countries using a composite index of ICT diffusion (the Infodensity index). This study reports that the ICT elasticity with respect to economic growth is between 0.1 and 0.3 (note that this is also very much the range of estimates we find in this paper below). Last, but not least, we highlight the recent paper by Waverman et al. (2005) in which estimates are provided for standard as well as endogenous growth models (which is the econometric strategy we replicate in what follows) in a large sample of developing and developed countries. Waverman et al. (2005) also innovate by considering mobiles lines (in addition to the standard fixed phone lines) as an ICT measure and report that the impact of ICT on growth seems larger in developed than in developing countries.[2]

On the basis of this brief overview of the literature, what are the lessons one should take on board? More specifically, if one wants to contribute to this literature, what are the issues one has to be mindful of and what are the most desirable extensions to pursue? The first lesson seems to be that in order to progress, the construction of panel datasets is crucial. The majority of existing studies is restricted to exploring the cross-country variation of the data and we believe the existing results can be improved substantially by also taking into account the time-series variation in the data. In short, one way to further advance this literature seems to be to generate panel estimates of the effect of ICT on growth. Second, this should be accomplished without losing sight of the cross-country variability: it is important to try to use large samples of countries inter alia in order to try to get at the issue of inter-regional differences (which is one of the main concerns in this paper). Third, it seems important to be attentive to the likelihood of reverse causality bias. This is an issue that has received, understandably, a great deal of attention in the literature and advancement is unlikely without coming to grips with this issue.

For this paper we put together an extensive panel dataset organized in five-year averages (so as to make use of the panel framework developed by, among others, Islam, 1995, and which has become now standard in the growth literature). The standard reason given for such design is to try to isolate business cycle fluctuations and concentrate on the long-term impact of ICT diffusion on growth. We try to improve upon the sizable literature on this issue by: (1) putting together a comprehensive dataset with more than 150 developed and developing countries covering the period from 1960 to 2004; (2) present standard Granger-causality evidence supporting the view that causality seems to flow from ICT diffusion to economic growth and, more importantly, not the other way around; and (3) estimate, using panel econometric techniques, the effects of ICT for all countries as well as for each regional group (that is, OECD, Latin America, Asia, Middle East, Africa and transition economies). As noted, one recurring concern of the existing literature is the lack of robustness of the econometric estimates, driven mainly by the twin facts that although endogeneity has been an important and difficult source of bias to deal with, the standard solutions to tackle it have been shown to be equally sensitive to other sources of bias (more specifically, the resulting system generalized method of moments [GMM] estimates in relatively small and highly heterogeneous samples has unfortunately turned out to be much more fragile than initially thought). Our Granger-results are encouraging as they suggest this concern does not seem to be sufficiently severe in the five-year averages panel design we adopted.

Our main finding is that the effect of ICT (fixed and mobile lines) on growth is positive, statistically significant and robust to different measures of ICT, different econometric estimators, different specifications (standard aggregate production and endogenous growth frameworks), as well as different ways of measuring key control variables. We also find the impact of ICT on growth in Latin America to be smaller than that impact in the OECD and Asian countries, but larger than that in Middle Eastern, African and transition economies. In terms of suggestions for future research we echo the literature in calling for the need to tackle an important source of omitted variable bias by putting forward indexes of economic reforms (quality of institutions and of the regulatory framework) as well as to try to construct composite indexes of ICT that better reflect their multifaceted nature.

This paper is organized as follows. Section 2 lays out the basic theoretical framework informing the estimation. Section 3 describes in detail the dataset put together for this exercise, while Section 4 has our econometric results. Section 5 concludes.

2   THEORETICAL FRAMEWORK

In order to answer the question 'Does ICT matter vis-à-vis economic growth?', in this section we articulate one way of adding our indexes of ICT to an otherwise standard Solow growth model, and then use that model to explain variations in growth rates across a large sample of countries over the last four decades or so. The use of the Solow model is motivated primarily by the fact that it contains a shift parameter that 'reflects not just technology, but resource endowments, climate, institutions and so on' (Mankiw et al., 1992, pp. 410–11), thereby allowing for an explicit link between ICT and economic growth. Additional advantages of the Solow model in this context are: (1) the comparisons it affords with the many other studies that use this framework; (2) its ability to test some other important hypotheses such as (a) that income per capita should be positively related to investment and negatively related to population growth rates, and (b) that countries converge to their steady-state levels of income per capita; and (3) that it works especially well in samples of relatively homogeneous countries, maybe like those of Latin America.[3]

The central piece in this model is an aggregate production function with positive and diminishing marginal products and constant returns to scale. It relates output (Y) to a pair of essential inputs, capital and labour (K and L), and to a shift parameter (A), usually representing technology. For a Cobb-Douglas production function, output in period t is:

$$Y_t = K_t^{\alpha}(A_t L_t)^{1-\alpha} \qquad 0 < \alpha < 1. \tag{6.1}$$

Standard assumptions are that technological progress is labour-augmenting and that the rates of growth of population (n), technological or institutional progress (g) and depreciation (δ) are constant and exogenous for any period.[4] If k is the capital–labour ratio and y is income per worker, the assumptions about the growth of population and technology imply that, in the steady-state (i.e., when the various quantities grow at constant rates), k_t would converge (for small values of n, g and δ) to a value $k*$ given by:

$$k* = \left[\frac{s}{n + g + \delta}\right]^{\frac{1}{(1-\alpha)}} \tag{6.2}$$

Substituting (6.2) into the production function and taking logs, the steady-state income per worker becomes:

$$\ln\left[\frac{Y_t}{L_t}\right] = \ln A_0 + gt + \frac{\alpha}{1-\alpha}\ln(s) - \frac{\alpha}{1-\alpha}\ln(n + g + \delta) \tag{6.3}$$

This yields the well-known hypotheses of the Solow model: the higher the rate of savings (investment), the richer the country; and the higher the rates of population growth, labour-augmented technological change and depreciation, the poorer the country will be. The model not only predicts that income per capita in each country will converge to its steady-state value, but also yields estimates of the speed at which this convergence will occur. Let y^* be the steady-state level of income per worker from (6.3), and y_t be the actual value at time t. In the neighbourhood of the steady-state, an approximation of the speed of convergence β is given by:

$$\frac{d\ln(y_t)}{dt} = \beta[\ln(y_{t-1}^*) - (\ln(y_{t-1}))] \qquad (6.4)$$

where $\beta = -(n+g+\delta)(1-\alpha)$. Notice that the speed of convergence depends on the determinants of the steady-state as well as on the level of income per worker at the beginning of the period.[5]

There are a few good reasons to expect that this model would perform better for samples that are relatively homogeneous (in the sense of having similar rates of capital depreciation and labour force growth). For example, Mankiw et al. (1992) obtain quite different parameter estimates for OECD countries than for non-oil exporting less developed countries. They found evidence of 'unconditional convergence' among the OECD countries,[6] but little or no such evidence for their larger and much less homogeneous samples. Given that our interest is focused on the Latin American countries, this framework would seem quite appropriate for our investigation.

In this light, we follow Waverman et al. (2005) in estimating two basic versions of the model. One corresponds more closely to the standard aggregate production function delineated above, while the second follows the endogenous growth approach. In terms of the former, the econometric model we estimate is as follows:

$$growth_{tc} = \alpha + \beta_1 K_{tc} + \beta_2 L_{tc} + \beta_3 E_{tc} + \beta_4 ICT_{tc} + \varepsilon_{tc} \qquad (6.5)$$

where $growth_{tc}$ is per capita real GDP growth rates in the relevant five-year period t in country c, K_{tc} stands for physical capital in country c at time t, L_{tc} stands for the labour input in country c at time t, E_{tc} reflects the quality of institutions (in our baseline model, legislative effectiveness, more on this below) and ICT_{tc} reflects the information and communication technologies (in our baseline results, we follow the literature in measuring them as either fixed or mobile phone lines).

The one Waverman et al. (2005) call the endogenous specification obtain by adding two important variables to equation (6.5) above, namely, human capital and initial income:

$$growth_{tc} = \alpha + \beta_1 K_{tc} + \beta_2 L_{tc} + \beta_3 E_{tc} + \beta_4 ICT_{tc} + \beta_5 Y_{0tc} + \beta_6 HK_{tc} + \varepsilon_{tc} \qquad (6.6)$$

where HK_{tc} stands for the stock of human capital in country c at time t and Y_{0tc} stands for the level of initial income at the start of each five-year period. These two variables are important because the former may reflect minimum absorptive capacity requirements for the successful adoption of ICT (that is, a minimum level of average education in the labour force above which ICT can be adopted more effectively), while the latter may capture differences in the economic development levels.

3   DATA

For this paper, we put together a comprehensive panel dataset covering more than 150 developing and developed countries. The time coverage is from 1960 to 2004 and our observations were calculated for the following five-year periods: 1960–64, 1965–69, 1970–74, 1975–79, 1980–84, 1985–89, 1990–94, 1995–99 and 2000–04. Note that the observations in the dataset are averages for each country for each of these periods, the availability of the underlying data provided. The time coverage represents an improvement upon existing studies, which tend to focus on the period from 1980 onwards, both for fixed and mobile lines.

The country coverage by region is as follows: OECD (25 countries), Latin America and the Caribbean (24 countries), Asia (21 countries), Sub-Saharan Africa (43 countries), Middle East and North Africa (hereafter MENA, 15 countries) and transition economies (26 countries). These add up to a grand total of 154 countries. Note that because of data availability not all countries can be included in all the specifications in our econometric analysis. However, for the exercises with best country coverage, the total number of countries reaches 153 (for a total of more than 1000 observations) which represent an improvement upon previous analyses, in which samples rarely exceed 100 countries.

In terms of the variables used, the dependent variable is the average growth rate of GDP per capita in purchasing power parity basis in constant 2000 dollars (Table 6A.1 in the Appendix has basic statistics, definitions and sources). Among the independent variables we use are the level of initial GDP per capita on a PPP basis (this is measured at the beginning of each five-year period, for example, for 1960–64 it refers to year 1960), gross capital formation as a share of GDP, number of main telephone lines per 100 inhabitants, number of cellular mobile telephone subscribers per 100 inhabitants (as well as the absolute number of fixed and mobile telephone lines in operation), percentage of 'primary school complete' in the total population, total population and size of labour force.

Examining our dataset, we can see, for instance, that the average annual per capita GDP growth rate over the whole period is 1.8 per cent with 0.04 standard deviation, maximum value of 49 per cent (for Equatorial Guinea in 1995–99) and a minimum of 44 per cent (for Lebanon during the civil war years of 1985–89), which are clearly outliers in view of the relatively small standard deviation. The average per capita GDP growth rates for each region over the whole period of analysis are as follows (standard deviations in parenthesis): for the OECD it is 2.8 per cent (0.02), for Latin America it is 1.6 per cent (0.26), for Asia it is 3.3 per cent (0.027), for the Middle East and North Africa it is 1 per cent (0.06), for Sub-Saharan Africa it is slightly less than 1 per cent (0.04), and for the transition economies it is 0.5 per cent (0.07).

Just for comparison purposes and focusing on the extent of ICT diffusion, our data show that ICT diffusion has been somewhat slower in Latin American Countries (LAC) than in the OECD countries and in some parts of the developing world. For example, while the OECD averages for fixed and mobile lines are approximately 33 and 22 per 100 inhabitants, respectively, the same averages in LAC are 9 and 7, in transition economies 12 and 9 and in Sub-Saharan Africa 1 and 2.[7]

4   ECONOMETRIC RESULTS

The main objective of this section is to discuss our econometric results. One crucial consideration here is to try to take on board the lessons from our brief overview of the literature above. More specifically, if one wishes to contribute to this literature, what are the issues one has to be mindful of and what are the desirable extensions? The first lesson we learn is that the construction of panel datasets is a desirable extension. The vast majority of existing studies is restricted to exploring the cross-country variation of the data and it seems natural to expect that the results can be improved substantially by taking into account the cross-country as well as the time-series variation in the data. Second, this should be accomplished without losing sight of the cross-country variability: it is important to try to use large samples of countries inter alia to try to get at the issue of inter-regional differences (which is one of our main concerns in this paper). Our focus here is on trying to compare the impact of ICT on growth in Latin America with the same impact in other regions (OECD, Asia, Africa, Middle East, etc.). One way of directly comparing these impacts is to run the same econometric model for each region, using the same variables as well as the same time frame. The resulting estimated impacts (that is, the coefficients on ICT on per capita growth) are thus comparable. Third, it is very important to be careful with respect to the possibility of reverse

causality bias (that is, whether growth causes ICT use while simultaneously ICT use causes growth). This is an issue that has received, understandably, attention in the literature and advancement is unlikely without
coming to grips with this issue. The results below are presented in three
main groups: we first report estimates based on the aggregate production
function approach; then we report estimates based on the endogenous
growth model; and finally we discuss various sensitivity checks. Note that
in our estimations, all variables also enter in logs.

As noted, one major issue we have to clarify at the outset regards the possibility of endogeneity bias arising in our data. Because the data comprise
five-year averages between 1960 and 2004, we are able to apply standard
Granger-causality tests for the significance and direction of a relationship
between ICT and growth.[8] We find there is very little evidence in our data
of Granger-causality running from economic growth to ICT: countries that
grow faster do not systematically invest more in information and communication technologies over five-year periods. On the other hand, there is some
encouraging evidence supporting the notion that mobile phone penetration
(and to a much lesser extent, fixed phone lines) Granger-cause economic
growth in our data. These results provide some support to estimate growth
equations using our data and treating the two ICT variables as exogenous.

Our aggregate production function and endogenous growth model specifications are based on Waverman et al. (2005, p. 16) but have a few differentiating features that are worth discussing. The specification we use for
the aggregate production function has fixed-effects for regions and time
periods (instead of two dummy variables capturing the level of external
indebtedness), which we believe should make the panel estimates we report
below at least equally robust to these effects. One important additional
change (vis-à-vis Waverman et al.) we should note is that we could not find
sufficient data on the institutional variable originally used (namely, 'rule of
law') and therefore we chose to use instead legislative effectiveness in the
understanding that this would play a similar role vis-à-vis the determination of cross-country economic performance. Also note that in the set of
results below we recognize the importance of checking for the implications
of data poolability across regions on the results and, as a consequence, we
report the results by region (which is usually not the case in this literature,
which when the issue is dealt with at all, tends to focus on the broad differ-
entiation between developing versus developed countries). This allows for
a more straightforward grasp of the substantial inter-regional differences
we find in our data. A last noteworthy difference is that in the number of
countries over which the estimations were carried out: in our case we use
more than 150 countries for the runs with best coverage with is larger than
any other study we know.

Table 6.1 contains our baseline aggregate production function results for all regions together. First, notice that the fit of the regression model is quite good, with relatively high R-squares throughout and in particular for those models involving fixed phone lines (columns 3 and 5). The coefficients for all the 'ICT variables' (namely, number of fixed and mobile lines, in absolute numbers as well as per 100 inhabitants) are positive and statistically significant. We naturally attach more weight to the per capita version of these ICT measures, yet it must be very reassuring to observe that not scaling these variables has no qualitative effect on our conclusions. Moreover, the coefficient estimates, especially in the case of fixed lines, are also economically meaningful. In other words, as Guatemala is the country closest to the Latin American average per capita growth rate of 0.9 per cent per year, if it would have experienced a 1 per cent greater number of fixed lines per capita it would have grown on average like Jamaica, which has experienced an average per capita growth rate of 1.3 per cent. As it can be seen from the table, the long-term impact of mobile lines, although equally statistically significant, has been considerably smaller than that of fixed lines.

As for the remaining explanatory variables, notice that the coefficient on physical capital always carries the expected positive sign, although it is statistically significant only when the fixed line variables are absent, while that on population is always statistically significant and carrying the negative sign predicted by the underlying theoretical model. As for the regional dummy variables, only the ones for the OECD and African countries turn out to be statistically significant throughout, with positive and negative signs, respectively (notice that the Middle East and North Africa [MENA] is the omitted category). Notice also that the dummy for Latin America is never statistically significant suggesting that the relation of the standard ICT variables in the aggregate production function model in the region as a whole is not systematically different from that in the comparator 'median' group (that is, MENA).

Table 6.2 shows the results by one region, namely Latin America. Interestingly, for the Latin American countries we obtain that all four coefficients on the standard ICT variables are still positive and all are statistically significant suggesting that these technologies do indeed have an important role to play in explaining economic performance in the continent, across countries as well as over time. Moreover, the economic significance of these effects essentially remains, as the size of the coefficients is very similar to those displayed in Table 6.1. Notice also that the fit of the model deteriorates rather dramatically, with the exception of those specifications containing fixed lines (columns 3 and 5) and this can be read in favour of the importance of the inter-regional variance in the adoption of mobile phones.

Table 6.1   *Aggregate production function model (dependent variable is average growth rate of real GDP per capita) panel fixed-effects estimates 153 countries, 1960–2004*

	(1)	(2)	(3)	(4)	(5)
Capital	0.132***	0.140***	−0.0201	0.165***	−0.0254
	[0.043]	[0.043]	[0.039]	[0.042]	[0.039]
Population	−0.197***	−0.175***	−0.485***	−0.144***	−0.114***
	[0.035]	[0.033]	[0.033]	[0.032]	[0.025]
Leg. effectiveness	−0.00215	−0.00168	−0.00044	−0.00074	−0.00031
	[0.0022]	[0.0021]	[0.0016]	[0.0017]	[0.0015]
OECD	1.209***	1.165***	0.464**	1.144***	0.422**
	[0.22]	[0.20]	[0.19]	[0.20]	[0.18]
Latin America	−0.067	−0.061	−0.112	−0.0589	−0.105
	[0.22]	[0.21]	[0.19]	[0.21]	[0.17]
Asia	−0.471*	−0.504**	−0.176	−0.519**	−0.173
	[0.25]	[0.23]	[0.20]	[0.23]	[0.18]
Transition	−0.103	−0.0879	−0.312	−0.0981	−0.383**
	[0.24]	[0.23]	[0.21]	[0.23]	[0.19]
Africa	−1.402***	−1.349***	−0.593***	−1.323***	−0.541***
	[0.22]	[0.21]	[0.21]	[0.21]	[0.19]
Mobile penetration		0.0209***			
		[0.0034]			
Fixed lines penetration			0.351***		
			[0.023]		
Mobile penetration (per 100 people)				0.0923***	
				[0.010]	
Fixed lines penetration (per 100 people)					0.371***
					[0.022]
Constant	10.67***	10.31***	11.71***	9.768***	9.779***
	[0.65]	[0.60]	[0.52]	[0.60]	[0.47]
Time dummies?	Yes	Yes	Yes	Yes	Yes
Observations	1110	1110	1035	1110	1035
Number of countries	153	153	153	153	153
R-squared	0.6328	0.6544	0.7972	0.6660	0.8155

Note: All variables in logs. Robust standard errors in brackets: *** p<0.01, ** p<0.05, * p<0.1.

Source: Author's estimates.

Table 6.2   *Aggregate production function model (dependent variable is average growth rate of real GDP per capita) panel fixed-effects estimates LAC countries, 1960–2004*

	(1)	(2)	(3)	(4)	(5)
Capital	−0.00725	0.00388	−0.0355	0.0234	−0.0266
	[0.090]	[0.089]	[0.081]	[0.081]	[0.081]
Population	−0.0958*	−0.0901*	−0.401***	−0.0809	−0.0431
	[0.055]	[0.048]	[0.060]	[0.052]	[0.036]
Leg.	−0.00391*	−0.00326	−0.00159	−0.00344*	−0.00154
effectiveness	[0.0022]	[0.0023]	[0.0015]	[0.0021]	[0.0015]
Mobile		0.0137**			
penetration		[0.0068]			
Fixed lines			0.362***		
penetration			[0.051]		
Mobile				0.101***	
penetration				[0.037]	
(per 100 people)					
Fixed lines					0.356***
penetration					[0.050]
(per 100 people)					
Constant	9.605***	9.486***	10.45***	9.292***	8.791***
	[0.85]	[0.77]	[0.66]	[0.79]	[0.62]
Time dummies?	Yes	Yes	Yes	Yes	Yes
Observations	214	214	188	214	188
Number of countries	24	24	24	24	24
R-squared	0.0924	0.1139	0.6306	0.1229	0.6240

Note: All variables in logs. Robust standard errors in brackets: *** $p<0.01$, ** $p<0.05$, * $p<0.1$

Source: Author's estimates.

In summary, our results show that ICT are an important growth determinant in the Latin American region: their adoption is positively and significantly associated with higher rates of per capita GDP growth. We also have uncovered some important evidence that shows that the impact of ICT on growth is larger in OECD and Asian countries (than in LAC countries), while for MENA and Africa this impact seems to be considerably smaller.

Tables 6.3 and 6.4 report our endogenous growth model results (we follow the same procedure as above by reporting first the results for the pooled data and then for Latin America). It must be noted at the outset

Table 6.3 *Endogenous growth model (dependent variable is average growth rate of real GDP per capita) panel fixed-effects estimates 105 countries, 1960–2004*

	(1)	(2)	(3)	(4)	(5)
Initial income	−0.0114***	−0.0133***	−0.0185***	−0.0115***	−0.0186***
	[0.0022]	[0.0023]	[0.0033]	[0.0022]	[0.0033]
Capital	0.0362***	0.0366***	0.0355***	0.0364***	0.0356***
	[0.0043]	[0.0042]	[0.0047]	[0.0043]	[0.0047]
Population	−0.00069	−0.0012	−0.0061***	−0.00064	−0.0003
	[0.00087]	[0.00088]	[0.0021]	[0.00085]	[0.00088]
Human capital	0.00183	0.00290*	0.00129	0.00216	0.00128
	[0.0015]	[0.0015]	[0.0018]	[0.0015]	[0.0018]
Leg.	0.000328**	0.00035***	0.000340**	0.000333**	0.000339**
effectiveness	[0.00014]	[0.00014]	[0.00015]	[0.00014]	[0.00015]
OECD	0.0275***	0.0259***	0.0242***	0.0269***	0.0243***
	[0.0072]	[0.0069]	[0.0069]	[0.0070]	[0.0069]
Latin America	0.00356	0.00251	0.00196	0.00327	0.00196
	[0.0065]	[0.0064]	[0.0064]	[0.0064]	[0.0064]
Asia	0.0174***	0.0152**	0.0176***	0.0170***	0.0176***
	[0.0063]	[0.0061]	[0.0061]	[0.0061]	[0.0061]
Transition	0.0229**	0.0199**	0.0218**	0.0220**	0.0219**
	[0.0097]	[0.0097]	[0.0093]	[0.0094]	[0.0094]
Africa	−0.00662	−0.00742	−0.00312	−0.0065	−0.00319
	[0.0068]	[0.0067]	[0.0069]	[0.0066]	[0.0069]
Mobile		0.00140***			
penetration		[0.00031]			
Fixed lines			0.00580***		
penetration			[0.0018]		
Mobile				0.000552	
penetration (per 100 people)				[0.00089]	
Fixed lines					0.00582***
penetration (per 100 people)					[0.0018]
Constant	0.0124	0.0328	0.0924**	0.0112	0.0657*
	[0.025]	[0.026]	[0.041]	[0.025]	[0.035]
Time dummies?	Yes	Yes	Yes	Yes	Yes
Observations	829	829	780	829	780
Number of countries	105	105	105	105	105
R-squared	0.3626	0.3816	0.3927	0.3647	0.3925

Note: Robust standard errors in brackets: *** $p<0.01$, ** $p<0.05$, * $p<0.1$

Source: Author's estimates.

Table 6.4   *Endogenous growth model (dependent variable is average growth rate of real GDP per capita) panel fixed-effects estimates LAC countries, 1960–2004*

	(1)	(2)	(3)	(4)	(5)
Initial income	0.00265	0.00198	−0.011	0.00139	−0.0107
	[0.0049]	[0.0050]	[0.0086]	[0.0048]	[0.0085]
Capital	0.0221***	0.0228***	0.0214**	0.0234***	0.0217**
	[0.0085]	[0.0086]	[0.0093]	[0.0085]	[0.0094]
Population	−0.00086	−0.00117	−0.00953*	−0.00079	0.000181
	[0.0015]	[0.0017]	[0.0051]	[0.0015]	[0.0017]
Human capital	−0.00047	−0.00077	6.32E-05	−0.00041	0.000228
	[0.0038]	[0.0038]	[0.0048]	[0.0037]	[0.0048]
Leg.	0.000307**	0.000318**	0.000308*	0.000316**	0.000312**
effectiveness	[0.00015]	[0.00016]	[0.00016]	[0.00015]	[0.00016]
Mobile		0.000563			
penetration		[0.0012]			
Fixed lines			0.00978*		
penetration			[0.0051]		
Mobile				0.00464	
penetration				[0.0030]	
(per 100 people)					
Fixed lines					0.00943*
penetration					[0.0051]
(per 100 people)					
Constant	−0.0493	−0.0402	0.0811	−0.0438	0.0323
	[0.041]	[0.041]	[0.082]	[0.041]	[0.063]
Time dummies?	Yes	Yes	Yes	Yes	Yes
Observations	204	204	180	204	180
Number of	23	23	23	23	23
countries					
R-squared	0.2677	0.2688	0.3014	0.2784	0.2987

Note: Robust standard errors in brackets: *** p<0.01, ** p<0.05, * p<0.1

Source: Author's estimates.

that although the improvements in terms of the country coverage in this case are somewhat modest (for instance, the number of countries increases to 105 as compared with 91 in Waverman et al., 2005), the use of five-year averages for panel estimation dramatically increases the available degrees of freedom, from below 80 to more than 800. The results for the pooled regions in Table 6.3 broadly confirm our previous findings: the coefficients on initial income, capital and institutions are all statistically significant throughout; in terms of the four standard ICT variables, we find that their coefficients are all positive and statistically significant, interestingly with the sole exception of that for mobile lines per capita.

The estimates from the endogenous growth model for each region are also interesting. For Latin America, we find support for growth payoffs of the standard ICT variables only for the case of fixed lines, while both capital and institutions show a statistically significant effect as well as expected signs. Furthermore, there is a noticeable reduction in the economic effects of fixed lines.[9]

In summary, once again our results show that ICT are an important growth determinant in Latin America: their use is positively and significantly associated with higher rates of per capita GDP growth. We also have uncovered evidence showing that the impact of ICT on growth is larger in OECD and Asian countries (than in LAC countries), while for MENA and Africa this impact seems to be somewhat smaller.

We have also subjected these results to a series of sensitivity checks.[10] We first investigated the results for the endogenous growth specification when we take out population and add in instead labour force (population is often used as a proxy for the labour input because of difference in statutory retirement dates across countries over time as well as differences in the extent of child labour). The results for the whole set of countries as well as for the Latin American sub-sample are very much the same: in the former case, the coefficients on mobile and fixed lines as well as that on fixed lines per capita are positive and statistically significant, while the coefficients on fixed lines are still positive and statistically significant for the Latin American sample.

In summary, we believe that our results suggest that the impact of ICT in Latin America has been substantial and that there are sufficient grounds to qualify it as robust.

5   CONCLUSIONS

The objective of this paper was to contribute to the econometric literature on the macroeconomic impacts of ICT diffusion with emphasis on the experience of Latin America.

We tried to improve upon the sizable related literature by putting together a comprehensive dataset with more than 150 developed and developing countries covering the period from 1960 to 2004, and by using it to test for exogeneity of the key ICT variables using the standard Granger-causality framework and estimating a variety of growth models that are supported by those tests. Overall, our estimates show that the effect of

ICT on growth is positive, statistically significant and robust to different measures of ICT, different econometric estimators, different specifications (standard aggregate production and endogenous growth frameworks), as well as different ways of measuring key control variables. We find the impact of ICT on growth in Latin America to be smaller than that impact in the OECD and Asian countries, but larger than that in Middle Eastern, African and transition economies.

In terms of suggestions for future research we echo most of the literature in calling for the need to tackle an important source of omitted variable bias by putting forward indexes of economic reforms (quality of institutions and of the regulatory framework) as well as to try to construct composite indexes of ICT that better reflect their multifaceted nature.

NOTES

*   I would like to thank Mario Cimoli, Nelson Correa, Alvaro Diaz, Joao Carlos Ferraz, Daniel Heymann, André Hofman, Michael Minges, Susan Teltscher, Gaaitzen De Vries, Leonard Waverman, Marcio Wohlers and seminar participants at the LBS/ITU 'Digital Transformations in the Information Society' Conference (Geneva) and CEPAL 'ICTs, Economic Growth, and Productivity' Workshop (Santiago) for valuable comments on previous versions of this paper. Mariela Dal Borgo provided superb data assistance. The views expressed in this paper are entirely mine.

1. In our view, the growth accounting and econometric approaches are complementary ways of assessing the macroeconomic impact of ICT on growth. One important objective of growth accounting is to decompose economic growth rates in order to quantify the relative contribution of each of the components. It is, however, an accounting exercise in the sense that the contributions of the various production factors can be obtained disregarding whether or not there is a statistically strong relationship between them and growth rates. On the other hand, the econometric approach is almost defined by the search of such statistically (as well as economically) meaningful relationships at the cost of decompositions becoming less straightforward.

2. In this paper, we follow the existing literature in proxying the diffusion of ICT by increases in the per capita penetration of fixed and mobile telephone lines. We are fully aware that ICT encompass various other technologies (Internet, PCs, etc.) but the fact that these technologies are very recent reflects upon the availability of data. We have also tried to circumvent this concern by constructing a simple composite index of ICT involving mobile penetration (per capita), imports of telecom equipment (as a percentage of GDP), number of outgoing international calls (per capita), number of Internet hosts (per capita), price of Internet connection and high-technology exports (percentage of GDP) (this is not reported in this version of the paper for the sake of space, but is available from the author upon request).

3. There are various well-known limitations of this model, such as the lack of institutional detail, the exogenous role of technology and the requirement of perfectly competitive markets.

4. See also Artus (1993) and Barro and Sala-i-Martin (1995).

5. Note that the concept of conditional convergence does not imply a tendency for the dispersion of per capita incomes to decrease (the latter is often referred to as 'σ convergence') (Barro and Sala-i-Martin, pp. 1995, 383–7).

6. The importance of homogeneous samples can be appreciated by pointing out that Barro and Sala-i-Martin (1995) present similar findings (unconditional convergence) for the states in the US, regions within Europe and prefectures within Japan.

7. Notice that for the sake of space we only analyse the results for fixed and mobile lines in this paper (we put together a dataset with more than 30 ICT variables and tried to replicate these econometric results for these other variables with mixed success, which we associate with the fact that the time coverage is much shorter for these other variables).

8. It is important to highlight that some of the caveats surrounding Granger-causality tests refer to the determination of the number of lags, the issue of the information set (possibility of omitted variables) and the somewhat narrow definition of causality based exclusively on temporal precedence. We are aware that the five-year averages may be too long to finely capture a feedback system between these two variables, yet this length is justified because our main concern in this paper is with long-term economic growth (shorter windows, say two to three years, will likely reflect a great deal of business cycle fluctuations).

9. The results for the other regions are as follows (they are not reported for the sake of space but are available from the author upon request). For OECD countries, we find little evidence of a significant impact of the standard ICT variables, although the coefficients on capital and initial income are both statistically significant and carry their expected (positive and negative, respectively) signs. Interestingly, the effect of institutions is statistically significant but carries a rather surprising negative sign. For the Asian countries, this pattern of results with respect to the ICT variables is repeated; although institutions once again appear to carry a rather surprising negative sign (while the results for capital and initial income are very much what one should expect). A rather different pattern of results emerges for Africa, with initial income, capital and now human capital mostly responsible for explaining the variation in growth rates while only the absolute number of mobile lines seems to play an important role with respect to the ICT variables. With exception of capital the results for the MENA countries are directly comparable to those for the African countries. Note that because of the insufficient degrees of freedom available, estimation in the case of the transition economies could not be carried out for this model.

10. These are not reported here for the sake of space, but are available upon request from the author including: using population density instead of population, using average years of education per worker instead of primary school enrolment, using the summation of fixed and mobile phone lines, comparing the impacts for the early versus later (1990–2004) years, using the (absolute and per capita) number of personal computers instead of fixed and mobile lines, and splitting the LAC sample between poorer and richer countries.

REFERENCES

Artus, Patrick (1993), *Théorie de la Croissance et des Fluctuations*, Paris: Presses Universitaires de France.

Barro, Robert and Jong-Wha Lee (2001), 'International Data on Educational Attainment: Updates and Implications', *Oxford Economic Papers*, **53**(3), 541–63.

Barro, Robert and Xavier Sala-i-Martin (1995), *Economic Growth*, New York: McGraw-Hill.

Brynjolfsson, Erik and Lorin M. Hitt (2003), 'Computing Productivity: Firm-level Evidence', *Review of Economics and Statistics*, **85**(4), 793–808.

Cronin, F., E. Parker, E. Colleran and M. Gold (1991), 'Telecommunications

Infrastructure and Economic Growth: An Analysis of Causality', *Telecommunications Policy*, **15**(6), 529–35.

Dolton, P. and G. Makepeace (2004), 'Computer Use and Earnings in Britain', *Economic Journal*, **114**(494), C117–129.

Doppelhofer, G., R. Miller and X. Sala-i-Martin (2004), 'Determinants of Long-term Growth: A Bayesian Averaging of Classical Estimates (BACE) Approach', *American Economic Review*, **94**(4), 813–35.

Durlauf, S.N., P.A. Johnson and J.R.W. Temple (2005), 'Growth Econometrics', in P. Aghion and S.N. Durlauf (eds), *Handbook of Economic Growth*, Volume 1A, Amsterdam: North-Holland, pp. 555–677.

Hardy, A. (1980), 'The Role of the Telephone in Economic Development', *Telecommunications Policy*, **4**(4), 278–86.

Indjikian, Rouben and Donald S. Siegel (2005), 'The Impact of Investment in IT on Economic Performance: Implications for Developing Countries', *World Development*, **33**(5), 681–700, May.

Islam, N. (1995), 'Growth Empirics: A Panel Data Approach', *Quarterly Journal of Economics*, **110**(4), 1127–70.

Jipp, A. (1963), 'Wealth of Nations and Telephone Density', *Telecommunications Journal*, July, 199–201.

Jorgenson, D. (2005), 'Accounting for Growth in the Information Age', in Philippe Aghion and Steven Durlauf (eds), *Handbook of Economic Growth*, Volume 1A, Amsterdam: North-Holland, pp. 743–815.

Levine, Ross and David Renelt (1992), 'A Sensitivity Analysis of Cross-country Growth Regressions', *American Economic Review*, **82**(4), 942–63, September.

Mankiw, Gregory, David Romer and David Weil (1992), 'A Contribution to the Empirics of Economic Growth', *Quarterly Journal of Economics*, **107**(2), 407–37, May.

Polity IV (2002), 'Political Regime Characteristics and Transitions, 1800–2002', available at http://www.systemicpeace.org/polity/polity4.htm; accessed 29 March 2010.

Qiang, C., A. Pitt and S. Ayres (2004), *Contribution of Information and Communication Technologies to Growth*, World Bank Working Paper No. 24, Washington DC.

Röller, L.-H. and L. Waverman (2001), 'Telecommunications Infrastructure and Economic Development: A Simultaneous Approach', *American Economic Review*, **91**(4), 909–23.

Sridhar, K.S. and V. Sridhar (2004), 'Telecom Infrastructure and Economic Growth: Evidence from Developing Countries', paper presented at a WIDER conference.

Stiroh, Kevin (2004), 'Reassessing the Impact of IT in the Production Function: A Meta-Analysis and Sensitivity Tests', Federal Reserve Bank of New York, Working Paper.

Teltscher, Susan and Diana Korka (2005), 'Macroeconomic Impacts', in G. Sciadas (ed.), *From the Digital Divide to Digital Opportunities: Measuring Infostates for Development*, UNCTAD/Orbicon.

Waverman, L., M. Mescchi and M. Fuss (2005), 'The Impact of Telecoms on Economic Growth in Developing Countries', in *Africa: The Impact of Mobile Phones*, Vodafone Policy Paper Series, No. 2, March.

APPENDIX 6A.1

Table 6A.1   Variable definitions, sources and basic statistics

Variable	Mean	Std. Dev.	Min	Max	Definition
Economic growth	0.0183	0.043	−0.44	0.49	Average growth rate of GDP per capita (PPP)[a]
Initial income level	7155.1	7665.4	336	58446	Level of GDP per capita (PPP)[b]
Fixed phone lines per 100	11.48	15.97	0.02	86.68	Number of main telephone lines in operation per 100 inhabitants[c]
Mobile phone lines per 100	10.33	19.823	0.0	97.71	Number of mobile telephone lines in operation per 100 inhabitants[d]
Capital	21.44	7.324	2.53	86.79	Gross fixed capital formation (% of GDP)[e]
Population	32295.85	113534.5	40.88	1258821	Total population[f]
Legislative effectiveness	1.761	0.817	0.0	3.0	Institutional quality variable that reflects on a 0-to-3 scale the degree of effectiveness of the legislative power with higher values indicating more effectiveness[g]
Human capital	14.76	10.63	0.1	65.2	Percentage of 'primary school complete' in the total pop: estimates for the age group over 15 years[h]

Sources: a. World Bank, World Development Indicators; b. ibid.; c. ITU, World Telecommunications Indicators 2005; d. ibid.; e. World Bank, World Development Indicators; f. ibid.; g. Polity IV (2002); h. Barro and Lee (2001).

7. ICT, learning and growth: an evolutionary perspective

Mario Cimoli and Nelson Correa

1 INTRODUCTION

The recent changes in international – political and economic – relations and the ongoing 'ICT revolution' are reshaping the opportunities and constraints facing policy-making and institutional engineering, although they have by no means decreased their importance. On the technological side, for example, the characteristics of today's productive knowledge have changed relative to, say, the electromechanical paradigms within which countries like Germany and the United States caught up with and overtook the UK nearly a century ago. They might also be partly different from the type of knowledge – largely centred on first-generation information and communication technologies (ICT) – through which, more recently, Korea and Taiwan approached the technological frontier. In turn, changes in the type of knowledge that countries need to accumulate and improve upon are often accompanied by changes in the production system and in the most appropriate policy packages concerning innovation, for example, the support to the national incumbent, the type of education offered and the role of public training and research centres.

A paradigm-based theory of production and innovation seems to be highly consistent with the evidence on the patterned and cumulative nature of technical change, as well as with the evidence on microeconomic heterogeneity and technological gaps. Even if micro-paradigms present considerable invariance across countries, the ways various paradigms are combined in broader technological systems and, more so, in national production and innovation systems highlight a considerable variety, shaped by country-specific institutions, policies and social factors. The hypothesis here is that evolutionary micro-foundations are a fruitful starting point for a theory on how technological gaps and national institutional diversities can jointly reproduce themselves over rather long time spans in ways that are easily compatible with the patterns of incentives and opportunities facing individual agents, even when they turn out to be profoundly suboptimal from a collective point of view.

The steps leading from a microeconomic theory of innovation and production to more aggregate analyses are clearly numerous and complex. A first obvious question concerns the possibility of identifying relative coherence and structures at these broader levels of observation. Historians of technology – including Hughes, Gilles and David – highlight the importance of technological systems, which, in the terminology of this paper, are structured combinations of micro-technological paradigms (see, for example, the fascinating reconstructions of the emerging system of electrification and electrical standards in David, 1990; for ICT, see Freeman and Louçã, 2001). At an even higher level of generality, Freeman and Pérez (1988) suggest the notion of techno-economic paradigms as a synthetic definition of macro-level systems of production, innovation and governance of social relations.

This approach can also be applied to the analysis of the differences and similarities in the patterns of ICT adoption and diffusion. The next section introduces the concept of technological paradigms and presents an empirical exercise that evaluates the ICT impact across countries. Section 3 then analyses the impact of ICT on Latin American countries. Here, the emphasis is on those variables that define, for each country, the capabilities of adopting and diffusing the ICT paradigm, such as learning, spillovers and specialization. The importance on the growth and development of specific combinations of ICT impacts and the economic governance of production and innovation systems in Latin America is underscored in Section 4. The last section concludes.

2 TECHNOLOGICAL PARADIGMS AND GAPS

A variety of concepts have recently been put forward to define the nature of innovative activities: technological regimes, paradigms, trajectories, salients, guideposts, dominant designs, general-purpose technologies, and so on. These concepts overlap in that they try to capture a few common features of the procedures and direction of technical change. The notion of technological paradigms is based on a view of technology grounded on the following three fundamental ideas (Cimoli and Dosi, 1995).

First, it suggests that any satisfactory description of 'what technology is' and how it changes must also embody the representation of the specific forms of knowledge on which a particular activity is based. This means that technology cannot be reduced to the standard view of a set of well-defined blueprints. Technology primarily concerns problem-solving activities and involves those tacit forms of knowledge embodied in individuals and organizational procedures.

Second, paradigms define basic artefacts that are progressively modified and improved over time. These artefacts can be described in terms of some fundamental technological and economic characteristics. In the case of an aircraft, for example, the basic attributes can be described not only in terms of the inputs and production costs, but also in terms of technological features such as wing-load, take-off weight, speed, refuelling distance and so forth. Technical progress often displays patterns of order and invariance with regard to these product characteristics. Technological invariance has been found in semiconductors, agricultural equipment and cars, as well as in micro-technological studies.[1]

Third, paradigms entail the idea that learning is possible only in the limited spectrum of techniques within which firms have been practising (Atkinson and Stiglitz, 1969). This property, now widely acknowledged in the innovation literature, is that learning is both local and cumulative. Local implies that the exploration and development of new techniques is likely to occur in the vicinity of the techniques already in use. Cumulative means that current technological development builds on past experience of production and innovation; it evolves via sequences of specific problem-solving junctures (Vincenti, 1990). This fits with the ideas of paradigmatic knowledge and the ensuing trajectories. An important implication is that, at any point in time, there is little scope for substitution between techniques because of the limited availability of blueprints that differ from those in use.

Paradigms, and particularly the idea of learning, may be also associated with production theories that allow for increasing returns – from those put forward by Young (1928) and Kaldor (1966, 1975) to the recent, more rigorous formalizations of path-dependent models of innovation diffusion. In the latter, interactions between microeconomic decisions and some form of adaptive learning (or externalities) produce unique technological paths that may be reinforced by lock-in effects with respect to technologies. Although some technological choices may well be inferior to others, they still prosper and become dominant because of the advantages of being first and the quirks of their history. These kinds of models have been proposed by Arthur (1989) and David (1985).

The concept of paradigm, or equivalent concepts, thus has clear foundations at a micro-technological level and explains the persistence of heterogeneity among firms and sectors. A paradigm-based theory of innovation and production also seems to be highly consistent with observed patterns of technical change and technological gaps.

Figure 7.1 illustrates how ICT has impacted productivity across

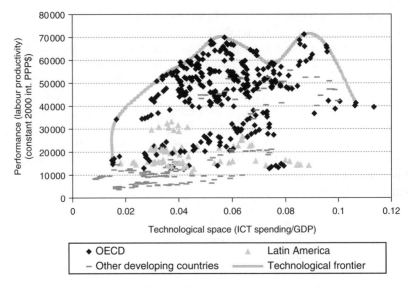

Source: Authors' elaboration, on the basis of the Observatory for the Information Society in Latin America and the Caribbean (OSILAC) database.

Figure 7.1   ICT paradigm and technological gaps, 1993–2004

countries. The technological space is proxied by ICT spending as a per-centage of GDP; each point indicates a country's location in terms of ICT spending and labour productivity. The technological trajectory (ICT spending–labour productivity) for each of the 44 countries included can be traced from 1993 to 2004.[2] The solid line indicates the technological frontier.

Figure 7.1 shows that the same level of performance can be obtained for different levels of ICT expenditure. This implies that a higher ICT expend-iture does not always lead to a higher level of productivity. In addition, the technological frontier describes a non-linear process, which means that an increase in ICT spending does not necessarily lead to a higher level of productivity.

In Figure 7.1, we can identify two groups of countries. The first group includes the countries that define the technological frontier or are close to it in terms of labour productivity (for example, Belgium, Italy, the Netherlands, Norway and the United States). These countries reach a higher level of productivity for each point in the technological space, and their ICT expenditures lead to an increase in productivity. In fact, the trace of technological trajectory for most of these countries has a positive slope: an increase in ICT spending is associated with higher

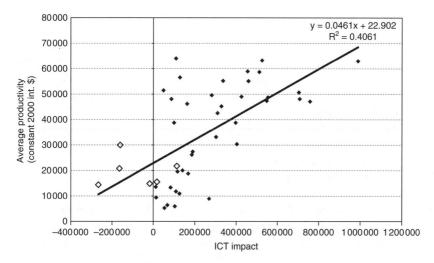

Source: Authors' elaboration, on the basis of OSILAC database.

Figure 7.2   ICT impact and productivity levels, 1993–2004

labour productivity. Beneath this group, the figure features is a white space, below which lie those countries that perform poorly in terms of productivity and face a large gap with the technological frontier. This is the second group, which includes the Latin American countries. The technological trajectories of most of the countries in this group show that the ICT spending does not lead to an increase in productivity. Finally, a few countries are situated between the two groups. These have improved their technological capabilities and accelerated the process of catching up with the international frontier (for example, New Zealand, Portugal Singapore and South Korea).

In the previous paragraph, we argue that the slope of the technological trajectory was different for the two groups of countries, suggesting that ICT spending would have higher effects in developed economies than developing economies. Figure 7.2 shows the linear regression between the ICT impact and the average level of labour productivity. The positive slope indicates that countries with higher levels of labour productivity have a higher ICT impact, while countries with lower productivity levels display a clear falling behind process in the adoption of these technologies.

The open diamonds in Figure 7.2's lower-left corner depict the Latin American economies. This set of countries presents the lowest ICT impact of the sample, posting even negative values.

An important implication of this view regards the persistent asymmetries among countries in their capabilities for ICT adoption and diffusion. Thus, at any point in time, one can draw two major conjectures:

1. Different countries might well be unequivocally ranked according to the efficiencies in the technological ICT space and different time lags in adopting technologies after they have been introduced into the world economy, irrespective of relative prices.
2. There is no significant relationship between these gaps and international differences in ICT expenditures. Wide differences apply to the mismatch between other structural determinants of technological capabilities and ICT. The development process and industrialization are strictly linked to the inter- and intra-national diffusion of 'superior' techniques. Thus, at any point in time, there is likely to be only one or, at most, very few 'best practice' techniques of production, which correspond to the technological frontier.

The industrialization process in developing countries is thus closely linked to the borrowing, imitation and adaptation of established technologies from more advanced economies. These processes of adoption and adaptation of technologies, in turn, are influenced by the specific capabilities of each economy. Empirical evidence strongly suggests that establishing proper technological dynamism in developing countries is impossible without first achieving major structural changes and the sequential construction of a widening manufacturing sector that includes local skills in a set of 'core' technologies. These core technologies often also imply basic infrastructures and networks common to a wide range of activities (such as the electricity grid, the road system, telecommunications and, more recently, the information network).

This suggests that there are technologies whose domains of application are so wide and whose role has been so critical that the pattern of technical change in each country largely depends on national capabilities in mastering production, innovation and imitation in a set of crucial knowledge areas (e.g., in the past, these crucial areas included mechanical engineering, electricity and electrical devices; today, they are centred on ICT). The modification of the adopted technology implies learning new production skills that grow through the adaptation of these capabilities to local specificities.

Furthermore, learning patterns and overall national capabilities are dynamically coupled via input–output flows, knowledge spillovers, complementarities and context-specific externalities. Together, they contribute to shape the organizational and technological context within which each economic activity takes place. Note, however, that the learning-by-doing process is not automatic; on the contrary, it requires adequate organizational conditions within each firm and sector and within the institutional environment.

3 LEARNING, SPILLOVERS AND HETEROGENEITY

This section establishes the impact of ICT on productivity and growth in Latin American countries. The emphasis is on learning in ICT as one of the activities that can improve productivity and thus growth. Heterogeneity among countries and sectors is included to capture the asymmetrical impact of these technologies.

Table 7.1 reports a cross-section regression including 12 Latin American countries (Argentina, Bolivia, Brazil, Chile, Colombia, Costa Rica, Ecuador, Mexico, Panama, Peru, Uruguay and Venezuela as the constant) and nine sectors (agriculture, mining, manufacturing, utilities, construction, wholesale/retail trade, transport/communication and finance/business services and other services as the constant). Labour productivity is the dependent variable, while the independent variables are lagged productivity, learning, specialization, rule of law and a set of dummy variables that captures the heterogeneity among sectors.

Learning is proxied by cumulative ICT expenditure in the last five years. The specialization variable is approximated by the Pearson coefficient, which is calculated on the differences in sectoral productivities. It implies that greater distances in productivity across sectors reflect a higher value of the specialization variable. The rule-of-law index is introduced here as a proxy of the institutional variable (Kaufmann et al., 2005). The learning dummies, calculated as the product between each of the sectoral dummies and the learning variable, capture the differences in learning patterns across sectors.

Higher ICT expenditure and, hence, improved learning capabilities in these technologies positively affect labour productivity. Furthermore, the lagged labour productivity variable shows the expected positive sign, and it is significant in all four regressions. This result indicates that country performance is largely explained by cumulative ICT learning and performance in previous periods.

The specialization variable is positive and significant in the three regressions in which it was included. This suggests that the most productive sectors are those that strongly reinforce increasing aggregate productivity. Not surprisingly, these sectors are manufacturing and services. Increasing productivity in these sectors diffuses learning through the rest of the

Table 7.1   Learning as cumulative ICT spending

Explanatory Variable	(1)	(2)	(3)	(4)
Labour productivity	1.016***	1.016***	1.012***	1.040***
(previous period)	(0.011)	(0.011)	(0.011)	(0.017)
Learning	0.014**	0.014**	0.016**	0.019**
	(0.007)	(0.007)	(0.007)	(0.008)
Specialization		5.74E–07**	8.65E–07***	8.41E–07***
		(0.000)	(0.000)	(0.000)
Rule of law			0.055**	0.047*
			(0.025)	(0.026)
Learning dummies				
Agriculture				0.023**
				(0.010)
Mining				−0.010
				(0.012)
Manufacturing				0.004
				(0.007)
Utilities				0.000
				(0.010)
Construction				0.016*
				(0.009)
Wholesale/retail				0.009
trade				(0.006)
Transport/				0.002
communications				(0.007)
Finance/business				−0.006
services				(0.007)
Constant	−0.243**	−0.275**	−0.259**	−0.566
	(0.116)	(0.114)	(0.112)	(0.152)
R-squared	0.987	0.988	0.989	0.990
Adjusted R-squared	0.987	0.988	0.988	0.989

Notes:
* Statistically significant at the 10% level.
** Statistically significant at the 5% level.
*** Statistically significant at the 1% level.
This is a cross-section regression estimated by ordinary least squares. The dependent variable is labour productivity in the present period. Labour productivity and learning are in log form. Learning is the cumulative ICT spending in the last five years. The specialization variable represents the differences in productivity across all sectors for each country. The institutions variable is represented by the rule-of-law index. The regression includes 108 observations (one year, 12 countries and nine sectors). Standard errors are in parentheses.

Source: Authors' calculations, on the basis of OSILAC database.

Table 7.2 Spillovers: regression analysis

Explanatory Variable	OLS			
	Aggregate impact	Sectoral impact	Aggregate impact	Sectoral impact
ICT	0.973***	0.677***	0.960***	0.668***
	(0.045)	(0.019)	(0.042)	(0.018)
Specialization			2.46E–06***	3.19E–06***
			(8.08E–07)	(5.42E–07)
R-squared	0.890	0.702	0.905	0.720
Adjusted R-squared	0.888	0.702	0.902	0.719
	IV			
	Aggregate impact	Sectoral impact	Aggregate impact	Sectoral impact
ICT	0.999***	0.683***	0.980***	0.670***
	(0.046)	(0.021)	(0.042)	(0.020)
Specialization			2.40E–06***	3.36E–06***
			(7.64E–07)	(5.77E–07)
R-squared	0.913	0.708	0.929	0.730
Adjusted R-squared	0.911	0.708	0.925	0.728

Notes: *** Statistically significant at the 1% level.
OLS: ordinary least squares; IV: instrumental variables. The dependent variable is GDP. Lagged ICT expenditure was used as an instrumental variable. GDP and ICT are in real values and in log form. The specialization variable represents the differences in productivity across all sectors for each country. Aggregate regressions include 60 observations (48 using IV); sectoral regressions include 540 observations (438 using IV) (five years, 12 countries and nine sectors). Standard errors are in parentheses.

Source: Authors' calculations, on the basis of OSILAC database.

economy and thus positively impact aggregate productivity. The construction and agriculture sectors have significantly different learning patterns. The rule-of-law variable is positive and significant, suggesting a positive link between the strength of a country's institutions and its performance.

Table 7.2 presents the results from the exercise using OLS and instrumental variables to assess the aggregate impact of ICT on GDP (that is, total ICT expenditures and total GDP). The aggregate effect is higher than the impact of sectoral ICT expenditures on sectoral GDP (that is, sectoral GDP and ICT expenditures for each of the nine sectors considered). In all the regressions, the ICT coefficient has the expected positive sign and is

Table 7.3   Growth, ICT and sectoral heterogeneity

Explanatory Variable	(1)	(2)
ICT	0.976	0.962
	(0.016)	(0.015)
Specialization		2.47E-06
		(0.000)
Dummies		
Agriculture	3.282	3.220
	(0.124)	(0.118)
Mining	2.609	2.543
	(0.127)	(0.121)
Manufacturing	1.215	1.193
	(0.105)	(0.099)
Utilities	1.016	0.971
	(0.114)	(0.108)
Construction	2.341	2.288
	(0.118)	(0.113)
Wholesale/Retail Trade	1.047	1.026
	(0.105)	(0.099)
Transport/	0.700	0.679
Communications	(0.105)	(0.099)
Finance/Business Services	1.206	1.186
	(0.105)	(0.099)
Constant	1.679	1.648
	(0.146)	(0.139)
R-squared	0.895	0.905
Adjusted R-squared	0.893	0.903

Note: The estimation method is ordinary least squares (OLS). The dependent variable is GDP. GDP and ICT are in real values and in log form. The specialization variable represents the productive heterogeneity across all sectors for each particular country. All values are significant at the 1% level. All regressions include 540 observations (five years, 12 countries and nine sectors). Standard errors are in parentheses.

Source: Authors' calculations, on the basis of OSILAC database.

significant at the 1 per cent level, even after controlling for specialization. The aggregate impact is always higher than the sectoral impact. This suggests the existence of spillovers associated with ICT.

The next three exercises analyse the sensitivity of the ICT coefficient to country and sectoral heterogeneity. Table 7.3 presents the results of an exercise that evaluates the impact of ICT expenditure and specialization, controlled only by sectoral heterogeneity. All coefficients are always significant at the 1 per cent level and show the expected signs.[3] These results suggest a very strong linear correlation between ICT and GDP, even after controlling for specialization. Nevertheless, the ICT coefficient seems too high.

Table 7.4 evaluates the impact of ICT expenditure and specialization when we control for country heterogeneity. All the ICT coefficients are always significant at the 1 per cent level, and they have the expected signs.[4] These results suggest a very strong linear correlation between ICT and GDP. Nevertheless, the ICT coefficient again seems too high. Finally, the ICT coefficient decreases by more than half, from 0.9 to 0.4, when country and sectoral heterogeneities are considered separately.

Table 7.5 presents the results of an exercise that considers sectoral and country heterogeneities jointly. The ICT coefficient has the expected positive sign and is always significant at the 1 per cent level, even after controlling for specialization and institutions. This suggests a positive linear correlation between ICT spending and GDP.[5] Table 7.5 differs from the previous two tables, however, in the value of the ICT coefficient. The ICT coefficient falls from 0.9 in the sectoral analysis to 0.4 in the country analysis and, finally, to 0.1 when the two effects are considered jointly. This implies that the omission of one of these two effects leads to an overestimation of the ICT impact on GDP. The specialization and institutions coefficients have the expected positive signs, and they are always significant in explaining the level of GDP, suggesting that both should be included in the analysis. In other words, when a country is more specialized and has stronger institutions, it will also have a higher level of income.

To sum up, ICT has a positive impact on productivity and growth, which is displayed through learning activities in these technologies. Lagged productivity, specialization and spillovers are the channels through which ICT affects the rest of the economy. Lagged productivity incorporates the learning accumulated in the past. Specialization is related to the driver effect of those sectors that lead the economy in terms of productivity and diffuse their capabilities to other sectors. The presence of spillovers reflects the ICT impact on linkages and interactions between different actors in the economy.

Two overlapping mechanisms can explain these results. The first recalls the technological push mechanisms. In this case, lagged and current expenditures on ICT improve competencies and capabilities in using those technologies and, consequently, productivity. The second explanation is related to the demand pull effect. ICT expenditure increases effective demand, thereby increasing spillovers, sectoral productivity, the scale of production capacities and, hence, aggregate productivity. In this case, a general Verdoon-Kaldor effect should prevail as the dominant explanation of productivity growth (Kaldor, 1966, 1975; Vernon, 1966; Pigeon and Wray, 1999).

The impact of ICT may be overestimated, however, if both country and

Table 7.4 Growth, ICT and country heterogeneity

Explanatory Variable	(1)	(2)
ICT	0.428***	0.428***
	(0.016)	(0.016)
Specialization		2.17E–07
		(0.000)
Dummies		
Argentina	0.406***	0.434**
	(0.126)	(0.209)
Bolivia	−1.632***	−1.580***
	(0.130)	(0.338)
Brazil	0.663***	0.713**
	(0.130)	(0.324)
Chile	−0.463***	−0.413
	(0.125)	(0.320)
Colombia	−0.473***	−0.424
	(0.126)	(0.317)
Costa Rica	−1.684***	−1.630***
	(0.127)	(0.343)
Ecuador	−1.336***	−1.304***
	(0.128)	(0.227)
Mexico	0.799***	0.844***
	(0.127)	(0.293)
Panama	−1.765***	−1.720***
	(0.128)	(0.296)
Peru	−0.724***	−0.673**
	(0.125)	(0.322)
Uruguay	−1.253***	−1.202***
	(0.128)	(0.328)
Constant	6.770***	6.715***
	(0.126)	(0.346)
R-squared	0.881	0.881
Adjusted R-squared	0.8783	0.8781

Notes:
**   Statistically significant at the 5% level.
***   Statistically significant at the 1% level.
The estimation method is ordinary least squares (OLS). The dependent variable is GDP. GDP and ICT are in real values and in log form. The specialization variable represents the productive heterogeneity across all sectors for each particular country. All regressions include 540 observations (five years, 12 countries and nine sectors). Standard errors are in parentheses.

Source: Authors' calculations, on the basis of OSILAC database.

Table 7.5 *Growth, ICT and sectoral and country heterogeneity: panel data regression*

Explanatory Variable	(1)	(2)	(3)	(4)	(5)	(6)
	Fixed Effects	Random Effects	Fixed Effects	Random Effects	Fixed Effects	Random Effects
ICT	0.107***	0.125***	0.104***	0.123***	0.115***	0.131***
	(0.007)	(0.009)	(0.007)	(0.008)	(0.008)	(0.009)
Specialization			6.72E–07***	7.05E–07***	3.25E–07*	3.90E–07**
			(1.46E–07)	(1.70E–07)	(1.73E–07)	(1.99E–07)
Institutions					0.109***	0.102***
					(0.030)	(0.034)
Constant	7.891***	7.793***	7.865***	7.765***	7.849***	7.753***
	(0.041)	(0.112)	(0.040)	(0.110)	(0.040)	(0.110)
Within R-squared	0.322	0.3222	0.354	0.354	0.373	0.3720
Hausman test	Fixed effects		Fixed effects		Fixed effects	
No. observations	540					
No. groups	108					

Notes:
* Statistically significant at the 10% level.
** Statistically significant at the 5% level.
*** Statistically significant at the 1% level.
The dependent variable is GDP. GDP and ICT are in real values and in log form. The specialization variable represents the productive heterogeneity across all sectors for each particular country. The institutions variable is represented by the rule-of-law index. All regressions include 540 observations (five years, 12 countries and nine sectors). Standard errors are in parentheses.

Source: Authors' calculations, on the basis of OSILAC database.

sectoral heterogeneity are not included. This clearly recalls the arguments of the above sections. Country and sectoral heterogeneity play a central role in explaining the pervasiveness of ICT in the economic system.

4 ICT IMPACTS ON PRODUCTION AND INNOVATION SYSTEMS

The importance of the institutional dimension for evolutionary theories of production and innovation is supported by growing evidence from both micro- and macroeconomic patterns of technological change. After all, at the microeconomic level, technologies are, to a fair extent, incorporated in particular institutions (the firms), whose characteristics, decision rules, capabilities and behaviours are fundamental in shaping the rates and directions of technological advance. Firms, in turn, are embedded in rich networks of relations with each other and with other institutional actors, ranging from government agencies to universities, research laboratories and civil organizations, among others.

As an intermediate step towards the identification of national socioeconomic regimes, we consider the anatomy and development of particular innovation and production systems at the national level, which embody distinctive mechanisms and directions of learning and are grounded in the microeconomic theory of production and innovation sketched above. To detail this hypothesis, however, we must analyse the composing elements and properties of these national systems. The recent literature uses a variety of largely overlapping concepts to refer to these properties, including a country's global technological capability, national innovation systems, national technological capabilities and national systems of production (Cimoli, 2000).

Latin American countries made significant changes to their macroeconomic policies and regulatory regimes in the 1980s. Trade and financial liberalization, the deregulation of markets and the privatization of economic activities were implemented as part of a wide structural reform package.[6] This strongly influenced the institutional context and, consequently, microeconomic behaviours, in particular with regard to firms. Firms are a crucial (although not exclusive) repository of knowledge, which is largely embodied in their operational routines and modified over time through their higher-level rules of behaviour and strategies (such as their search behaviours and their decisions concerning vertical integration and horizontal diversification). Moreover, their networks of linkages with other firms and with non-profit organizations (such as public agencies) enhance or limit the opportunities each firm faces to improve their problem-solving capabilities.

ICT diffusion in Latin America has jointly evolved with the impact of radical changes introduced in the 1980s. The region has essentially been affected by two simultaneous shocks: economic reforms and ICT. Some major features of these impacts are summarized in Table 7.6.

The specialization pattern in Latin America can be mapped out on the basis of comparative advantages and access to abundant factors of production, namely, natural resource endowment and cheap labour. Geographically, two separate patterns appear to have emerged. On the one hand, the South American countries have intensified their specialization

Table 7.6   ICT impact in the post-reform period

	Production and Adoption	Access and Diffusion
Opportunities	Modernization (incorporated in capital goods and production processes) and reduction of transaction costs	Profited by natural-resource-processing and low-skill industries and services
	Enhanced linkages and efficiency with world technology centres and multinational corporations	Increased efficiency and reduction of transaction costs in approaching input market for developed and industrializing economies
Constraints	Structural inertia and sticky diversification pattern	Reduced capabilities in R&D and engineering-intensive industries
	Polarized production systems and scant density of domestic linkages	Persistence of informal activities and income distribution

in natural resources and standardized commodities. On the other hand, Mexico and the Central American countries have globalized their manufacturing and assembly activities on the back of relatively abundant cheap labour (Mortimore and Peres, 2001).

ICT not only affects all industries and services, but also influences every function within each firm and industry. The pervasiveness of ICT has changed the production process, increasing the share of capital and the incorporated technologies, particularly in sectors with high export shares and services. ICT impacts are also felt in other essential activities, such as research and development (R&D), design, production, marketing and transport.

Capital-intensive natural-resource-processing industries have taken the lead in this case, together with the highly protected vehicle industry. The industrial structure showed structural weaknesses in the local linkages with other local firms and institutions, together with a diffused modernization of production process within firms. Standardization of production activities and improved quality are visible results. The aforementioned changes have two implications: first, firms are strongly dependent on foreign technology in the development of new products and processes; second, firms have gained competitiveness through activities targeted at existing products, rather than by creating new products (Cimoli, 2005; Cimoli and Correa, 2005).

Natural-resource-processing industries producing commodities for competitive world markets are now highly capital intensive, with incorporated technologies that are mainly imported. They are among the industries with the strongest performance in terms of relative labour productivity. These industries are highly automated and incorporate an intensive level of ICT in capital goods and in the production process. It is in these activities, as well as in non-tradables sectors such as telecommunications or energy and transport services, that Latin American countries have partially closed up the relative productivity gap with more mature industrial economies. In contrast, R&D and engineering-intensive activities (such as the production of pharmaceutical raw materials and capital goods) and unskilled-labour-intensive industries (such as the manufacture of shoes, garments or furniture for the domestic markets) appear to have done worse, rapidly losing ground vis-à-vis the evolving international efficiency frontier. ICT also have important consequences in these industries.

To explain the effects of ICT, we have to recall that most of the knowledge production centres are located in advanced economies (including research on new material, research on basic science, product design and so on). ICT clearly make the exchange of information easier and faster, which does not necessarily support the relocation of the above activities to Latin American economies. On the contrary, these technologies facilitate the process of information exchange and communications, but they do not necessarily support the local creation and diffusion of knowledge. In the case of the automobile industry, for example, quality control and certification are evaluated online, with information being exchanged from one part of the world to another. Subsidiaries of multinational corporations and domestic large firms tend to operate in real time, planning their production activities online with their external licensors and technological services. In effect, controlling companies, which are mainly located in advanced economies, benefit from comparative advantages in technology and innovation and the real-time exchange of information to operate production and R&D activities. Multinational companies concentrate the bulk of their research and development activities in their countries of origin or, as recent trends suggest, in strongly dynamic economies that specialize in highly technology-intensive industries and that represent huge potential markets for technological products, like China.

In the extreme case of the in-bond assembly, or *maquila*, industries, which are intensive users of low-skilled labour, ICT are abundantly incorporated in capitals goods and production processes (Capdevielle, 2005). The firms and plants in these industries match the efficiency of those on the technological frontier. However, these industries have neither increased their productivity nor displayed strong linkages with the rest of the economy; in fact, increasing integration with international markets has not implied increasing dynamism in all domestic technological activities.[7] Conversely, in Korea and Malaysia the most dynamic export sectors have the highest share in total manufacturing value-added, revealing stronger linkages between exports, domestic production and institutions promoting R&D and technological capabilities.

Regional technological capabilities in hardware and artefacts associated with ICT are mainly explained by policies that promote foreign direct investment (FDI), as in the case of *maquila* industries, programmes facilitating temporary imports of inputs used to produce export goods (like Mexico's Programa de Importación Temporal para Producir Artículos de Exportación, or PITEX) and free trade zones. Most of the regional production capacity installed locally involves subsidiaries of multinational corporations, which are leaders in electronics, semiconductors, printed circuits, microprocessors, mobile phones, televisions (LCD and plasma) and personal computers. Not surprisingly, those multinational corporations are from countries (such as Japan, Korea, Singapore, the United States and members of the European Union) that have radically transformed their industrial structure to promote the expansion of firms and sectors that develop technological capabilities associated with the ICT paradigms. The regional software industry is mainly restricted to four countries: Argentina, Brazil, Mexico and Uruguay. These countries have shown an increasing trend in their share of world exports in software products, accompanied by a higher share of employment in domestic firms with respect to the larger multinational corporations (including Hewlett-Packard, IBM, Microsoft and Oracle). However, the share of this industry within the GDP remains relatively low, at 0.4 per cent in Mexico, 0.7 per cent in Argentina, 1.6 per cent in Brazil and 1.8 per cent in Uruguay.

These microeconomic behaviours of firms, combined with the specialization pattern, explain the undermining of endogenous technological capabilities. They reduce the domestic production linkages and labour absorption capacity of the formal manufacturing sector, thereby diminishing the sector's capacity to act as a driver of development for the whole economy. The simultaneous existence of an outward-oriented modern sector that consistently fails to provide enough employment and of a low-productivity informal sector that accounts for a large share of jobs can thus be seen as a peculiar manifestation of structural heterogeneity. The weight of the informal sector in urban labour markets is fairly even across the region's countries, ranging from 39 per cent in Chile to 67 per cent in Bolivia (Cimoli et al., 2005).

Informality is an increasingly entrenched feature of Latin American economies. Informal activities are unproductive, and the concentration of the workforce in the least productive sector drags down overall productivity. It is estimated that in the late 1990s, labour productivity in the informal sector was just 20 per cent of that in the formal sector, and the informal sector accounted for about half of total employment. Not only does informality have adverse effects on economic performance in terms of exclusion, marginalization, income inequality and access to ICT, but it directly affects overall productivity – and thus growth – by reducing average productivity in the economy.

5 CONCLUSIONS

A paradigm-based theory of innovation and production is highly consistent with the evidence on the patterned and cumulative nature of ICT and on the gaps in producing and adopting these technologies. Countries are unequivocally ranked according to efficiencies in ICT adoption, and its impact therefore shows a large diversity across countries.

In Latin America, ICT have a positive effect on productivity and growth. Learning, spillovers and specialization are central for explaining the impact of ICT, but this impact is differentiated according to country and sectoral heterogeneities. In fact, the impact is overestimated when these variables are omitted.

When Latin American countries are compared with developed and industrializing economies, they show a large gap in their capabilities for absorbing and diffusing ICT. These processes of technological adoption and adaptation are influenced by the specific capabilities of each economy. The configuration of production and innovation systems is closely linked with the borrowing, imitation and adaptation of established technologies from more advanced economies. The empirical evidence strongly suggests that establishing proper technological dynamism in Latin American countries is impossible without first achieving major changes and the sequential construction of widening opportunities for firms, sectors and institutions, including indigenous skills in a set of 'core' technologies and production capacities.

The overlap between the ICT impact and the configuration of Latin American production and innovation systems have diffused opportunities on the one hand, and raised barriers, on the other. Some sectors and activities have clearly benefited from the incorporation of ICT and expanded their participation in international markets. Others have been constrained in creating capabilities and acceding to these technologies.

NOTES

1. The interpretation of technical change and a number of historical examples can be found in pioneering works on the economics of technical change, such as those by Chris Freeman, Nathan Rosenberg, Richard Nelson, Sidney Winter, Thomas Hughes, Paul David, Joel Mokyr, Paolo Saviotti and others; for a partial survey, see Dosi (1988).
2. Figure 7.1 plots all the performances for all technological combinations known in 2004; that is, it represents the actual, not the theoretical, patterns of ICT.
3. The ICT coefficient is the same coefficient that can be obtained using a panel data regression with fixed effects. The only difference regards the sector dummies, which are included explicitly in the OLS regression to control for sectoral differences.
4. The ICT coefficient is the same coefficient that can be obtained using a panel data regression with fixed effects. The only difference regards the country dummies, which are included explicitly in the OLS regression to control for country differences.
5. It shows the coefficients and levels of significance for ICT, specialization and institutions in explaining GDP using random and fixed effects, even if the Hausman test always prefers fixed effects. This table differs from the previous two (Tables 7.3 and 7.4), in the perspective of analysis: the first table considered only sectoral effects (we used sectoral dummies); the second table considered only country effects (we used country dummies); and the present table uses both sectoral and country effects.
6. National systems also entail a broader notion of embeddedness in a set of social relationships, rules and policy incentives and constraints. Metcalfe (1995) provides the following policy-oriented definition of a national innovation system: a 'set of institutions which jointly and individually contribute to the development and diffusion of new technologies and which provide the framework within which governments form and implement policies to influence the innovation process'.
7. Ciarli and Giuliani (2005) reach a similar conclusion for the case of Costa Rica. The diversification of exports towards the electronics components and medical instruments sectors, as a result of the attraction of foreign direct investments, has not been accompanied by significant technological and production linkages with domestic companies.

REFERENCES

Arthur, W.B. (1989), 'Competing technologies, increasing returns and lock-in by historical events', *Economic Journal*, **99**(394), 116–31.

Atkinson, A.B. and J.E. Stiglitz (1969), 'A new view of technological change', *Economic Journal*, **79**(315), 572–8.

Capdevielle, M. (2005), 'Globalización, especialización y heterogeneidad estructural en México', in M. Cimoli (ed.), *Heterogeneidad estructural, asimetrías tecnológicas y crecimiento en América Latina*, Santiago: Economic Commission for Latin America and the Caribbean (ECLAC) and Inter-American Development Bank (IDB), pp. 101–26.

Ciarli, T. and E. Giuliani. (2005), 'Inversion extranjera directa y encadenamientos productivos en Costa Rica', in M. Cimoli (ed.), *Heterogeneidad estructural, asimetrías tecnológicas y crecimiento en América Latina*, Santiago: Economic Commission for Latin America and the Caribbean (ECLAC) and Inter-American Development Bank (IDB), pp. 101–26.

Cimoli, M. (2000), *Developing Innovation Systems: Mexico in the Global Context*, New York and London: Continuum-Pinter Publishers.

Cimoli, M. (ed.) (2005), *Heterogeneidad structural, asimetrías tecnológicas y crecimiento en América Latina*, Santiago: Economic Commission for Latin America and the Caribbean (ECLAC) and Inter-American Development Bank (IDB).

Cimoli, M. and N. Correa (2005) 'Trade openness and technology gaps in Latin America: a low-growth trap', in J.A. Ocampo (ed.), *Beyond Reforms: Structural Dynamics and Macroeconomic Theory*, Palo Alto: Stanford University Press.

Cimoli, M. and G. Dosi (1995), 'Technological paradigms, patterns of learning and development: an introductory roadmap', *Journal of Evolutionary Economics*, **5**(3), 243–68.

Cimoli, M., A. Primi and M. Pugno (2005), 'An enclave-led model of growth: the structural problem of informality persistence in Latin America', *Department of Economics Working Paper*, No. 0504, University of Trento.

David, P.A. (1985), 'Clio and the economics of QWERTY', *American Economic Review*, **75**(2), 332–7.

David, P.A. (1990), 'The dynamo and the computer: an historical perspective on the modern productivity paradox', *American Economic Review*, **80**(2), 355–61.

Dosi, G. (1988), 'Sources, procedures, and microeconomic effects of innovation', *Journal of Economic Literature*, **26**(3), 1120–71.

Freeman, C. and F. Louçã (2001), *As Time Goes By: From the Industrial Revolutions to the Information Revolution*, Oxford: Oxford University Press.

Freeman, C. and C. Pérez (1988), 'Structural crises of adjustment: business cycles and investment behavior', in G. Dosi and others (eds), *Technical Change and Economic Theory*, London: Continuum International Publishing, pp. 38–66.

Kaldor, N. (1966), *Causes of the Slow Rate of Economic Growth in the United Kingdom*, Cambridge, UK: Cambridge University Press.

Kaldor, N. (1975), 'What is wrong with economic theory?', *Quarterly Journal of Economics*, **89**(3), 347–57.

Kaufmann, D., A. Kraay and M. Mastruzzi (2005), 'Governance matters IV: governance indicators for 1996–2004', draft, Washington: World Bank.

Metcalfe, J.S. (1995), 'Technology systems and technology policy in an evolutionary frame-work', *Cambridge Journal of Economics*, **19**(1), 25–46.

Mortimore, M. and W. Peres (2001), 'Corporate competitiveness in Latin America and the Caribbean', *CEPAL Review*, No. 74, August, 35–57.

Pigeon, M.-A. and L.R. Wray (1999), 'Demand constraints and economic growth', *Macroeconomics Paper*, No. 9905004, EconWPA.

Vernon, R. (1966), 'International investment and international trade in the product cycle', *Quarterly Journal of Economics*, **80**(2), 190–207.

Vincenti, W.G. (1990), *What Engineers Know and How They Know It*, Baltimore: Johns Hopkins University Press.

Young, A. (1928), 'Increasing returns and economic progress', *Economic Journal*, **38**(152), 527–42.

8. ICT and knowledge complementarities: a factor analysis on growth

Marco Capasso and Nelson Correa*

1 INTRODUCTION

Many studies have tried to measure the impact of information and communication technologies (ICT) on economic growth. There are several ways to determine this impact: growth accounting exercises, panel data regressions, mathematical simulations and so forth. Most of them consider ICT as having a direct impact on growth. They assume that the simple accumulation of ICT goods leads to a direct positive impact on some income measure. This way of measuring is not precise, however, as it neglects the contribution to the knowledge base. ICT should not be considered a mere capital input, but rather both a capital good and an input to knowledge creation.

In this paper, we focus on measuring the impact of ICT on economic growth only through their contribution to knowledge. Hence, instead of concentrating our attention on the accumulation of ICT goods, we assess the contribution of ICT use to the knowledge base and then the contribution of the knowledge base to economic growth. We thus study two important links to evaluate the impact of ICT use on economic growth. The first link acts between ICT and knowledge, while the second connects knowledge and GDP growth. After measuring both effects, we determine the part of the contribution of ICT to economic growth that operates through knowledge.

While nobody today is discussing the importance of knowledge for economic growth, the mathematical formalization is still a point of conflict. In the following section, we introduce knowledge as an input in the classical production function, thereby deviating from the typical exercise that considers a Cobb-Douglas production function with only two inputs (capital and labour). The main difference from the typical exercise lies exactly in our need for measuring an unobserved variable that represents the stock of knowledge of each country. After building the knowledge indicator, we determine its impact on economic growth.

New technologies have undoubtedly encouraged the diffusion of knowledge. The rise of radio, television and the Internet and the development of many means of mass communication have reduced the cost of access to all kinds of information, facilitating the spread of codified knowledge around the whole economic system. This broader access to information not only helps the diffusion of codified knowledge, but it also allows the creation of new knowledge. A clear example is the creation of scientific knowledge, where the newest works are created on the basis of previous ideas. Thus, the knowledge frontier could not be expanded without access to the old codified knowledge contained in previous works. Since ICT provide access to previously codified knowledge, they enforce the creation of new knowledge. This argument takes for granted the cumulative characteristic of knowledge, which implies that knowledge creation depends on the existing knowledge base. Access to a larger knowledge base thus facilitates the creation of new ideas.

ICT use contributes positively first to the expansion of the knowledge base and then to economic growth. Nonetheless, the magnitude of this impact depends on other factors that also contribute to the creation and diffusion of knowledge, such as expenditures on research and development (R&D), level of education and the number of scientific works. We test for the existence of complementarity among these four proxies of knowledge (that is, ICT use, publications, tertiary enrolment and R&D) and identify a specific proportion at which the knowledge proxies work best in producing economic growth. We call this the golden proportion and elaborate a measure of distance from it, which represents the inefficiency in the distribution of the knowledge proxies. This variable is then incorporated in the original production function to correct the knowledge impact for such inefficiency. Therefore, a change in ICT use in a country acts on GDP both by changing the knowledge indicator and by changing the efficiency in the interaction between ICT and the other knowledge proxies.

Summing up, the present paper has the ambitious goal of addressing two issues simultaneously. Our first aim is to evaluate the impact of ICT use on knowledge and economic growth. Our second goal is to analyse knowledge complementarities.

The structure of the paper is as follows. Sections 2 and 3 analyse the relation between knowledge and growth, on the one hand, and ICT and growth, on the other. Section 4 reviews the concepts of complementarity and supermodularity. Section 5 explains the construction of the knowledge indicator, while Section 6 reports the results of the empirical analysis.

In Section 7, we perform a number of exercises to infer policy implications. Section 8 concludes.

2 KNOWLEDGE AND GROWTH

Knowledge has generally not been treated explicitly in textbook production functions. Scholars prefer to work with technical change instead of knowledge. Knowledge is never mentioned, for example, in the following production function introduced by Solow (1957):

$$Y = AK^{\alpha}L^{\beta}, \tag{8.1}$$

where $\alpha + \beta = 1$ and where Y represents gross domestic product, A is the level of technical change, K is the capital amount and L is the labour force. In this case, technical change is Hicks-neutral, since A affects capital and labour in the same way in the production function. Although some authors associate A with knowledge (for example, D. Romer, 1996), Solow (1957) himself labelled it technical change. The reason is clear: this function does not include knowledge. If we accept that it does, we must admit that it is a very peculiar kind of knowledge, because it is treated as a public good that is completely free to everybody. It receives no compensation, and there is thus no economic incentive to invest in knowledge.

To illustrate the striking difference between the previous function and other functions that treat knowledge as a production input, we need to introduce the following function:

$$Y = AK^{\alpha}L^{\beta}C^{\gamma} \tag{8.2}$$

where C is the stock of knowledge.

There are two important differences between equations (8.1) and (8.2). First, in equation (8.2) the sum of all input parameters does not necessarily equal one (that is, $\alpha + \beta + \gamma \neq 1$). Second, the two equations differ in their technical change: while in equation (8.1) A could be considered knowledge under some strong assumptions, in equation (8.2) knowledge and technical change are two different things. The rest of this section clarifies these two statements.

The literature provides an interesting discussion on introducing knowledge as an input in the production process. Carlaw and Lipsey (2002) and Lipsey et al. (2005) discuss imposing constant returns to scale on equation (8.2), that is, imposing $\alpha + \beta + \gamma = 1$. They argue that it does not make much sense, since it implies that when a firm wants to increase its output by replicating an existing plant, it needs to duplicate the stock of capital, labour and also knowledge. The duplication of knowledge requires the creation of new knowledge, but once new knowledge is created, then the new plant cannot be a replication of the previous one, assuming constant technology.

Since forcing constant returns to scale on all factors of production does not fit well when knowledge is considered a factor of production, it seems more reasonable to maintain constant returns in capital and labour and allow for increasing returns in the three factors of production. The endogenous growth literature is full of models with increasing returns. One of the pioneers of this line of thought was Lucas (1988), who presents a model with accumulation of physical and human capital. He allows for increasing returns by considering spillovers in the accumulation of human capital. Barro (1990) presents a function with three inputs: labour, capital and government purchases. He considers constant returns in private inputs and increasing returns in all factors of production. Paul Romer (1996) assumes a production function with three factors of production: knowledge state of the firm, aggregate knowledge and other inputs. He considers constant returns in the inputs the firms can control and increasing returns in all factors of production.

The problem with assuming increasing returns as in equation (8.2) is that we must drop the assumption of perfect competition, since in this case all inputs cannot be paid with the value of their marginal product without causing the firm to suffer losses. It is for this reason that scholars disagree on explicitly adopting a function with increasing returns. However, dropping the perfect competition assumption in a study intended for Latin American economies does not seem a great loss. Rather, it seems more realistic to work without it.

To illustrate the different treatment of technical change and knowledge in the two equations, it is useful to point out the differences among all factors of production. Cornes and Sandler (1986) and Romer (1990) claim that any economic good, and then any factor of production, can be classified by the extent to which it is a rival good and its degree of excludability. A good is purely rival if its use by an agent precludes its use by any other agent; it is purely non-rival good if its use by one agent does not limit its use by other agents. Most goods are rival: for example, if you eat an apple, no one can eat that same apple. Examples of non-rival goods include public goods, which are by definition non-rival and non-excludable. For example, the street lights installed by the state or the military force of any country are public goods. In both cases, an individual can use the goods without precluding their use by another individual. A good is purely excludable if an agent, often the owner of the good, can prevent other agents from using it. In contrast, a good is non-excludable if no agent can prevent others from using the good. An interesting example for economic growth is the degree of excludability of different kinds of scientific research. In the case of applied scientific research, innovations can very often be patented, precluding the possibility of other individuals benefiting from them. Applied scientific research therefore has a high degree of excludability. In the case of basic scientific research, even great innovations can seldom be patented (for example, Albert Einstein never patented his theory of relativity). Therefore, basic scientific research often has the characteristics of a non-excludable good.

In the economic growth literature, the capital amount (K) and the labour force (L) are considered rival and excludable goods. Capital is rival because when a firm uses its capital in a productive process, the same capital generally cannot be used, at the same time, in other productive processes. Moreover, a firm can perfectly prevent other firms from using its capital, so capital is excludable. Labour is considered a rival good since one person cannot be in two places at the same time and thus cannot be working in two enterprises at the same moment. Since firms can set contracts in such a way to prevent other firms from using their human capital, then labour can also be considered excludable.

The technical change (A) is an exogenously provided public input, and as such it is non-excludable and non-rival. There is no compensation for the input A; private interests have no influence on the generation of new technical change. All the firms can use all the stock of A without precluding other firms from doing the same.

Knowledge (C) represents the union of truths, beliefs and wisdom that can be labelled as the things that the economic agents have learned. It is idiosyncratic for all individuals. It represents what the agents know or what they understand about a particular subject, understanding that can be used in a productive process. The concept of knowledge we are describing is non-rivalrous and excludable. Notice that considering knowledge to be a rival good only reinforces our point about why knowledge is different from technical change. In this sense, if knowledge is an excludable good, it should receive compensation, and knowledge should therefore be included as an input in the production function.

Knowledge is non-rival because its consumption by an individual does not reduce the amount available for consumption by others. In other words, knowledge is non-rival because there is a zero marginal cost from an additional individual enjoying the benefits of it. In our example, the amount of knowledge does not depend on the number of plants we want to build: knowledge is not spent when we replicate one plant a thousand times. Nevertheless, it is excludable: not everybody can have access to the same knowledge because some forms of knowledge are individual-specific; that is, some agents will have more knowledge than others. One of the reasons to think that knowledge is excludable is the acceptance that it can be tacit. Tacit knowledge is the component that is inherent to a particular individual, to his or her own experience, and it cannot be transferred, except through the sharing of the same experiences (Polanyi, 1966). Experience sharing depends at least partially on the will of the owner of the experience. Thus, the recognition of the tacit component of knowledge implies the recognition that knowledge is an excludable good, and, consequently, it produces knowledge heterogeneity among economic agents and an incentive to pay compensation for this input.

Taking knowledge as an excludable and non-rival good perfectly matches with the idea of increasing returns in the production function. Thus, if it is possible to double output using the same amount of knowledge, by simply doubling capital and labour, then we have constant returns to scale in capital and labour. Indeed, it would be necessary to increase the knowledge base only slightly to increase output more than twofold and, therefore, to have increasing returns to scale in our three inputs.

3   ICT AND GROWTH

The relation between ICT and economic growth has generally been examined in the simple context of a GDP depending only on capital and labour. Consequently, ICT is considered part of the capital stock, as well as a factor influencing labour productivity. This theoretical assessment was not initially supported by empirical data, as Robert Solow remarked in 1987: 'You can see the computer age everywhere but in the productivity statistics'. Economists have given several explanations to the Solow productivity paradox (for a review, see Triplett, 1999). For example, Oliner and Sichel (1994) estimate the contribution of ICT to growth to have been modest through the early 1990s because computing equipment still represented an extremely small fraction of the capital stock. After 1995, however, the growth of labour productivity showed a clear rebound. Oliner and Sichel (2000) identify information and communication technology as the key variable for this rebound, in that the stocks of computers and network infrastructures increased rapidly, while their producers gained efficiency in the production process. Jorgenson and Stiroh (2000) confirm that productivity gains in high-technology industries (including the ICT sector) have been a direct source of capital deepening and labour productivity gains, while the same industries are also responsible for the observed total factor productivity (TFP) growth. Jorgenson (2001) summarizes the whole story by stating that the faster productivity growth in ICT-producing industries provoked the accelerated information and communication technology price decline. This price decline, in turn, has provided incentives for the ongoing substitution of information and communication technology for other productive inputs, thus giving much additional weight to components of capital input with higher marginal products. Jorgenson and Stiroh (1999) emphasize the conceptual difference between the afore described substitution and the different interpretation involving 'technical change'. In the case of substitution, the benefits deriving from the introduction of computer-intensive equipment are fully internalized by the users of information and communication technology and their suppliers. In the case of technical change, more output is produced from the same inputs; that is, a spillover phenomenon occurs by which third parties also receive benefits.

David (2000, p. 54) considers the coexistence of the rise of labour productivity with the process of transition to a 'new, information-intensive techno-economic regime'. The idea that the progress of technology is not continuous would explain the productivity paradox of the late 1980s and early 1990s. Moreover, only the coordination between technological and organizational change and labour force training can allow the full exploitation of ICT in terms of economic growth. This suggestion summarizes our thesis about the importance of ICT as complementary to other knowledge variables for best influencing economic growth. Carlaw and Oxley (2004) also stress the importance of complementarity when analysing the contribution of ICT to economic growth. When new general-purpose technologies (GPTs) emerge, they lack many of the complementary technologies that enable them to become productive. Moreover, all technological knowledge must become embodied in some real physical component of the work, whether it is physical or human capital (including all tacit skills), laws and legal institutions, or social and cultural norms. A reskilling of human capital and organizational changes are needed for GPTs to make a positive contribution to growth, and their initial lack can translate into a delay between the introduction of the GPT and the evidence of a positive contribution to growth. From a growth accounting perspective, this means that total factor productivity cannot represent technical change, and may even be negatively correlated with it, when that change is driven by a transforming GPT such as ICT.

Doms et al. (1997) investigate the relation between human capital and technology, following the intuition that if technology and workers' skills are complements, then firms with above-average workers' skills may have an advantage in adopting the latest technologies, thereby reinforcing their lead over rivals. Bresnahan et al. (2002) find that information and communication technology is complementary to a new workplace organization that includes broader responsibilities for line workers, more decentralized decision-making and more self-managing teams. The cluster of complementary changes involving ICT, workplace organization and services thus constitutes a key skill-biased technical change. Freeman (1995) expresses a similar idea at the country level. He reports that countries that had an educational and training system capable of a rapid and effective response to the huge demands for new skills stemming from the ICT techno-economic regime had a big comparative advantage in the efficient implementation of ICT itself. Finally, Fagerberg and Hildrum (2002) suggest that the impact of ICT on the knowledge–growth relationship should be analysed only after a full understanding has been achieved of how different forms of knowledge and capabilities interact in the knowledge-creating process.

We think that taking into account the relation between ICT and knowledge is essential to fully capture the contribution of ICT on economic growth. Moreover, we suggest the existence of knowledge complementarities, where ICT use is complementary to other knowledge proxies, in the sense that they need one another to be fully exploited in terms of GDP growth. In the next section, we focus on the concept of complementarity and how the economic literature has dealt with it.

4   COMPLEMENTARITY AND SUPERMODULARITY

The concept of complementarity has figured in economic theory for centuries, for example, as a relation between a pair of production inputs. Complementarity holds when the marginal returns to one variable increase the level of another variable. From a marginal point of view, this is equivalent to saying that the cross-partial derivatives of the function are positive. If we could efficiently estimate a linear production function like the following,

$$y = \beta_0 + \beta_1 x_1 + \beta_2 x_2 + \beta_3 x_1 x_2, \qquad (8.3)$$

then complementarity between x_1 and x_2 would be signalled by a positive estimated value of β_3. A more intuitive way of understanding complementarity resides in the definition of supermodularity, which represents a dual definition of complementarity itself. Following Milgrom and Roberts (1990), we define a function $f: R^n \to R$ as supermodular if

$$f(x_1) + f(x_2) \leq f(\min(x_1, x_2)) + f(\max(x_1, x_2)), \qquad \forall\, x_1, x_2 \in R^n \quad (8.4)$$

which can be rewritten as

$$[f(x_1) - f(\min(x_1, x_2))] + [f(x_2) - f(\min(x_1, x_2))] \leq f(\max(x_1, x_2))$$
$$- f(\min(x_1, x_2)) \quad (8.5)$$

Inequality equation (8.5) means that the sum of the changes in the function when several arguments are increased separately is less than the change resulting from increasing all the arguments together (that is, the 'the whole is more than the sum of parts'). For the simple case of two activities, x_1 and x_2, that the firm can either carry out can be done by the firm ($x_i = 1$) or not ($x_i = 0$) with consequent overall profit $f(x_1, x_2)$, complementarity holds between x_1 and x_2 if

$$f(1,0) + f(0,1) \leq f(1,1) + f(0,0) \quad (8.6)$$

Supermodularity is not necessarily related to the properties of convexity or increasing returns to scale. For example, the Cobb-Douglas function, $f(x_1, x_2) = x_1^a x_2^b$, is supermodular for all values of a and b, that is, independently of its increasing or decreasing returns to scale. For a detailed description of the logical links between complementarity and supermodularity, see Topkis (1998).

Milgrom and Roberts (1990) extend the original idea of complementarity of production inputs to the case of a relation among economic activities. If there is complementarity, then an increase in the level of any subset of activities translates into an increase of the marginal return of all the remaining activities. Consequently, if the marginal costs associated with some activities fall, it is optimal to increase the level of all of the activities in the grouping. Organizational practices may often show complementary relations, in the sense that the implementation of one practice increases the marginal return to other practices. Several other works are based on this intuition. Arora and Gambardella (1990), who study a sample of large chemical and pharmaceutical producers, report complementarity among the firms' strategies of external linkage with other parties. Ichniowski et al. (1997) find evidence that clusters of complementary human resource management practices have large effects on productivity, while changes in individual work practices have little or no effect on productivity. Athey and Stern (2002) analyse the positive impact on emergency response of an enhanced form of 911 emergency number that is capable of digitally identifying the caller's location; the authors thus stress the importance of complementarities between the adoption of different information and communication technologies in emergency health care. Miravete and Pernias (2004) find significant complementarity between product and process innovation for the case of the Spanish ceramic tile industry. Belderbos et al. (2006) indicate that different types of R&D cooperation (with competitors, clients, suppliers and universities and research institutes) may act as complements in improving productivity, especially when the firm size is large. Dosi (1988) claims that public knowledge is complementary to more specific and tacit forms of knowledge generated within the innovating units. Mohnen and Röller (2005) find evidence of the existence of complementarity in innovation policies, in the sense that it is necessary to adopt a package of policies to make firms innovate. Finally, Cimoli and Dosi (1995) assert that a country's pattern of technological change in core technologies (which in the past would have included mechanical engineering, electricity and electrical devices and today also covers information and communication technologies) does not average out with technological capabilities in other activities, but rather is complementary to them.

The literature uses different methods to test for complementarity. First of all, two complementary variables should present a positive and significant correlation. In other words, if we believe that in reality agents try to exploit complementarities, the logical outcome would be an empirical sign of the contemporaneous use of complementary inputs. The main problem resides in the possible dependence of both inputs on other variables. Arora and Gambardella (1990) therefore regress the possibly complementary variables onto other variables representing each firm's characteristics, and they then analyse the correlation coefficients among the residuals. Another approach, following the idea arising from equation (8.3), is to perform a regression in which interactions among the variables of interests are explicitly invoked by cross-products of regressors. This procedure can be based either on a theoretically founded model, as in Milgrom and Roberts (1990), or on extending the simplest linear model to a quadratic one, as in Lokshin et al. (2006).

Another possibility is to divide the overall sample into different subsamples, each of which includes all the observations that share the same particular combination of the variables of interest. For the case of k dichotomic variables, as described by Mohnen and Röller (2005), we have 2^k possible states for each individual, so $2^k - 1$ dummy variables must be included in our model to catch the influence exerted by each particular combination on a dependent product variable. When the variables of interest are not dichotomic, as in the case of Bresnahan et al. (2002), cut-off points must be identified to operate a sub-sample procedure. This can entail simply distinguishing high and low values for each variable (thus creating four quadrants in the case of two variables); looking at the combinations that most often recur in the whole sample; or applying scaling algorithms (see Ichniowski et al., 1997, for the last case).

In our work, we use factor analysis to connect some of the intuitions lying behind the described approaches. We construct a knowledge indicator based on the correlation matrix of the four observable variables we think have a link with knowledge. The construction of a knowledge indicator draws on the first eigenvalue of the correlation matrix, that is, on the sub-dimension that best sums up the co-movements among the knowledge proxies. The knowledge factor can thus be understood as a way to express the proportion of the four proxy variables that all the countries tend to have. This proportion is important for two reasons: first, we use it to identify the level of knowledge present in each country; second, it may express the optimal complementarity proportion of the knowledge proxies (that is, the proportion at which complementarity has its strongest effects). The knowledge level is approximated by our knowledge indicator, which provides – for each country and given the level of observable variables – the closest level of the same variables should they be in the so-called 'golden' proportion. We then see the effect on economic growth of the knowledge variable we have built, linking our work to the literature of economic growth described in the previous section. We then consider the effect of complementarity explicitly, as we include in our model a measure of each country's distance from the closest 'optimal complementarity' proportion of the knowledge proxies. Roughly speaking, we use the correlation approach (as in Arora and Gambardella, 1990) in that we apply a procedure based on the correlation matrix. We then focus on the final effect on GDP of different combinations of knowledge proxies, thus reinterpreting the intuition behind the procedure used by Bresnahan et al. (2002).

5   CONSTRUCTION OF THE KNOWLEDGE INDICATOR

In the empirical part of this paper, we consider the time span from 1996 to 2001 (inclusive), and we examine 73 countries, 15 of which are from Latin America and the Caribbean. We use the following data series from the World Bank, World Development Indicators database: gross fixed capital formation (in current United States dollars), gross domestic product (in current United States dollars), gross domestic product (in constant 2000 United States dollars), labour force (total), and scientific and technical journal articles. We use the data series for gross enrolment rate (per cent, tertiary, total), from the World Bank Group's GenderStats database. We use the data series for gross domestic expenditure on R&D (GERD) as a percentage of gross domestic product (GDP), from the United Nations Educational, Scientific and Cultural Organization (UNESCO) Institute for Statistics. Finally, we use the Info-use index, constructed by Orbicom, a network of UNESCO Chairs in Communications. The Info-use index summarizes the ICT uptake and intensity of use within each country for each year. ICT uptake includes the following: television-equipped households per 100 households; residential phone lines per 100 households; personal computers per 100 inhabitants; and Internet users per 100 inhabitants. For ICT intensity, we use the following: broadband users/Internet users; international outgoing telephone traffic minutes per capita; and international incoming telephone traffic minutes per capita. For details on the construction of the index, we recommend reading the original report edited by Sciadas (2005). Here, we just note that the Info-use index (henceforth, 'ICT index') refers only to the use of ICT. To catch one-year-lagged relations among the variables, we compute a two-year average for each series. Thus, for example, the value of enrolment in 2001 is actually the geometric mean of the values observed in 2000 and 2001.

We want to unify the different proxies for knowledge into one indicator that can identify the stock of knowledge present within each country. Information and communication technology acts as a complement of the other means of production of knowledge, and it therefore should have a strong link with the other knowledge proxies: namely, the number of scientific publications (weighted for each country's population), the percentage of inhabitants with completed tertiary education and the percentage of GDP invested in R&D. These three proxies, together with ICT, have a relation with knowledge, in the sense that they can be considered either inputs or outputs of the knowledge creation process. We translate all the relations among the knowledge proxies into approximately linear relations by taking the natural logarithms of publications and R&D actually, $\log(1 + x)$ to avoid negative values. We then standardize the final four proxy series (see Figure 8.1).[1] The correlations among the four variables are presented in Table 8.1, which clearly shows that the linear relations among the variables are sufficiently high for applying a factor model.

In particular, we apply a static factor model, as in the following:

$$x_{it} = \Lambda C_{it} + \xi_{it} \tag{8.7}$$

That is, the four knowledge proxies contained in the 4×1 vector x are assumed to be linearly related to our knowledge indicator, C, while still keeping an idiosyncratic part, x_i. Equation (8.7) holds for each country and each year. The way in which the observable variables are linked to the knowledge indicator is contained in the 4×1 vector Λ, written in the last

Table 8.1   Correlations and factor weights of the knowledge proxies

	ICT	Log(Publications)	Enrolment	Log(R&D)
ICT	1.0000			
Log(Publications)	0.8409	1.0000		
Enrolment	0.7188	0.7917	1.0000	
Log(R&D)	0.7434	0.8448	0.7109	1.0000
Factor weights	0.8667	0.9701	0.8220	0.8650

Sources: World Bank, World Development Indicators; World Bank Group's GenderStats; United Nations Educational, Scientific and Cultural Organization (UNESCO) Institute for Statistics; Orbicom.

row of Table 8.1 and estimated by the principal factor procedure. In other words, a one-point rise in the knowledge indicator, at time t for country i, means that the observable knowledge proxies should rise by 0.87, 0.97, 0.82 and 0.87 points, respectively. The final row of Table 8.1 thus identifies the proportion of the knowledge proxies that countries tend to approximate. In the following sections, this proportion is shown to be 'golden' in that it drives the country to the best complementary fit – that is, it guarantees the highest exploitation of knowledge proxies in terms of GDP. Once the weights Λ have been obtained, we estimate the knowledge indicator by generalized least squares; the resulting ranking is presented in Table 8.1. The first positions are held by Northern European countries, together with Israel, Singapore and some English-speaking countries. Among the Latin American countries, Argentina and Chile lead the ranking, followed closely by Uruguay and Brazil, while the last positions are held by Ecuador and Paraguay. However, the lower correlations among the proxies of the poor countries negatively affect the precision of the indicator in the last part of the ranking (see Figure 8.1).

The linearization of the publications and R&D variables (operated through the log transformation to calculate the golden proportion) has strong economic implications. The existence of a best complementarity proportion among the transformed variables implies that an increase in the knowledge indicator generally requires far fewer publications and less R&D in countries with low levels of knowledge relative to countries with higher initial knowledge. For example, to increase the knowledge indicator, a country with the right proportion among knowledge proxies but with a low initial knowledge indicator should devote stronger efforts to increasing the enrolment rate and ICT use than to increasing publications or R&D. As the country raises its knowledge level, however, the intensity of efforts should reverse. Thus, to increase the knowledge indicator, a

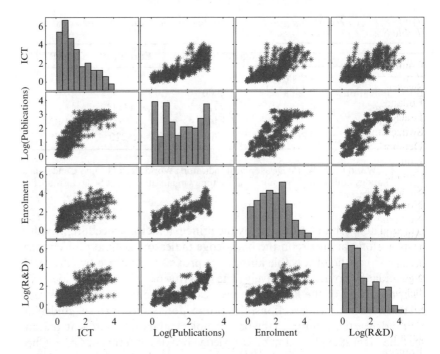

Sources: World Bank, World Development Indicators; World Bank Group's GenderStats;
United Nations Educational, Scientific and Cultural Organization (UNESCO) Institute for
Statistics; Orbicom.

Figure 8.1   Knowledge proxies and ICT use: scatter plots and histograms

country with the right proportion and with a high initial level of knowledge should aim for relatively greater increases in publications and R&D
rather than increases in ICT use or enrolment.

In reality, no country lies in an ideal state where the golden proportion
exactly holds. Consequently, for the same level of knowledge, a country
could better approximate the golden proportion by simply rebalancing
the levels of its knowledge proxies. This intuition is illustrated in Table
8.3, which describes the situation of Latin America and the Caribbean
by means of the standardized knowledge proxies and our knowledge
indicator.

Argentina obtains the first position of this sub-ranking, although
its relative power in terms of ICT and R&D does not seem very high.
Nevertheless, the enrolment proxy is much higher than for Chile, which
ranks just behind Argentina. We find the opposite in the case of Brazil,
where enrolment is very low and investment in R&D is relatively high.

Table 8.2 Knowledge index, 2001

Country	Index	Country	Index	Country	Index
Sweden	3.6582	Estonia	2.3251	Tunisia	1.0440
Finland	3.5339	Greece	2.2619	*Venezuela*	0.9821
Israel	3.3908	Czech Republic	2.2038	*Costa Rica*	0.9793
Switzerland	3.3802	Portugal	2.1833	*Panama*	0.9681
Denmark	3.3641	Hungary	2.1346	Georgia	0.9678
United States	3.3298	Croatia	1.9968	Moldova	0.9561
Canada	3.2835	Slovak Republic	1.9487	Egypt	0.9417
Singapore	3.2066	Poland	1.9259	*Trinidad and*	0.8374
Norway	3.1858	Russia	1.7900	*Tobago*	
Netherlands	3.1756	Bulgaria	1.6789	China	0.8358
Australia	3.1370	Lithuania	1.6681	*Jamaica*	0.7882
United Kingdom	3.1271	*Argentina*	1.6409	Thailand	0.7598
Iceland	3.1157	Latvia	1.6211	India	0.6551
New Zealand	3.0945	*Chile*	1.6015	*Bolivia*	0.6189
Belgium	3.0266	Cyprus	1.5955	*Colombia*	0.5868
Germany	3.0030	Kuwait	1.5934	*Peru*	0.4738
Austria	2.9992	Ukraine	1.4555	Mongolia	0.4291
Japan	2.9244	Turkey	1.3354	Kyrgyzstan	0.3902
France	2.8964	*Uruguay*	1.3183	Uganda	0.3692
Korea (Rep.)	2.8366	*Brazil*	1.2514	*Ecuador*	0.2786
Slovenia	2.7395	South Africa	1.2432	*Paraguay*	0.2140
Ireland	2.6788	Romania	1.1958	Pakistan	0.2012
Italy	2.5599	Armenia	1.1329	Burkina Faso	0.1861
Spain	2.5510	Malaysia	1.0730	Zambia	0.1632
Hong Kong	2.3998	*Mexico*	1.0595		

Source: Authors' elaboration.

Ecuador and Paraguay are driven to the bottom of the ranking by their very low number of scientific publications, while Peru compensates a similar phenomenon through very high enrolment. Enrolment is also high in Panama, which shows a high ICT use like Caribbean countries including Costa Rica, Trinidad and Tobago and Jamaica.

6 ESTIMATION OF THE GROWTH MODEL

Our empirical analysis shows approximately constant returns to scale for capital and labour and slightly increasing returns after the introduction of knowledge as a production input. Moreover, the knowledge

Table 8.3   Latin America and Caribbean: knowledge proxies and indicator, 2001

Country	ICT	Log(Publ.)	Enrolment	Log(R&D)	Knowledge
Argentina	1.4902	1.4623	2.8481	0.8653	1.6409
Chile	1.8043	1.4392	1.9658	1.0325	1.6015
Uruguay	1.6698	1.1716	1.8885	0.5261	1.3183
Brazil	1.1833	1.0617	0.8699	1.8288	1.2514
Mexico	1.2727	0.9571	1.0259	0.7819	1.0595
Venezuela	1.1628	0.7701	1.5710	0.8453	0.9821
Costa Rica	1.5534	0.7830	0.9280	0.8422	0.9793
Panama	1.0165	0.6932	2.2462	0.7659	0.9681
Trinidad and Tobago	1.4392	0.8221	0.3068	0.2355	0.8374
Jamaica	1.0696	0.7666	0.8591	0.1244	0.7882
Bolivia	0.6363	0.3484	1.8946	0.6192	0.6189
Colombia	0.9919	0.3812	1.2116	0.3807	0.5868
Peru	0.9793	0.1893	1.5818	0.2489	0.4738
Ecuador	0.7899	0.0661	0.8495	0.2049	0.2786
Paraguay	0.5934	0.0170	0.8622	0.1779	0.2140

Sources: World Bank, World Development Indicators; World Bank Group's GenderStats; United Nations Educational, Scientific and Cultural Organization (UNESCO) Institute for Statistics; Orbicom; authors' elaboration.

base was revealed as one of the major components explaining economic development.

Following Carlaw and Lipsey (2002), we assume the following form of the GDP function:

$$Y_{it} = A K_{it}^{\alpha} L_{it}^{\beta} C_{it}^{\gamma} \qquad (8.8)$$

where Y is the gross domestic product, A is the level of technical change, K is the capital amount expressed in real terms, L is the labour force and C is the country-specific knowledge, as approximated by the indicator built in the previous section. Taking logarithms and explicitly considering errors, we obtain:

$$y_{it} = a + \alpha k_{it} + \beta l_{it} + \gamma c_{it} + \varepsilon_{it} \qquad (8.9)$$

We compute equation (8.9) with the same panel of countries used to build the knowledge estimator. Table 8.4 reports our results for both the random effects regression and the fixed effects regression.

If we sum the coefficients corresponding to capital and labour, then

Table 8.4   GLS regression: knowledge as input[a]

Explanatory Variable	Random Effects	Fixed Effects
Constant	6.012651	7.238315
	(0.4547444)	(1.456096)
Log(Capital)	0.493339	0.2540511
	(0.0202843)	(0.0158064)
Log(Labour)	0.4619885	0.7423928
	(0.0306431)	(0.0877113)
Log(Knowledge)	0.3748997	0.2151168
	(0.0311708)	(0.0292003)
Within R-squared	0.6687	0.7199
Between R-squared	0.9501	0.7968
Overall R-squared	0.9496	0.7968
Hausman Test	Fixed effects is preferred	

Note: a. The dependent variable is log(GDP). All coefficients are significant at the 1% level; standard errors are in parentheses.

Source: Authors' elaboration.

$\alpha + \beta \cong 1$. That is, there are constant returns to scale when capital and labour are increased in proportion. If we add the coefficient corresponding to knowledge, then $\alpha + \beta + \gamma$ is significatively greater than one. That is, there are increasing returns to scale when capital, labour and knowledge are increased in proportion.

As discussed above, for each level of the knowledge indicator, we would expect to have a given amount for each of the four knowledge proxies used in building the indicator. This given amount should satisfy the 'golden' proportion we described. All the countries tend to have this proportion among the knowledge proxies, but the proportion does not hold exactly for any country. Following the typical factor analysis lexicon, we use the term 'common part' to refer to the expected level of the proxy ($X_{jit} = \lambda_j C_{jit}$, where j is the proxy, i the country and t time), given the level of the common factor (in our case, the knowledge indicator), and we use the term 'idiosyncratic part' for the difference between the observable series of the knowledge proxy and its 'common part' ($\xi_{jit} = x_{jit} - X_{jit}$). If we sum the squares of all the idiosyncratic parts of each country and take the square root of the sum, we obtain a Euclidean measure of the country's distance from the golden proportion – that is, a measure of the country's distance from the proportion for which complementarity would work best, according to our thesis. The absolute distance tends to suffer from a scale problem, in the sense that countries that have more knowledge also tend to

Table 8.5   GLS regression of residuals on relative distance from complementarity[a]

Explanatory Variable	Random Effects	Fixed Effects
Constant	0.0009384	0.0195978*
	(0.0021359)	(0.0080722)
Distance	−0.0010996	−0.0229635*
	(0.0018342)	(0.0092692)
Within R-squared	0.0207	0.0207
Between R-squared	0.003	0.003
Overall R-squared	0.001	0.001
Hausman Test	Fixed effects is preferred	

Notes:

*   Statistically significant at the 5% level.
a.   The dependent variable is the residuals of equation (8.9); standard errors are in parentheses.

Source: Authors' elaboration.

have larger idiosyncratic parts. We therefore have to weight the absolute distance with the corresponding level of the knowledge indicator, in order to eliminate this scale effect and obtain a measure of relative distance that is comparable across countries. Recalling equation (8.7), we define the relative distance from the 'best complementarity' proportion as follows:

$$D_{it} = \frac{(\xi_{1it}^2 + \xi_{2it}^2 + \xi_{3it}^2 + \xi_{4it}^2)^{\frac{1}{2}}}{C_{it}} \qquad (8.10)$$

If we regress the residuals of regression (8.9) on the previous measure of distance,

$$\hat{\varepsilon}_{it} = \omega D_{it} + u_{it}, \qquad (8.11)$$

we see that distance from perfect complementarity might be a useful regressor in equation (8.9), as its significance against the residuals is high (see Table 8.5).

We therefore add the distance to the logarithmic form of the growth function:

$$y_{it} = a + \alpha k_{it} + \beta l_{it} + \gamma c_{it} + \theta D_{it} + \varepsilon_{it} \qquad (8.12)$$

We thus obtain new estimates of the parameters, while taking into account the effect that the distance from perfect complementarity has on the

Table 8.6   GLS regression: knowledge as input and distance from complementarity as regressor[a]

Explanatory Variable	Random Effects	Fixed Effects
Constant	6.137605*	6.726404*
	(0.4512438)	(1.456409)
Log(Capital)	0.4782307*	0.2544124*
	(0.0201774)	(0.0156591)
Log(Labour)	0.4793055*	0.7758344*
	(0.0305475)	(0.0878772)
Log(Knowledge)	0.3820925*	0.2188085*
	(0.0306708)	(0.0289633)
Distance	−0.0540603*	−0.0244841**
	(0.0151134)	(0.0096142)
Within R-squared	0.6708	0.7261
Between R-squared	0.9489	0.7954
Overall R-squared	0.9484	0.7954
Hausman Test	Fixed effects is preferred	

Notes:
*   Statistically significant at the 1% level.
**   Statistically significant at the 5% level.
a.   The dependent variable is log(GDP); standard errors are in parentheses.

Source: Authors' elaboration.

country's performance in terms of GDP. Results are reported in Table 8.6. The parameters of capital, labour and knowledge are very similar to what we already found. However, we have a new regressor, the distance from the 'perfect complementarity proportion', for which we get a parameter that is significant and negative.

We now sum up our results. For each country, we analyse the levels of the knowledge proxies and infer the country's level of knowledge. However, although we infer from the data an ideal path that links the unobservable knowledge to the observable proxies, in reality such observable proxies are not linked to the knowledge indicator in this ideal way. Rather, they present some idiosyncratic parts that cause them to be closer or farther from the levels than we would predict from the level of the knowledge indicator. In other words, we first identify each country's unobservable knowledge level. We then predict that for this knowledge level, the knowledge proxies will be at given amounts for which a 'golden' proportion holds, and we measure the overall relative distance from these predicted or expected amounts. In the technical context of a Cobb-Douglas function linking capital, labour and economic growth, we use both the knowledge indicator and the distance from the perfect complementarity fit of the knowledge proxies. Our results indicate a positive influence of knowledge, which drives the growth function towards increasing returns to scale, and a negative influence of the distance, which means that for the same level of knowledge, the country would benefit from a more efficient relation among the knowledge proxies.

7   POLICY IMPLICATIONS

We now provide some examples of the effect of an ICT policy according to our model. In particular, we analyse the effect of an equal relative increase, namely a 10 per cent increase, of the ICT use index. The starting point is comparing two countries for which our indicator shows a similar knowledge level, namely, Bolivia and Colombia (see Table 8.3). For the case of Bolivia, such 10 per cent increase in ICT causes a shift of the knowledge indicator from 0.6189 to 0.6282. On the other hand, the relative distance from the optimal complementarity fit falls from 2.2857 to 2.2500. From equation 8.12, we obtain the corresponding variation in the logarithm of GDP:

$$\Delta y_{it+1} = \gamma(\log(C_{it+1}) - \log(C_{it+1})) + \theta(D_{it+1} - D_{it})$$

that is, for the case of Bolivia,

$$\Delta y_{it+1} = 0.2188(\log(0.6282) - \log(0.6189)) - 0.0245(2.2500 - 2.2857)$$

$$= 0.0041, \quad (8.13)$$

Proceeding in the same way, we obtain Colombia's log(GDP) variation as

$$\Delta y_{it+1} = 0.2188(\log(0.6011) - \log(0.5868)) - 0.0245(1.5781 - 1.5402)$$

$$= 0.0044 \quad (8.14)$$

The percentage increase in Bolivia's GDP is slightly lower than Colombia's, after we increased both ICT indexes by the same 10 per cent. However, this equal percentage increase corresponds to an absolute increase in standardized ICT use, which is much higher for Colombia than for Bolivia, as Colombia's current level of ICT use is relatively high (see Table 8.3). The similar effect on GDP of two different absolute increases in ICT use stems from the different proportions of the knowledge proxies that the two countries have, although their knowledge indicator is approximately the same. In the case of Bolivia, the new amount of ICT use will complement other proxies like enrolment, and it will then contribute more to overall knowledge. Colombia, in turn, already has a relatively high ICT use. The new amount will mostly be considered idiosyncratic and not linked to knowledge, thus increasing the relative distance from the optimal complementarity proportion. It is important to bear in mind that, here, we are only concerned with the effects of ICT through the knowledge channel, and we are thus ignoring all questions related to capital.

The results for ECLAC countries of a relative ICT increase of 10 per cent are shown in Table 8.7. The table provides a clear sense of the role that complementarity plays for our model, especially when compared with Table 8.3. We already discussed Bolivia and Colombia. Comparing other two countries that share a similar value of the knowledge indicator – namely, Argentina and Chile – reveals the different effects on GDP of an equal variation of ICT use. In the initial 2001 position, Chile shows higher ICT use than Argentina, but a lower enrolment ratio. If we raise the ICT use index of both countries, the percentage increase in GDP will be higher for Argentina than for Chile, because in Argentina the increase in the knowledge indicator reduces the distance from the optimal complementarity fit position. We would see the same phenomenon in Panama, where

Table 8.7   Effect on GDP of a 10% increase in ICT use

Country	Δ ICT	Δ Log(Knowledge)	Δ (Distance)	Δ Log(GDP)
Argentina	10%	0.0131	−0.0111	0.0031
Chile	10%	0.0162	0.0433	0.0025
Uruguay	10%	0.0182	0.0395	0.0030
Brazil	10%	0.0136	0.0011	0.0029
Mexico	10%	0.0173	0.0870	0.0016
Venezuela	10%	0.0170	0.0199	0.0032
Costa Rica	10%	0.0227	0.1165	0.0021
Panama	10%	0.0151	−0.0183	0.0038
Trinidad and Tobago	10%	0.0246	0.1044	0.0028
Jamaica	10%	0.0195	0.0591	0.0028
Bolivia	10%	0.0148	−0.0355	0.0041
Colombia	10%	0.0242	0.0377	0.0044
Peru	10%	0.0295	−0.0171	0.0069
Ecuador	10%	0.0403	0.0257	0.0082
Paraguay	10%	0.0394	−0.0435	0.0097

Source: Authors' elaboration.

the initial levels of enrolment and R&D are similar to or greater than the levels of Costa Rica, Trinidad and Tobago and Jamaica, while the 2001 ICT use index is lower. If the ICT index rises in all these countries, which share a similar initial level of the knowledge indicator, then the effect on GDP should be much higher for Panama, because here ICT better complements the other knowledge proxies. The opposite would occur in Mexico, whose ICT use in 2001 seems to be high relative to the other knowledge proxies. Consequently, an increase in ICT use would translate into a modest GDP increase, compared with countries like Brazil and Venezuela. As for the lowest part of the knowledge ranking, we mentioned above that the factor procedure did not work well enough at the lower extreme of the sample, so we do not consider the last rows of the table.

8   CONCLUSIONS

We have analysed the impact of ICT use on economic growth through knowledge, together with the role of complementarities in this process. We assumed a Cobb-Douglas production function with three inputs: capital, labour and knowledge. The unobservable variable, knowledge, was generated by a static factor analysis that considered four observable knowledge proxies: ICT use, the number of publications in technical and scientific journals, enrolment in tertiary education and expenditure in research and development.

Econometric regressions on a panel of 73 countries suggested the presence of constant returns to scale in capital and labour and increasing returns for all three factors of production. Moreover, we found that an intensification of ICT use leads to a positive impact on GDP because it helps to increase the stock of knowledge. Nevertheless, the extent of this effect highly depends on having the right balance of ICT with the other knowledge components.

Knowledge complementarities are a fundamental factor influencing the final effect of ICT on economic growth. The effect of ICT through the knowledge channel is maximum when all the knowledge proxies, including ICT use, are distributed in the right proportion, which we call the 'golden' or 'best complementarity' proportion. Even though current ICT use is often above this golden proportion in Latin American economies, an ICT use increment still produces a positive impact on knowledge and economic growth. However, the magnitude of this positive impact depends on the current level of ICT use with respect to the ICT level predicted by the golden proportion. In other words, if the increased ICT use drives the country to a position that is closer to the golden proportion, then ICT use will better complement the other knowledge proxies, and the corresponding increase in GDP will be higher. In contrast, a country whose ICT use level is already relatively high relative to the other knowledge proxies would benefit less from a further increase in ICT use.

NOTES

* At the time of writing this chapter, Marco Capasso was a researcher at the Division of Production, Productivity and Management at the Economic Commission for Latin America and the Caribbean (ECLAC), Santiago, Chile. We thank Mario Cimoli, Giovanni Dosi and all the participants to the 'Growth, Productivity and ICT' conference held at ECLAC, Santiago, Chile, on 29–30 March 2007, for helpful comments and suggestions.
1. Standardization uses the following standard deviations of the panel of transformed data: 60.683 for ICT use, 1.4804 for $\log(1 + \text{publications})$, 19.425 for enrolment and 0.41472 for $\log(1 + \text{R\&D})$.

REFERENCES

Arora, A. and A. Gambardella (1990), 'Complementarity and external linkages: the strategies of the large firms in biotechnology', *Journal of Industrial Economics*, **38**(4), 361–79.

Athey, S. and S. Stern (2002), 'The impact of information technology on emergency health care outcomes', *RAND Journal of Economics*, **33**(3), 399–432.

Barro, R.J. (1990), 'Government spending in a simple model of endogenous growth', *Journal of Political Economy*, **98**(5), S103–S126.

Belderbos, R., M. Carree and B. Lokshin (2006), 'Complementarity in R&D cooperation strategies', *Review of Industrial Organization*, **28**(4), 401–26.

Bresnahan, T., E. Brynjolfsson and L. Hitt (2002), 'Information technology, workplace organization and the demand for skilled labor: firm-level evidence', *Quarterly Journal of Economics*, **117**(1) 339–76.

Carlaw, K.I. and R.G. Lipsey (2002), 'Externalities, technological complementarities and sustained economic growth', *Research Policy*, **31**(8), 1305–15.

Carlaw, K.I. and L.T. Oxley (2004), 'ICT diffusion and economic growth in New Zealand', Econometric Society 2004 Australasian Meetings Paper, No. 167, Econometric Society.

Cimoli, M. and G. Dosi (1995), 'Technological paradigms, patterns of learning and development: an introductory map', *Evolutionary Economics*, **5**(3), 243–68.

Cornes, R. and T. Sandler (1986), *The Theory of Externalities, Public Goods and Club Goods*, New York: Cambridge University Press.

David, P. (2000), 'Understanding digital technology's evolution and the path of measured productivity growth: present and future in the mirror of the past', in E. Brynjolfsson and B. Kahin (eds), *Understanding the Digital Economy*, Cambridge, MA: MIT Press.

Doms, M., T. Dunne and K.R. Troske (1997), 'Workers, wages, and technology' *Quarterly Journal of Economics*, **112**(1), 253–90.

Dosi, G. (1988), 'Sources, procedures, and microeconomic effects of innovation', *Journal of Economic Literature*, **26**(3) 1120–71.

Fagerberg, J. and J. Hildrum (2002), 'Mobility of knowledge, ICT and growth', University of Oslo, Centre for Technology, Innovation and Culture, Paper prepared for the DRUID 2002 Conference, Copenhagen.

Freeman, C. (1995), 'Technological revolutions and catching-up: ICT and the NICs' in J. Fagerberg, B. Verspagen and N. Von Tunzelmann (eds), *The Dynamics of Technology, Trade and Growth*, Aldershot, UK and Brookfield, VT, USA: Edward Elgar.

Ichniowski, C., K. Shaw and G. Prennushi (1997), 'The effects of human resource management practices on productivity', *American Economic Review*, **87**(3), 291–313.

Jorgenson, D.W. (2001), 'Information technology and the U.S. economy', Working Paper, No. 1911, Harvard University, Institute of Economic Research.

Jorgenson, D.W. and K.J. Stiroh (1999), 'Information technology and growth', *American Economic Review*, **89**(2), 109–15.

Jorgenson, D.W. and K.J. Stiroh (2000), 'Raising the speed limit: U.S. economic growth in the information age', *Brookings Papers on Economic Activity*, No. 1, pp. 125–236.

Lipsey, R., K. Carlaw and C. Bekar (2005), *Economic Transformations*, Oxford: Oxford University Press.

Lokshin, B., R. Belderbos and M. Carree (2006), 'Internal and external R&D: complements or substitutes? Evidence from a dynamic panel data model', Hi-Stat Discussion Paper Series, No. d06-163, Hitotsubashi University, Institute of Economic Research.

Lucas, R.E. (1988), 'On the mechanics of economic development', *Journal of Monetary Economics*, **22**(1), 3–42.

Milgrom, P. and J. Roberts (1990), 'The economics of modern manufacturing: technology, strategy and organization', *American Economic Review*, **80**(3), 511–28.

Miravete, E. and J. Pernias (2004), 'Innovation complementarity and scale of production', CEPR Discussion Paper, No. 4483, London, Centre for Economic Policy Research.

Mohnen, P. and L.H. Röller (2005), 'Complementarities in innovation policy', *European Economic Review*, **49**(6), 1431–50.

Oliner, S.D. and D.E. Sichel (1994), 'Computer and output growth revisited: how big is the puzzle?', *Brookings Papers on Economic Activity*, No. 2, pp. 273–334.

Oliner, S.D. and D.E. Sichel (2000), 'The resurgence in growth in the late 1990s: is information technology the story?', *Journal of Economic Perspectives*, **14**(4), 3–22.

Polanyi, M. (1966), 'The tacit dimension', in L. Prusak (ed.), *Knowledge in Organizations*, Oxford: Butterworth-Heinemann.

Romer, D. (1996), *Advanced Macroeconomics*, New York: McGraw-Hill.

Romer, P. (1990), 'Endogenous technological change', *Journal of Political Economy*, **98**(5), S71–S102.

Romer, P. (1996), 'Increasing returns and long-run growth', *Journal of Political Economy*, **94**(3), 1002–37.

Sciadas, G. (ed.) (2005), *From the Digital Divide to Digital Opportunities: Measuring Infostates for Development*, Montreal: Orbicom.

Solow, R. (1957), 'Technical change and the aggregate production function', *Review of Economics and Statistics*, **39**(3), 312–20.

Solow, R. (1987), 'We'd better watch out', *New York Times Book Review*, 12 July.

Topkis, D.M. (1998), *Supermodularity and Complementarity*, Princeton, NJ: Princeton University Press.

Triplett, J. (1999), 'The Solow productivity paradox: what do computers do to productivity?', *Canadian Journal of Economics*, **32**(2), 309–34.

9. A dynamic input–output simulation analysis of the impact of ICT diffusion in the Brazilian economy

Fabio Freitas, David Kupfer and Esther Dweck*

1 RESEARCH PURPOSES

Information and communication technologies (ICT) are considered a general-purpose technology. Until the mid-1990s, however, the economic impact of ICT diffusion seemed small. This perspective underlies Solow's famous (1987) observation that 'we see computers everywhere except in the statistics on productivity growth'. In the second half of the 1990s, opinions began to change as several studies pointed to the important contribution of ICT to the resurgence of GDP and productivity growth in the United States. Nevertheless, several analysts questioned whether ICT would have a similar positive impact in countries with different structural features than the US economy.

This questioning inspired the construction of a research agenda on the impact of ICT diffusion in various countries around the world. This chapter contributes to this agenda by analysing the impact of ICT diffusion on the Brazilian economy. We develop and apply an input–output (hereafter IO) methodology, which involved the following tasks:

1. updating the last official IO matrix available (IBGE,[1] 1996) with partial information from the Brazilian System of National Accounts (mainly from the 2003 make-and-use tables);
2. disaggregating the IO matrix obtained in order to isolate the ICT-producing sectors; and
3. developing a dynamic IO simulation model to analyse the future impact of different ICT-diffusion scenarios on the Brazilian economy.

The chapter is organized as follows. The next section provides some methodological background on the use of IO matrices to measure and analyse the diffusion impact of new technologies. It also presents the main features of the dynamic IO simulation model we developed for Brazilian economy. The third section describes the implementation of the model, including updating and disaggregating the Brazilian IO matrix and feeding in the initial conditions related to Brazilian economy. Section 4 discusses current ICT impacts and some simulation findings generated by the simulation exercise. A short comment ends the chapter.

2 METHODOLOGICAL REMARKS

2.1 Previous Contributions

Most studies analysing the impact of ICT diffusion on economic growth are conducted within a growth accounting framework. Growth accounting is a non-parametric methodology[2] that tries to separate the contribution to economic growth of capital inputs, labour inputs and multi-factor productivity (MFP). From this perspective, ICT contribute to economic growth through their effects on both capital accumulation and MFP growth.[3] Growth accounting exercises have been performed at the macroeconomic[4] and sectoral levels. In the latter case, some studies try to quantify the separate contribution of the ICT-producing and ICT-using sectors.[5] Other studies try to address the difficult task of quantitatively evaluating the influence of spillover effects associated with ICT diffusion.[6]

Here we adopt a different methodological perspective, applying an IO approach to investigate the impact of ICT diffusion on the Brazilian economy. The well-established IO approach provides a basic framework for technological diffusion impact studies. This framework is especially suited to evaluating the systemic effects of technological change at a multi-sectoral level of analysis, which allows the investigation of the interaction between producers and users of new technologies.

Leontief and Duchin (1986) is the seminal work in this line of research. Their work is based on extensive field studies, which they use to elaborate prospective (20 years) scenarios for computer and computer-based equipment diffusion. The impact of the different diffusion scenarios on employment (by industry and type of occupation) are then analysed within the framework of a dynamic IO model for the United States economy. They employ a comparative dynamic methodology to evaluate these impacts; that is, the paths generated by the different technological diffusion scenarios are compared with a reference scenario characterized by no technical change.

The use of a dynamic IO model is justified by the need to ensure the consistency between the production of investment commodities and their subsequent availability in the economy (Duchin and Szyld, 1985, p. 269; Leontief and Duchin, 1986, p. 5). This is done by making fixed investment an endogenous variable in the model through the use of a multi-sectoral version of a flexible accelerator investment function.[7] This is the core theoretical relation underlying the model, characterized by the following features: (1) installed capacity is not necessarily fully utilized and is not reversible; (2) sectoral capacity-expansion decisions are based on recently observed growth rates; (3) the sectoral capacity variation is constrained by a zero value floor;[8] (4) the capacity growth in each sector is limited by an exogenously determined growth rate; (5) there is a time lag between the order and delivery of capital equipment; and (6) replacement investment is separately and explicitly analysed, and it depends positively on the sectoral output level. The other components of final demand, including household consumption, are considered to be exogenous to the model.

In contrast with the methodologies inspired by neoclassical theory, the IO approach used by Leontief and Duchin (1986) views economic growth as a demand-led process. In fact, Leontief and Duchin consider the demand expansion as a proximate cause of economic growth. Technical change and other supply factors can also influence economic growth, but only through their effects on the demand side. The analytical framework proposed here considers some but not all of these supply effects. This limitation matters, because the incorporation of this effect is a major difficulty associated with using the IO approach to analyse the impact of technological diffusion, in particular for treating the compensation effects that may counterbalance the negative impact of labour productivity growth on employment. From a demand-led growth perspective, full (or high) employment is not automatically ensured by the functioning of the price system, as presumed by the neoclassical-based methodologies. To offset (partially or not) the labour displacement effect of productivity growth, technical change has to induce the expansion of expenditures on domestically produced commodities.

Kalmbach and Kurz (1990) use the same type of IO framework in their work on the impact of the diffusion of micro-electronic-based new technologies on the West German economy. They propose a modified investment function, which allows them to overcome what they consider to be the most important problems of Leontief and Duchin's model: (1) the inability to analyse declining industries; (2) the implausibly high variability of output growth rates; (3) the frequent tendency to achieve the maximum capacity growth ceiling; (4) the implausibly high amplitude of the fluctuation of capacity utilization; and (5) the unrealistically large duration of the cycles generated by the model. The modification introduced by Kalmbach and Kurz in the investment function is related to the modelling of the capacity expansion decision. In their model, desired capacity depends not only on the most recent output growth rates, but also on sectoral trend growth rates. Short-run and long-run orientations are combined in such a way that the weight given to the trend growth rates is endogenous to the model and positively related to the variability of the most recently observed output growth rates. By using this formulation of the capacity expansion decision, they manage to address the last four problems mentioned above. The first problem (the inability to analyse declining industries) is solved by relaxing the assumption of a zero value floor for the desired output capacity variation.

Kalmbach and Kurz's model also differs from Leontief and Duchin in the treatment of final demand components other than fixed investment and in the modelling of the diffusion process. With respect to the former, they regard as endogenous all final demand components other than investment – except exports, which are considered to be the only source of autonomous demand. Household consumption is modelled by an econometrically estimated disaggregated Keynesian consumption function. Total government expenditures equal a fixed share of GDP of the preceding period. With regard to modelling the diffusion process, the elaboration of alternative diffusion scenarios involved extensive field studies – a feature shared with the work of Leontief and Duchin – oriented toward identifying the micro-electronic-based best-practices techniques. In contrast with Leontief and Duchin's work, however, Kalmbach and Kurz consider these techniques to be immutable throughout the diffusion process, conceived as the transition between the techniques in use in 1980 and the best-practice techniques defined by field studies. The economic impacts of alternative diffusion scenarios are also evaluated by means of a comparative dynamic method, evaluating each path associated with a different diffusion scenario against a no-technical-change reference scenario. The diffusion scenarios are differentiated by the time period required to complete the transition from the old to the new techniques.

To analyse compensation effects, Kalmbach and Kurz adopt an approach that deals implicitly with the issue. Since exports are considered the main determinant of economic growth, compensation effects should operate through it. That is, labour productivity growth induced by technical change should affect the external competitiveness of domestic producers and thus the growth rate of exports. The authors treat compensation effects implicitly by evaluating what the export growth rate should be to guarantee the full compensation of employment loss provoked by labour productivity growth. The required export growth rate calculated this way can be assessed in terms of its likelihood.

Verspagen (2002) also uses a dynamic IO approach to analyse the impact of technological diffusion. His contribution is more theoretical, as his empirical analysis only serves to illustrate the fruitfulness of the proposed theoretical framework. Conversely, by incorporating a rigid accelerator investment function, Verspagen's model resembles Leontief's original model (Leontief, 1953 and 1970) and it should be subjected to the same type of problems encountered in that model.[9]

The novelty of Verspagen's work resides in the combination of the dynamic IO approach with theoretical elements from post-Keynesian and evolutionary economics. From the post-Keynesian theoretical background, he uses the idea of a demand-led growth process.[10] He also follows the balance-of-payments constrained growth literature (cf. McCombie and Thirlwall, 1994). The model includes a balance-of-payments equilibrium condition that implies that throughout the trajectories generated by the model, the value of aggregate government and household consumption is endogenous in order to guarantee the equilibrium between total exports and imports. Further, this equilibrium condition implies that exports are the only autonomous demand component,[11] so export expansion determines the rate of economic growth. Nevertheless, the balance-of-payments equilibrium condition used by Verspagen is excessively restrictive. First, the equality between exports and imports is a very simplified balance-of-payments equilibrium condition for economies characterized by a relatively high degree of international financial integration. Second, the two situations of balance-of-payments disequilibrium are asymmetrical and some economies persistently grow at levels of activity below those associated with the balance-of-payments constraint.

From evolutionary economics, Verspagen takes the replicator equations that are used for modelling the structural dynamics of final demand components and the effects of competitiveness in foreign trade. With regard to the former, this implies that sectors with above-average attractiveness increase their shares of total expenditures. Verspagen applies this reasoning to analyse the dynamics of sectoral shares in total fixed investment, in total government and household consumption and in total world exports. Verspagen uses a different version of the replicator equation when modelling the effects of foreign trade competitiveness. In his version, the share of domestic sectoral exports in external markets increases (decreases) as the ratio of competitiveness between domestic and foreign producers takes a value above (below) unity. Similarly, the share of sectoral imports in domestic markets (measured as sectoral domestic demand) decreases (increases) as the ratio of competitiveness between domestic and foreign producers takes a value below (above) unity.

The use of replicator equations with reference to foreign competitiveness is interesting because it provides a way to deal with the effects of the process of technical change on demand and, through demand, on economic growth. In particular, this application provides a methodology for modelling compensation effects on demand caused by competitiveness gains associated with productivity growth induced by technical change. Nevertheless, Verspagen's paper does not fully explore the potential of this methodology for dealing with compensation effects. The ratio of competitiveness is exogenously defined, and it is not explicitly related to any performance criteria (such as price or quality). Much of the evolutionary flavour of the model is lost as a result, and the replicator equation serves only to implement exogenously specified competitiveness scenarios, but this simplification permits a first incursion in the field.

The application of the replicator equations for modelling the structural dynamics of final demand components also has an important shortcoming, related to the sectoral level of analysis. The sectors themselves are conceived as the competitors for shares in total expenditures. If fully applied, this methodology would make attractiveness a function of relative prices, implying an unreasonable hypothesis of gross substitutability between sectoral outputs. Since the ratio of attractiveness is exogenously determined, however, the application of the replicator equation in question is equivalent to the assumption of different sectoral growth rates of final demand. As such, the methodology used by the author simply represents a special way to incorporate scenarios covering the change in the sectoral composition of final demand.

The empirical part of Verspagen's paper applies the above framework to the analysis of the prospective growth patterns of the Dutch economy. Like the other IO-based works discussed earlier, Verspagen elaborates different technical change scenarios, but the scenarios are not specifically constructed to analyse the impact of the diffusion of a given technology. The reference (or base) scenario in Verspagen's paper is based on a projection of the past pattern of technical change in the Dutch economy, obtained from historical IO data. Two other scenarios are built around the reference scenario by assuming a faster and a slower velocity of technical change. Finally, there is also a no-technical-change scenario. Verspagen uses the replicator equations to elaborate two types of scenarios: the composition of demand and the competitiveness scenarios. Based on various combinations of the above scenarios, Verspagen explores the future patterns of the Netherlands' economic growth and investment shares using comparative dynamics simulation exercises.

2.2 The Model

The dynamic IO simulation model proposed in this chapter combines various features of the above IO-based works. This section presents the main characteristics of the model, as well as some of its similarities and differences with the models discussed above. A more detailed description of the model is given in the Appendix.

The model determines at each period the output level of each sector of the economy, given its total demand. The total demand is composed of intermediate consumption and final demand. Final demand comprises five components: (1) personal consumption expenditures (PCE); (2) gross fixed investment (GFI); (3) the change in private inventories; (4) exports of goods and services; and (5) government consumption expenditures. Two of those components, personal consumption and gross fixed investment, are described by some behavioural assumptions and are thus treated as partially endogenous variables, while the other components are considered exogenous.

2.2.1 Personal consumption expenditures

A common extension of the IO model, which is also found in Kalmbach and Kurz's and Verspagen's models,[12] is the integration of the Keynesian-Kaleckian multiplier within the Leontief multiplier. This allows income effects to be incorporated in the impact analysis using the IO model. We tested a few different ways to deal with endogenous consumption, given the available data. We chose the simplest alternative, since the results were not very different.

Personal consumption expenditures were divided between imported and domestic demand and between durable and non-durable consumption goods and services. The latter is important because the behaviour of demand is markedly different for durable and non-durable consumption. It is possible to express the non-durable consumption value as a positive function of total wages, which can be justified by the fact that the wage bill is the only income directly generated by the production decision. In fact, the relationship between the value of non-durable consumption and the wage bill is quite stable through time in the Brazilian economy. Assuming a stable relationship between wages and total output by industry, we can also define wage-output coefficients by industry and hence to express personal consumption expenditures as a function of total output by industry.

Consumption expenditures on non-durables are related to domestic and foreign-produced commodities. Nonetheless, the contribution of non-durables consumption to the determination of sectoral output depends only on the consumption demand for domestic commodities. This is obtained by subtracting the consumption demand for foreign commodities (imports) from total consumption demand. We applied the same method to divide the demand vector of imported durables (exogenous demand) and non-durables (endogenous demand) consumption. This step was important for the elaboration of simulation scenarios related to trade patterns, as discussed in Section 4.2 below.

2.2.2 Gross fixed investment

The investment demand vector by industry or by commodity depends on the estimated capital flow matrix and each industry's desired productive capacity, which results in investment decisions by industry. The gross fixed investment vector includes investment not only by the corporate sectors, but also by households and the government. Therefore, it can also be divided into two components: an exogenous part related to household and government investments and an endogenous part related to corporate investments, including both financial and non-financial corporations.

The endogenous part is modelled as an investment function based on a flexible accelerator. Sectoral investment is thus considered a function of the level of sectoral output.[13] If the actual degree of utilization is equal to its normal or desired level, sectoral investment is proportional to sectoral output, implying that they grow at the same rate and consequently that the investment-to-output ratio is constant. If the actual degree of utilization is above (below) its normal level, sectoral investment grows at a higher (lower) rate than sectoral output. As a result, the growth of sectoral output capacity is governed by the rate of sectoral demand expansion, and output capacity tends to adjust to demand requirements while the actual degree of utilization tends to adjust to its normal level. This tendency requires, however, that the value of the parameter relating the sectoral investment and the deviation between the actual and normal degree of sectoral capacity utilization is maintained within a certain range. This requirement is accomplished by hypothesis in the simulation exercises.

The investment function is directly defined at the sectoral level to avoid an implicit representative agent assumption usually encountered in the literature. Investment in the above function actually represents the existing opportunities for sectoral investment, and we assume that the aggregated individual investment decisions by sector follow these opportunities. This can be justified by the hypothesis that competitive interactions are sufficient to constrain the behaviour of the aggregated result of individual investment decisions. We therefore suppose that a deviation between the actual and normal degree of capacity utilization will tend to be eliminated by the pressure of competition, entailing the type of adjustment described above.

The investment function discussed above concerns the demand for investment of either domestic or foreign origin. As in the analysis of consumption expenditures, investment expenditures on domestically produced commodities are obtained by subtracting imported investment goods from total demand, given the capital imports coefficients.

Finally, three assumptions underlie the investment function. First, the installation of desired capacity is always possible. Second, the scrapping of fixed capital items is described by a rigid parameter by industry, which is not affected by variations in capital utilization. Finally, the capital output relation is constant throughout the simulation period. Although these hypotheses are unrealistic (especially when applied to ICT sectors, given their high rate of technological innovation), these are commonly used procedures for simplifying the modelling of investment functions.

Table 9.1 highlights the connections between the proposed model and the previous works discussed in this section. The present model is still in an early stage of development. In particular, the treatment of the scenarios and of the compensation/feedback effects deserves to be enhanced. With regard to the former, we are waiting for the release of the United States 2002 IO benchmark matrix for the definition of a technological gap scenario. The idea is that the United States IO information, when translated into the Brazilian IO classification, can be used to define best practices for producing and using ICT industries. We also plan to introduce competitiveness scenarios to better analyse the behaviour of exports and imports throughout the technological diffusion processes. As for the compensation/feedback effects, it will be possible to introduce them in the model with the aid of the competitiveness scenarios for the Brazilian economy. For instance, this can be implemented in the model either directly or using the replicator methodology developed by Verspagen. In the latter case, a more ambitious task would be the full implementation of such a methodology, which would require endogenizing the ratio of external competitiveness in relation to price (or some non-price competitiveness performance indicators).

3 IMPLEMENTATION OF THE MODEL FOR THE BRAZILIAN ECONOMY

Before the application of the model to investigate ICT diffusion in the Brazilian economy, we had to overcome two problems related to the Brazilian IO database. First, Brazilian IO data are not available on a timely basis. Second, the level of disaggregation of the Brazilian IO database is inadequate for investigating ICT-producing industries. We overcame these problems by updating and disaggregating the Brazilian IO database, using the procedures discussed below.

Table 9.1   Model comparison scheme

Demand Component	Leontief and Duchin	Kalmbach and Kurz	Verspagen	The Present Model
Personal consumption expenditures	Exogenous	Endogenous	Endogenous aggregate consumption; exogenous sectoral composition	Endogenous only in the case of non-durable commodities
Investment	Flexible accelerator	Flexible accelerator	Rigid accelerator	Flexible accelerator
Exports	Exogenous	Exogenous	Exogenous	Exogenous
Government expenditures	Exogenous	Endogenous (fixed proportion of GDP)	Endogenous aggregate consumption; exogenous sectoral composition	Exogenous
Diffusion scenario	Field studies informing the range of intermediate prospective changes in input, capital and employment coefficients	Field studies for the definition of best practices; scenarios covering different convergence speeds to the best practice	Technical change scenarios built around a reference scenario obtained from an extrapolation of past tendencies; additional composition of demand and competitiveness scenarios	Provisional and extreme hypothetical scenarios for sensibility and exploratory analysis
Compensation/ feedback effects	No compensation effect explicitly considered	Compensation effects implicitly considered by the evaluation of the plausibility of the potential export expansion required to eliminate employment losses	Compensation effects incorporated through the use of replicator equations to model feedback effects associated with the competitiveness gains on domestic production of tradable commodities	No compensation effect considered

Source: Elaboration by the authors.

3.1 Matrix Updating

The latest official IO table for the Brazilian economy published by the Brazilian statistical office (IBGE) is based on 1996 data, but IBGE has published the make-and-use tables from the System of National Accounts with 2003 data. We were therefore able to update the IO matrix using partial information from the 2003 make-and-use tables and an appropriate updating methodology.

This study uses the updating methodology of Grijó and Bêrni (2005), transforming the use table measured in the System of National Accounts at consumers' prices into the domestic supply use table measured at basic prices. To transform consumer prices into basic prices, one first excludes trade and transportation margins,[14] then subtracts indirect taxes collected and remitted by producers and finally isolates the domestic demand from imports. We combined data of the last official IO database with 1996 data for the margins, taxes and imports by using industries, with the known 2003 total value of production at basic prices, trade and transportation margins, indirect taxes and imports by commodities.

The methodology has four steps:

1. Define a mark-down matrix for the use of domestic supply at basic prices and mark-up matrices for indirect taxes, trade and transportation margins and imports, based on the official 1996 IO database.
2. Given those mark-down and mark-up matrices, obtain a first estimation of the use table at basic prices, as well as the commodity-by-industry tables of indirect taxes, trade and transportation margins and imports for 2003.
3. In the case of structural changes in production, trade and transportation margins, imports or taxes from 1996 to 2003, make adjustments to fill possible blanks in the 1996 structure.
4. Use the RAS method[15] to reconcile the two sources of information, aiming to balance all five tables given the known 2003 values of the make-and-use tables of the System of National Accounts.

The updating results are indirectly presented in the next part, when we discuss the disaggregation of the updated matrix.

3.2 Matrix Disaggregation

The calculated Brazilian IO matrix is composed of 42 activities. However, this level of aggregation is not detailed enough to identify the ICT-producing sectors. To isolate both the direct and indirect effects of those sectors, we need to disaggregate the IO matrix. The methodology proposed here is derived from Wolsky (1984). The original method consists of two steps for disaggregating the technical coefficient matrix:

Step 1: simple disaggregation, based on the share of the sub-industries in the total gross output of the industry; and
Step 2: distinguishing matrix, based on additional information about sub-industries.

Both steps must fulfil some re-aggregation conditions.

This methodology presents two limitations given the current availability of data for the Brazilian economy and the model developed below. First, the direct disaggregation of the technical coefficient matrix prevents the use of additional information in terms of the flow data related to the make-and-use tables. Second, the disaggregation is only applied to intermediary consumption but not to the other components of the IO model (namely, value-added, final demand and employment).

We therefore use a methodology proposed by Freitas and Dweck (2006), which tries to overcome both limitations. This methodology disaggregates the flow data present in the make-and-use tables to obtain the technical coefficient matrix and the other components of the IO model. It is an indirect disaggregation method with regard to the IO model, because it is done at the commodity-by-industry structure rather than directly at the industry-by-industry relations, as in the Wolsky method. This methodology is implemented in four stages:

1. In the first stage, the market share matrix[16] is disaggregated in two steps similar to those proposed by Wolsky. The first step is a simple disaggregation based on the share of the sub-industries in the total gross output of the original industry. The second uses additional information about sub-industries to adjust the results subject to some re-aggregation conditions. These two steps can be applied directly to market share matrix or to the make matrix, depending on the information available.
2. The second stage also involves a two-step disaggregation, this time of the commodity-by-industry direct input coefficients matrix. The steps are the same as in the first stage, with some additional re-aggregation conditions. The two steps can be applied to the intermediate portion[17] of the use matrix in terms of flow value, or to the direct input coefficients matrix.[18] In this stage, the commodity-by-industry tables of indirect taxes, trade margins, transportation costs and imports are also disaggregated to guarantee the total value of production by

sub-industries. We thus obtain disaggregated data for the domestic and imported input coefficients separately, as well as for total value-added.

3. Once we have determined both the disaggregated market share and the disaggregated commodity-by-industry direct input coefficients matrix, we can calculate the disaggregated technical coefficient matrix. As for the regular industry-by-industry direct technical coefficient matrix, the third stage obtains the disaggregated matrix by pre-multiplying the input coefficients table by the market share matrix, both disaggregated.

4. In the final stage, we disaggregate the other components of the IO model. The value-added was disaggregated in the second stage, so only the final demand and employment are disaggregated in the fourth stage. The information about these components is available in the use table either by commodity, as in the case of final demand components, or by industry, as in the case of employment. The procedure for disaggregating the final demand portion of the use matrix is similar to the approach used in the third stage. That is, the final demand matrix was pre-multiplied by the disaggregated market share matrix. The components that are usually available by industry, such as employment, were disaggregated directly using specific information on the sub-industries.

3.2.1   The data used for disaggregation

The difficulties of establishing a list of ICT products led the Working Party on Indicators for the Information Society (WPIIS) to develop a separate classification of ICT goods before classifying ICT services (OECD, 2003, p. 2).[19] Following this approach, we first discuss the identification of the ICT manufacturing industries in the Brazilian economy and then the ICT services industries.

The current OECD ICT sector definition for manufacturing industries is shown in Table 9.2.[20] Since these industries are still too aggregated, we need to evaluate the weight of ICT products in each of them. A more detailed classification, presented in OECD (2003, pp. 8–13) following the 2002 Harmonized System (HS), can be converted into a product classification. Based on this classification, we calculated the weights of ICT products in each of these sub-industries, classified according to the National Classification of Economic Activity (CNAE). The results, shown in Table 9.3, indicate that the weight of ICT products is too small in two of the industries identified above, at only 1.7 per cent for the manufacture of office machinery production and 12.7 per cent for the manufacture of insulated wire, cable and electric conductors. We therefore excluded these two sectors from the ICT manufacturing sectors in the Brazilian economy.

Table 9.2   OECD classification of ICT goods

ISIC	Description	CNAE
3000	Office, accounting and computing machinery	30
3130	Insulated wire and cable	31.30
3210	Electronic valves and tubes and other electronic components	32.10
3220	Television and radio transmitters and apparatus for line telephony and line telegraphy	32.21 32.22
3230	Television and radio receivers, sound or video recording or reproducing apparatus and associated goods	32.30
3312	Instruments and appliances for measuring, checking, testing, navigating and other purposes, except industrial process equipment	33.20
3313	Industrial process equipment	33.30

Sources: OECD (2002); IBGE – http://www.ibge.gov.br/concla/default.php; accessed 31 March 2010; elaboration: authors.

Table 9.3   Brazilian classification of ICT goods

CNAE classification	Description	ICT (% of total)
30.1	Manufacture of office machinery production	1.70
30.2	Manufacture of equipment and machinery of electronic systems for data processing	100.00
31.3	Manufacture of insulated wire, cable and electric conductors	12.70
32.1	Manufacture of basic electronic components	82.80
32.2	Manufacture of television and radio transmitters and apparatus for line telephony and line telegraphy	99.70
32.3	Manufacture of television and radio receivers, sound or video recording or reproducing apparatus and associated goods	100.00
33.2	Instruments and appliances for measuring, checking, testing, navigating and other purposes, except industrial process equipment	85.70
33.3	Manufacture of electronic systems machinery, instruments and equipments related to industrial process control and automatization	100.00

Source: IBGE, Annual Industrial Survey 2003; elaboration: authors.

Table 9.4   OECD classification of ICT services

ISIC	Description	CNAE
5150	Wholesaling of machinery, equipment and supplies	51.65-9
7123	Renting of office machinery and equipment (including computers)	71.33-1
642	Telecommunications	64.2
72	Computer and related activities	72

Sources: OECD (2002); IBGE – http://www.ibge.gov.br/concla/default.php accessed 31 March 2010; elaboration: authors.

Table 9.5   Disaggregated activities

Aggregated Industries		Disaggregated Industries
System of National Accounts	Description	
11	Manufacture of electronic products equipment and machinery	30.2
		32.1
		32.2
		32.3
		33.3
		Other
37	Communications	64.2
		Other
40	Services to the business sector	72
		Other

Source: IBGE – http://www.ibge.gov.br/concla/default.php; accessed 31 March 2010; elaboration: authors.

We next adopted the same method for services industries. The OECD classification is shown in Table 9.4. We do not have enough data for the first two industries at this level of disaggregation, so they were not included in the Brazilian classification.

Based on this classification, we can identify seven ICT sub-industries in the Brazilian economy, of which five are manufacturing and two are services. As shown in Table 9.5, these seven ICT sub-industries are incorporated into three of the 42 industries of the IO matrix. The manufacturing sub-industries all correspond to the manufacture of electronic products equipment and machinery. The share of each manufacturing sub-industry

Table 9.6   Share of ICT manufacturing in total gross output value

System of National Accounts	Disaggregated Activities	Description	Share of Total Gross Output (%)
11	30.2	Manufacture of equipment and machinery of electronic systems for data processing	21.4
	32.1	Manufacture of basic electronic components	10.0
	32.2	Manufacture of television and radio transmitters and apparatus for line telephony and line telegraphy	39.7
	32.3	Manufacture of television and radio receivers, sound or video recording or reproducing apparatus and associated goods	23.0
	33.3	Manufacture of electronic systems machinery, instruments and equipments related to industrial process control	1.3
	Other		4.1

Source: IBGE, Annual Industrial Survey 2003; elaboration: authors.

Table 9.7   Share of ICT services in total gross output value

System of National Accounts	Aggregated Activities		Disaggregated Activities	Share of Total Gross Output (%)
37	Communications	64.2	Telecommunications	90.8
		Other		9.2
40	Services to the business sector	72	Computer and related activities	29.2
		Other		70.8

Source: IBGE, Annual Service Survey (2003); elaboration: authors.

in total gross output is shown in Table 9.6. The services industries fall under two different aggregated industries: communications and services to business sector. Their shares of total output are shown in Table 9.7. We discuss the results of the disaggregation together with the results from the simulations in Section 4.2.

3.3   Initial Conditions

The initial conditions of most of the variables (such as output, technical coefficients, the market share matrix and final demand), as well as the wage-related variables, were all drawn from the disaggregated input–output matrix for 2003, obtained as described in Sections 3.1and 3.2. In contrast, capital coefficients, such as the capital flow matrix and capital output ratio, were estimated.

The only capital flow matrix available for the Brazilian economy is not at the same level of disaggregation as the IO matrix. It is divided by institutional sectors, and the commodities are aggregated into three subsectors: machinery and equipment; construction; and other. This original matrix allowed for a separation of total investment into endogenous and exogenous investment, by institutional sector. The idea, as mentioned earlier, was to isolate corporate investment from household and government investment. However, part of household investment actually corresponds to the agriculture, forestry, fishing and hunting sector and part to autonomous producers; these shares should be included in the endogenous investment component.

We thus used the industries employed in this work to divide the investment matrix among aggregated sectors and not exactly institutional sectors. To distribute total investment by commodity, we complemented the Brazilian data with data from the 1997 United States capital flow table.

This United States table provides the most detailed view of investment by commodity and by using industry, showing flows of 180 commodities to 123 private sector industries. We aggregated these data into the Brazilian IO aggregation – that is, 80 commodities to 42 industries – and we then reaggregated them into five aggregate sectors: agriculture, forestry, fishing and hunting; non-financial and non-insurance services, mining and quarrying, manufacturing, utilities and construction; financial and insurance services; the general government sector; and (consumer) households. The United States data refer only to the first three sectors.

We used a different method to distribute the total investments of the last two sectors (that is, government and households). Based on the information available for the Brazilian economy, we were able to divide the general government sector and consumer household investments by the sub-sectors described above. These data can be complemented with the total investment by commodity available in the IO matrix. Each commodity is associated with one of the three sub-sectors, and we can calculate its share in the corresponding sub-sector. We used these shares to distribute the investment of the general government sector and consumer households by commodity, in order to complete the capital flow matrix.

We obtained the level of productive capacity and the capital-output ratio by aggregated industries based on capacity utilization data[21] and past levels of investment and output data for the Brazilian economy by industry, given in equations (9A.14) and (9A.15) in the Appendix.

4   PRELIMINARY RESULTS

The results are organized in two blocks. First, we analyse the current impact of the ICT-producing sectors on the Brazilian economy based on the results of the disaggregation method described above. Second, we present the results of the simulation model, with an emphasis on the future impact of different prospective ICT diffusion scenarios on the Brazilian economy.

4.1   Current ICT Impacts

The share of ICT sectors in the Brazilian economy in 2003 are presented in Tables 9.8, 9.9, and 9.10. Table 9.8 highlights the low participation of ICT sectors in the Brazilian economy in terms of output, value-added

Table 9.8   Share of ICT sectors in gross output, value-added and employment, Brazil 2003 (%)

ICT Sector	Gross Output	Value-added	Employment
Electronic systems machinery for data processing	0.13	0.10	0.04
Basic electronic components	0.07	0.05	0.06
Television and radio transmitters and apparatus for line telephony	0.25	0.19	0.03
Television and radio receivers, sound or video recording	0.14	0.11	0.04
Electronic systems machinery, instruments and equipments related to industrial process control and automation	0.01	0.01	0.01
Telecommunications	*2.11*	*2.65*	0.20
Computer and related activities	0.88	1.20	*1.51*
Total ICT	*3.60*	*4.30*	*1.90*

Source: Research project.

Table 9.9   Share of ICT sectors in final demand, Brazil 2003 (%)

ICT Sector	Gross Fixed Capital Formation	Exports	House-holds' Final Consump-tion	Total Final Demand	Total Final Demand Imports
Electronic systems machinery for data processing	0.83	0.55	0.28	0.35	3.98
Basic electronic components	0.40	0.27	0.14	0.17	1.94
Television and radio transmitters and apparatus for line telephony	1.53	1.02	0.51	0.66	*7.35*
Television and radio receivers, sound or video recording	0.89	0.59	0.30	0.38	4.26
Electronic systems machinery, instruments and equipments related to industrial process control and automation	0.05	0.03	0.02	0.02	0.25
Telecommunications	0.04	0.60	4.08	2.08	0.23
Computer and related activities	0.29	1.42	0.07	0.29	0.43
Total ICT	*4.02*	*4.48*	*5.39*	*3.96*	*18.44*

Source: Research project.

and employment, in which the ICT sectors represent only 1.90 per cent. Among the ICT sectors, services sectors represent a larger share than man-ufactures, with telecom having the greatest share in terms of gross output and value-added. This does not imply a high employment share, however: almost 80 per cent of ICT employment is in computer and related activi-ties, which represents less than 30 per cent in terms of value-added or gross output.

Table 9.9 focuses on the ICT shares in final demand components, for both domestic and imported goods. The share of households' final con-sumption is the greatest, followed by exports. However, the share of ICT

Table 9.10 Share of ICT in total imports, by demand component (%)

ICT Sector	Gross Fixed Capital Formation	Exports	House-holds' Final Consump-tion	Total Final Demand Imports	Total Inter-mediate Goods Imports	Total Imports
Electronic systems machinery for data processing	5.46	4.76	2.68	3.98	1.04	1.89
Basic electronic components	2.66	2.32	1.31	1.94	0.51	0.92
Television and radio transmitters and apparatus for line telephony	10.10	8.80	4.96	7.35	1.93	3.50
Television and radio receivers, sound or video recording	5.86	5.10	2.87	4.26	1.12	2.03
Electronic systems machinery, instruments and equipments related to industrial process control and automation	0.34	0.30	0.17	0.25	0.07	0.12
Telecommunications	0.29	0.00	0.19	0.23	0.20	0.71
Computer and related activities	0.57	0.00	0.34	0.43	0.16	2.86
Total ICT	*25.29*	*21.27*	*12.52*	*18.44*	*5.03*	*12.03*
Share in ICT imports[a]	*27.91*	*0.23*	*14.74*	*44.26*	*55.74*	*100.00*

Note: a. Share of ICT imports in total ICT imports, by demand component.

Source: Research project.

in final demand imports is quite high at almost 19 per cent, compared with its 4 per cent share in total final demand.

The highest import share of total final demand imports is related to television and radio transmitters and apparatus for line telephony, which is the most important component in gross fixed capital formation. This indicates a high ICT investment-related propensity to import, which is

Table 9.11   Static impact analysis: exogenous consumption

ICT Sector	Gross Output	Value-added	Employment
Electronic systems machinery for data processing	40 400	14 677	160
Basic electronic components	19 692	7 363	285
Television and radio transmitters and apparatus for line telephony	74 723	27 621	146
Television and radio receivers, sound or video recording	43 329	16 696	187
Electronic systems machinery, instruments and equipments related to industrial process control and automation	2 522	1 156	41
Telecommunications	639 812	388 919	885
Computer and related activities	267 589	176 047	6 655
Total ICT	*1 088 067*	*632 479*	*8 358*
Total	*30 261 669*	*14 702 650*	*439 867*

Source: Research Project.

underscored by the results for the share of ICT sectors in total imports by demand component (see Table 9.10). ICT commodities represent 25.3 per cent of investment-related imports, which correspond to 27.9 per cent of total ICT imports. As a simple comparison, both indicators for house-holds' final consumption are almost half of the investment indicators. On the other hand, the share of ICT in total imports, 12.03 per cent, is smaller than the weight in final demand, owing to the low share of intermediate demand, at only 5.03 per cent. Nevertheless, intermediate goods imports represent more than half of total ICT imports.

The next three tables are related to static impact analysis. Tables 9.11 and 9.12 present the results of a 1 per cent increase in the exogenous final demand of each sector, instead of the usual backward and forward linkages related to the same absolute variation in each sector. Table 9.11 considers consumption to be part of exogenous demand, while non-durable consumption is endogenous in Table 9.12, as explained above. As expected, the integration of the usual Keynesian-Kaleckian multiplier with the Leontief multiplier increases the multiplier and consequently the indirect effect of an increase in autonomous expenditures.

In Table 9.13, we compare backward and forward linkages of ICT sectors in Brazil with the United States. The data show relevant differences in the penetration pattern of ICT in the two economies. The backward

Table 9.12   Static impact analysis: endogenous consumption

ICT Sector	Gross Output	Value-added	Employment
Electronic systems machinery for data processing	76 022	27 618	301
Basic electronic components	37 054	13 855	536
Television and radio transmitters and apparatus for line telephony	140 608	51 975	276
Television and radio receivers, sound or video recording	81 532	31 417	351
Electronic systems machinery, instruments and equipments related to industrial process control and automation	4 746	2 175	77
Telecommunications	776 774	472 173	1 075
Computer and related activities	373 982	246 043	9 301
Total ICT	*1 490 718*	*845 256*	*11 915*
Total	*36 849 117*	*17 663 707*	*515 104*

Source: Research project.

Table 9.13   Backward and forward linkages: Brazil and the United States, 2003

Country and ICT Sector	Backward Linkages (Average)	Backward Linkages (Index)	Forward Linkages (Average)	Forward Linkages (Index)
Brazil				
ICT manufactures	0.050	1.030	0.027	0.558
Telecommunications	0.035	0.722	0.047	0.959
Information services	0.035	0.708	0.038	0.785
United States				
ICT manufactures	0.035	1.144	0.038	1.240
Telecommunications	0.031	1.035	0.050	1.644
Information services	0.028	0.913	0.024	0.796

Source: US IO Matrices and Research Project; elaboration: authors.

linkages, which indicate the effect of an increase in a specific sector's final demand, show a similar order of magnitude among Brazilian and US economies, particularly for ICT manufacturing and information services. Conversely, the forward linkages, which measure the impact on a specific sector of an increase in total exogenous final demand, present a divergent pattern in the two countries. Although ICT manufacturing and telecommunications show a very high forward linkage index in the United States economy, they are both below average in Brazil.

This result has an immediate policy implication. Given the US standard, the rate of ICT diffusion can probably be enhanced on the user side, which would promote more growth than simply favouring the acceleration of ICT production in the economy. It is important to keep in mind that the linkage refers to total production, without differentiating imports from domestic production. The greater the share of demand supplied by imports, the lesser would be the growth impact of any action promoting ICT use diffusion.

The role played by trade patterns in the final linkage is explored in the next section, where we use simulation exercises to assess two extreme hypotheses on ICT imports penetration in Brazil.

4.2 Simulation Results

The main objective of the simulation exercises is to quantify (in order of magnitude) the effects of the main causes underlying various scenarios by comparing the different trajectories generated by them. In other words, the model is not designed to make predictions about the future trajectories of an economy, but to implement a comparative dynamics methodology. We thus compare the trajectory of a reference scenario with two different simulation hypotheses:

The *reference scenario* (RS) assumes a constant and equal growth rate for each component of the exogenous final demand equal to 2 per cent for the next 20 years, starting in 2003.

Hypothesis 1 (H1) assumes different growth rates for ICT sectors with an unchanged pattern of international trade. It incorporates a growth rate 1 per cent higher than the reference scenario for each ICT sector separately and for all ICT sectors together for the 20 years following 2003.

Hypothesis 2 (H2) assumes diffusion of ICT with changes in the trade pattern. We test two extreme scenarios: in the first, the ICT sectors' ratios of all imports to total use tend to zero in ten years; in the second, they tend to one in ten years.

Figure 9.1 shows the results of H1, where each line refers to a 1 per cent higher growth rate for the respective ICT sector and the solid black line for

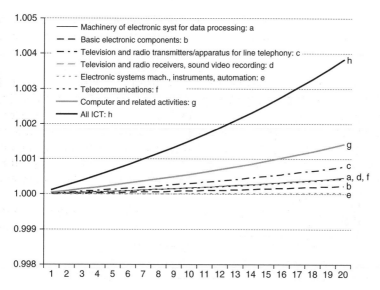

Source: Research project.

Figure 9.1   Growth rates with unchanged trade pattern (%)

all ICT sectors simultaneously. The figure shows the results relative to the base scenario for technological progress, such that a value above (below) one indicates a higher (lower) rate than in the base scenario. The highest rate, as expected, corresponds to all ICT sectors growing at a faster rate. This is followed by the computer and related activities sub-sector, which points to a high weighted backward linkage. Note that the linkages shown in Table 9.13 relate to total supply, while the results from the simulation runs are related to the impact on the Brazilian economy. Hence, even if the computer and related activities sub-sector does not have the highest index, it does have one of the lowest import rates, together with the other ICT service sector.

Figure 9.2 illustrates the impact of the two extreme trade pattern scenarios. The figure shows both scenarios, assuming a growth rate 1 per cent higher for all ICT sectors relative to the reference scenario, in which all sectors grow at the same rate. For purposes of comparison, the solid line in Figure 9.2 is the same as the solid black line of the Figure 9.1.

These results differ from those proposed initially. The original idea was to test a complete import substitution of ICT sectors, represented by a zero imports ratio of ICT products. The model became too explosive, however, when we also implemented this hypothesis for capital coefficients, given

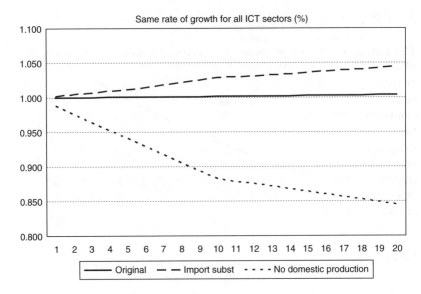

Source: Research project.

Figure 9.2   Growth rates with different trade pattern

the other parameters. The results presented in this figure thus relate to imports substitution or penetration for intermediate and consumption goods, as well as for the exogenous final demand components, but not for endogenous investments.

The dashed line represents the import substitution scenario, while the dotted line corresponds to the imports penetration scenario. We find that if ICT production was completely supplied by imports, the final growth rate of would be 15 per cent lower than the reference scenario. On the other hand, if ICT production was internalized, the growth rate would not increase at the same rate, but rather would only be 5 per cent higher than the reference scenario. This could reflect the low forward linkage of the ICT sectors in the economy relative to the United States, as mentioned in our discussion of current ICT impacts. None of the scenarios tested in the simulation dealt with changes in ICT on the user side. To do that, the best simulation scenario would be one of technical catching-up with the United States economy using United States IO information as a benchmark, which will probably be the next phase of our work.

5 FINAL COMMENTS

The simulation results presented in this chapter give a preliminary idea of possible trajectories generated by the model. The two scenarios are extreme, and results are simple to predict. Further data work will provide better simulation scenarios, which will contribute to a more systematic comparative analysis. The future research agenda may include a simulation of technical catching-up between the Brazilian and US economies using the United States IO information as a benchmark. We will also undertake complementary field studies aimed at improving the quality of empirical data on the Brazilian ICT diffusion process. The implementation of Verspagen's replicator methodology to model feedback supply effects is another task to be developed.

NOTES

* Federal University of Rio de Janeiro, Institute of Economics, Research Group on Industry and Competitiveness. We are grateful to Felipe Marques for his collaboration on the data work and to participants of two seminars held at ECLAC in November 2006 and March 2007 for helpful suggestions
1. Instituto Brasileiro de Geografia e Estatística.
2. Sometimes growth accounting methodologies are complemented by econometric techniques for parametric estimation and exploratory analysis of statistical relationships between relevant variables. See Hulten (2000, pp. 22–4) and OECD (2001, p. 19).
3. For more details on growth accounting, see OECD (2001), Hulten (2000) and Jorgenson et al. (1987).
4. See Jorgenson and Stiroh (2000), Oliner and Sichel (2000) and Jorgenson (2001).
5. See Stiroh (2002) and Jorgenson et al. (2006).
6. See Schreyer (2000) and Van Ark and Inklaar (2005).
7. The original dynamic IO model of Leontief (1953, 1970) used a rigid accelerator investment function. This version of the model suffered from instability problems, causal indeterminacy and possible negative solutions (cf, Kurz et al., 1998, introduction to part II). These problems may be solved through the use of an alternative formulation of the investment function (ibid.). This approach is followed by Duchin and Szyld (1985), being the theoretical background underlying Leontief and Duchin's (1986) empirical study.
8. This assumption implies that the model is not able to deal with declining industries.
9. See note 7.
10. Both Leontief and Duchin (1986) and Kalmbach and Kurz (1990) considered demand growth as the proximate cause of economic expansion.
11. Kalmbach and Kurz's and Verspagen's models are similar. In contrast with Kalmbach and Kurz, however, Verspagen justifies the exclusive exogenous character of exports through the use of the balance-of-payments equilibrium condition.
12. The extension introduced in this model is closer to the one presented in Kalmbach and Kurz than to Verspagen's approach. The main difference refers to parameter estimations: we use a non-parametric method to estimate the consumption function, while Kalmbach and Kurz use an econometric (parametric) method.
13. Sectoral investment is a function of the level of sectoral demand. To simplify the analysis, we assume that the short-run expectations underlying sectoral production decisions are realized, which implies that sectoral output is always equal to sectoral demand.

14. These margins are treated separately as commodities that are produced by industries and purchased by intermediate and final users.
15. Bacharach (1970); Bulmer-Thomas (1982); Miller and Blair (1985); Kurz et al. (1998); UN (1999).
16. A matrix in which entries in each column show, for a given commodity, the proportion of the total output of that commodity produced in each industry. Each commodity is assumed to be produced by the various industries in fixed proportions (industry technology assumption).
17. In this table, each column shows, for a given industry, the amount of each commodity the industry uses, in terms of value.
18. Here, the matrix entries in each column show the amount of a commodity used by an industry per dollar of output of that industry.
19. According to OECD (2003, p. 2) 'these difficulties were related to the rapidly changing character of ICT goods and services, and the dated nature of current standard classifications'.
20. The current definition was originally approved in 1998 and amended slightly in 2002 to reflect ISIC Rev 3.1 changes to wholesale (OECD, 2003, p. 1).
21. The capacity utilization data were obtained from the historical database of the Getúlio Vargas Foundation, accessed through the online economic databases provided by the Central Bank of Brazil.

REFERENCES

Bacharach, M. (1970) *Biproportional Matrices and Input–Output Change*, Cambridge, UK: Cambridge University Press.

Bulmer-Thomas, V. (1982), *Input–Output Analysis in Developing Countries: Sources, Methods and Applications*, London: John Wiley and Sons.

Duchin, F. and Szyld, D.B. (1985) 'A Dynamic Input–Output Model with Assured Positive Output', *Metroeconomica*, **XXXVII**(3), October, 269–82.

Freitas, F. and Dweck, E. (2006) 'Metodologia de Desagregação do Modelo Insumo-Produto para a Análise de Geração Setorial de Emprego' Instituto de Economia, GIC (mimeo).

Grijó, E. and Bêrni, D. de Avila (2005), 'Metodologia Completa para a Estimativa de Matrizes de Insumo-Produto', *VIII Encontro de Economia da Região Sul, ANPEC – SUL 2005*.

Hulten, C.R. (2000). 'Total Factor Productivity: A Short Biography', NBER Working Papers No. 7471.

Jorgenson, D.W. (2001) 'Information Technology and the U.S. Economy', *American Economic Review*, **91**(1).

Jorgenson, D.W. (2005), 'Accounting for Growth in the Information Age', in Aghion, P. and Durlauf, S. (eds) *Handbook of Economic Growth*, Amsterdam: North Holland.

Jorgenson, D.W. and Stiroh, K.J. (2000), 'Raising the Speed Limit: U.S. Economic Growth in the Information Age', *Brookings Papers on Economic Activity*, 1.

Jorgenson, D.W., Gollop, F.M. and Fraumeni, B.M. (1987), *Productivity and U.S. Economic Growth*, Cambridge, MA: Harvard University Press.

Jorgenson, D.W., Ho, M.S., Samuels, J. and Stiroh, K.J. (2006), 'The Industry Origins of the American Productivity Resurgence', downloadable at http://eco nomics.harvard.edu/faculty/jorgenson/files/IndustryOriginsAmerProdResurg_EconomicSystemsResearch.pdf; accessed 22 March 2010.

Kalmbach, P. and Kurz, H.D. (1990), 'Micro-electronics and Employment: A Dynamic Input–Output Study of the West German Economy', *Structural Change and Economic Dynamics*, **1**(2), December, 371–86.

Kurz, H.D., Dietzenbacher, E. and Lager, C. (1998), *Input–Output Analysis Volume I*, Cheltenham, UK and Lyme, NH, USA: Edward Elgar.

Leontief, W. (1953) 'Dynamic Analysis', in *Studies in the Structure of the American Economy*, Chapter 3, New York: Oxford University Press, pp. 53–90.

Leontief, W. (1970), 'The Dynamic Inversed', in A.P. Carter, and A. Brody (eds), *Contributions to Input–Output Analysis*, Vol. 1.

Leontief, W. and Duchin, F. (1986), *The Future Impact of Automation on Workers*, New York: Oxford University Press.

McCombie, J. and Thirlwall, A. (1994), *Economic Growth and the Balance of Payments Constraint*, New York: St. Martin's Press.

Miller, R.E. and Blair, P.D. (1985), *Input–Output Analysis: Foundation and Extensions*, New Jersey: Prentice Hall.

OECD (2001), *Measuring Productivity: Measurement of Aggregate and Industry-level Productivity Growth*, OECD, Paris, downloadable at http://www.oecd.org/dataoecd/59/29/2352458.pdf; accessed 27 March 2010.

OECD (2002), *Measuring the Information Economy*, OECD, Paris, downloadable at www.oecd.org/dataoecd/16/14/1835738.pdf; accessed 29 March 2010.

OECD (2003), *A Proposed Classification of ICT Goods*, OECD, Paris, downloadable at www.oecd.org/dataoecd/5/61/22343094.pdf; accessed 29 March 2010.

Oliner, S.D. and Sichel, D.E. (2000), 'The Resurgence of Growth in the Late 1990s: Is Information Technology the Story?', *Journal of Economic Perspectives*, **14**(4).

Schreyer, P. (2000), 'The Contribution of Information and Communication Technology to the Output Growth: a Study of the G7 Countries', *STI Working Paper*, OECD, Paris.

Solow, R. (1987), 'We'd better watch out', *New York Times Book Review*, 12 July.

Stiroh, K.J. (2002), 'Information Technology and U.S. Productivity Revival: What do the Industry Data Say?', *American Economic Review*, **92**(5).

United Nations (1999) *Handbook of Input–Output Table Compilation and Analysis*, New York: UN Statistical Division.

Van Ark, B. and Inklaar, R. (2005), 'Catching Up or Getting Stuck? Europe's Troubles to Exploit ICT's Productivity Potential', GGDC Research Memorandum, GD-79, downloadable at http://www.ggdc.net/publications/memorandum/gd79.pdf; accessed 27 March 2010.

Verspagen, B. (2002), 'Evolutionary Macroeconomics: A Synthesis Between Neo-Schumpeterian and Post-Keynesian Lines of Thought', *The Electronic Journal of Evolutionary Modeling and Economic Dynamics*, No. 1007, http://www.e-jemed.org/1007/index.php; accessed 29 March 2010.

Wolsky, A.M. (1984), 'Disaggregating Input–Output Models', *Review of Economics and Statistics*, **66**(2).

APPENDIX 9A.1   THE MODEL

9A.1.1   Main Variables

We define the following variables:

q: Total commodity output, a commodity-by-one vector.
g: Total industry output, an industry-by-one vector.
B: Direct input coefficients matrix in which entries in each column show the amount of a commodity used by an industry per unit value of output of that industry; it is a commodity-by-industry matrix.
A: Direct input coefficients matrix, an industry-by-industry matrix.
D: An industry-by-commodity matrix, also referred to as the market share matrix.
e: A column vector in which each entry shows the total final demand purchases for each commodity from the use table; it is a commodity-by-one vector.
f: A column vector in which each entry shows the total final demand purchases of each industry output; it is an industry-by-one vector.
^: A symbol that, when placed over a vector, indicates a square diagonal matrix in which the elements of the vector appear on the main diagonal and zeros elsewhere.
$\mathbf{i}_n$: Unit (summation) vector containing only ones; it is an n-by-one vector.
$\mathbf{I}_n$: Identity matrix of dimension n, where. $\mathbf{I}_n = \hat{\mathbf{i}}_n$

Bold capital letters indicate a matrix; bold lowercase letters indicate a vector.

9A.1.2   Equations

The basic IO model starts from the fundamental identity of national accounts between total supply and total demand.

$$\mathbf{g}_t + \mathbf{m}_t = \mathbf{A}\mathbf{g}_t + \mathbf{A}_t^m\mathbf{g}_t + \mathbf{f}_t + \mathbf{f}_t^m, \tag{9A.1}$$

where **m** is the industry-by-one vector of the supply of imported commodities by origin industry, $\mathbf{A}^m\mathbf{g}$ is the industry-by-one vector of the intermediate demand of imported commodities by origin industry and $\mathbf{f}^m$ is the industry-by-one vector of the final demand of imported commodities by origin industry. The above equation simply means that total supply corresponds to the sum of domestic production and imported goods and services available in the economy, which could also be expressed by the following equation:

$$\mathbf{g}_t^{Tot} = \mathbf{A}_t^{Tot}\mathbf{g}_t + \mathbf{f}_t^{Tot}, \tag{9A.1'}$$

where 'Tot' means the total value, which is obtained by summing the demand (or supply) for domestic production and imports. By definition, total imports are the sum of intermediate and final demand imports.

$$\mathbf{m}_t = \mathbf{A}_t^m\mathbf{g}_t + \mathbf{f}_t^m. \tag{9A.2}$$

This means that another important identity is

$$\mathbf{g}_t = \mathbf{A}\mathbf{g}_t + \mathbf{f}_t, \tag{9A.3}$$

which is the basis for the usual IO analysis, which relates exogenous change in final domestic demand and its impact on domestic production (total gross output by industry). However, in models like the one presented here, in which part of the final demand is endogenized, it is sometimes important to determine total demand independently from the trade pattern.

9A.1.2.1 Final demand
The value of final demand can be divided into five components: (1) personal consumption expenditures (PCE); (2) gross fixed investment; (3) the change in private inventories; (4) exports of goods and services; and (5) government consumption expenditures. Two of those components, personal consumption ($\mathbf{f}_{C,t}^{Tot}$) and gross fixed investment ($\mathbf{f}_{I,t}^{Tot}$), are described by some behavioural assumptions. Hence, it is possible to present total final demand divided into three vectors:

$$\mathbf{f}_t^{Tot} = \mathbf{f}_{C,t}^{Tot} + \mathbf{f}_{I,t}^{Tot} + \mathbf{f}_{o,t}^{Tot}. \tag{9A.4}$$

Personal consumption expenditures The PCE commodity-by-one vector ($\mathbf{e}_{C,t}^{Tot}$) was first divided between imported ($\mathbf{e}_{C,t}^m$) and domestic demand ($\mathbf{e}_{C,t}$), and then the domestic demand was divided between durable ($\mathbf{e}_{C,t}^d$) and non-durable ($\mathbf{e}_{C,t}^{nd}$) consumption goods and services. Thus, given the market share matrix ($\mathbf{D}$), we obtain the PCE industry-by-one vector:

$$\mathbf{f}_{C,t}^{Tot} = \mathbf{D} \cdot \mathbf{e}_{C,t}^{Tot} = \mathbf{D} \cdot \mathbf{e}_{C,t}^d + \mathbf{D} \cdot \mathbf{e}_{C,t}^{nd} + \mathbf{D} \cdot \mathbf{e}_{C,t}^m; \tag{9A.5}$$

or

$$\mathbf{f}_{C,t}^{Tot} = \mathbf{f}_{C,t}^{d} + \mathbf{f}_{C,t}^{nd} + \mathbf{f}_{C,t}^{m}. \qquad (9A.5')$$

The non-durable consumption value can be expressed as a positive function of total wages (W), so non-durable consumption can be expressed as

$$\mathbf{f}_{C,t}^{nd} = \mathbf{c}_{w}W. \qquad (9A.6)$$

where $\mathbf{c}_{w} = (1/W)\mathbf{f}_{C,t}^{nd}$ is an industry-by-one vector of propensities to consume in relation to total wages. Assuming a stable relation between wages and total output by industry, we can define

$$W_{t} = \omega'\mathbf{g}_{t}, \qquad (9A.7)$$

where ω is a vector of wage-output coefficients by industry. Therefore, the consumption vector can be expressed as a function of total output by industry:

$$\mathbf{f}_{C,t} = \mathbf{c}_{w}\omega'\mathbf{g}_{t} + \mathbf{f}_{C,t}^{d}, \qquad (9A.8)$$

or

$$\mathbf{f}_{C,t} = \mathbf{A}_{C,t}^{w}\mathbf{g}_{t} + \mathbf{f}_{C,t}^{d}, \qquad (9A.9)$$

where $\mathbf{f}_{C,t}^{d}$ will be added to the other components of final demand that were not endogenized. The same method was applied to divide the demand vector into imported durable (exogenous demand) and non-durable (endogenous demand) consumption. This step is important for the elaboration of simulation scenarios related to the trade pattern.

Gross fixed investment The investment demand vector by industry or by commodity depends on estimated capital flow matrix ($\mathbf{M}_{K,t}$) and each industry's desired productive capacity, which results in investment decisions by industry ($\mathbf{gi}_{t}$):

$$\mathbf{f}_{I,t}^{Tot} = \mathbf{D} \cdot \mathbf{e}_{I,t}^{Tot} = \mathbf{D} \cdot \mathbf{M}_{K,t}\mathbf{gi}_{t}. \qquad (9A.10)$$

The gross fixed investment vector includes not only investment by the corporate sectors, but also household and government investment. Therefore, it can also be divided into two components, an exogenous part, related to household and government sector investments, and an endogenous part, related to corporate investments, including both financial and non-financial corporations:

$$\mathbf{gi}_t = \mathbf{gi}_{\text{end},t} + \mathbf{gi}_{\text{exg},t}. \tag{9A.11}$$

The endogenous part is modelled as an investment function based on a flexible accelerator:

$$\mathbf{gi}_{\text{end},t} = \mathbf{\hat{h}}_t \mathbf{g}_t, \tag{9A.12}$$

where $\mathbf{\hat{h}}_t$ is a diagonal matrix with the sectoral propensities to invest that relates the levels of sectoral output with the levels of sectoral investments. The behaviour through time of the propensities to invest is given by the following equation:

$$\mathbf{\hat{h}}_t = \mathbf{\hat{h}}_{t-1}[\mathbf{I} + \mathbf{\hat{\gamma}}(\mathbf{u}_{t-1} - \mathbf{\bar{u}})], \tag{9A.13}$$

where $\mathbf{u}_t$ is the vector of the actual degree of capacity utilization, $\mathbf{\bar{u}}$ is the normal or desired degree of capacity utilization by industry and $\mathbf{\hat{\gamma}}$ is a diagonal matrix whose elements are the parameters of the sensitivity of sectoral investment to the deviation between the actual and the desired degree of capacity utilization.

The actual degree of capacity utilization is determined by the capacity level:

$$\mathbf{u}_t = \mathbf{\hat{\bar{g}}}_t^{-1} \mathbf{g}_t, \tag{9A.14}$$

where the actual productive capacity by industry, at the beginning of period t, can be derived by previous investment decisions:

$$\mathbf{\bar{g}}_t = \mathbf{\hat{\bar{g}}}_{t-1}(\mathbf{i}_n - \delta) + \mathbf{\hat{v}}^{-1} \mathbf{gi}_{\text{end},t-1}. \tag{9A.15}$$

There are two underlying assumptions: first, the installation of desired capacity is always possible; second, the scrapping of fixed capital items is described by a rigid parameter (δ) by industry, which is not affected by variations in capital utilization. Finally the capital output relation (v) is also constant throughout the simulation period.

The total investment demand by commodity is thus determined by:

$$\mathbf{e}_{I,t}^{\text{Tot}} = \mathbf{M}_{K,t}(\mathbf{\hat{h}}_t \mathbf{M}_{\text{end}} \mathbf{g}_t + \mathbf{gi}_{\text{exg},t}) = \mathbf{M}_{K,t} \mathbf{\hat{h}}_t \mathbf{M}_{\text{end}} \mathbf{g}_t + \mathbf{M}_{K,t} \mathbf{gi}_{\text{exg},t}, \tag{9A.16}$$

and the investment demand for domestically produced investment goods is obtained by subtracting imported investment goods from total demand, given the capital imports coefficients vector ($\mathbf{m}_{K,t}$).

$$e_{I,t} = (I - \hat{m}_{K,t})e_{I,t}^{Tot}. \tag{9A.17}$$

Therefore,

$$f_{I,t} = D \cdot e_{I,t} = f_{Iend,t} + f_{Iexg,t} = A_{I,t}g_t + f_{Iexg,t}, \tag{9A.18}$$

where $A_{I,t} = D \cdot (I - \hat{m}_{K,t})M_{K,t}\hat{h}_t M_{end}$ and $f_{Iexg,t} = D \cdot (I - \hat{m}_{K,t})M_{K,t}gi_{exg,t}$.

9A.1.2.2 Total domestically produced output

We can substitute equations (9A.9) and (9A.18) into (9A.4), adjusted for domestic production, and then into equation (9A.3), obtaining

$$g_t = Ag_t + A_{C,t}^w g_t + f_{C,t}^d + A_{I,t}g_t + f_{Iexg,t} + f_{O,t}. \tag{9A.19}$$

Redefining the vector of exogenous final demand as $f_{exg,t} = f_{C,t}^d + f_{Iexg,t} + f_{O,t}$, we can define total output as a function of $f_{exg,t}$:

$$g_t = [I - A - A_{C,t}^w - A_{I,t}]^{-1}f_{exg,t}. \tag{9A.20}$$

10. The relative impact of the regulatory framework on the diffusion of ICT: evidence from Latin America, 1989–2004

Nauro F. Campos*

1 INTRODUCTION

The diffusion of information and communication technologies (ICT) has recently received a great deal of attention. Many believe that this general-purpose technology has potential comparable with those that underpinned the Industrial Revolution of the middle of the nineteenth century. Indeed, fixed and mobile phones, personal computers and the Internet have diffused rapidly in the past ten or 15 years with massive (and still imperfectly understood) productivity, growth and welfare implications.

One argument is that privatization and de-regulation have played a major role in this process although, to date, there have few efforts to assess their relative importance. This paper contributes to this analysis. We provide a comprehensive assessment of the determinants of ICT diffusion in Latin America and the Caribbean (LAC). We study the diffusion processes of four types of ICT (fixed and mobile phones, personal computers and the Internet) and examine a comprehensive set of potential determinants (i.e., economic, political, technological and the institutional and regulatory framework dimensions) using a unique yearly panel dataset of 35 Latin American and Caribbean economies between 1989 and 2004. We tackle questions such as how fast have ICT diffused in this region? What are the main determinants of this process? Further, there is a widely held view by international organizations (IMF, 2001; OECD, 2004; World Bank, 2006;) that changes that occurred in the institutional and regulatory framework (IRF) in the early 1990s have played a major role in this process. Have they?

Our OLS fixed effects estimates support a ranking of determinants with levels of human capital and per capita GDP as main factors, followed in decreasing order of importance by the effectiveness of the regulatory framework (degree of competition in the domestic market and various characteristics of regulatory agencies), technical aspects (e.g., average price of call for phones, bandwidth for Internet and speed for computers) and political variables (democracy and durability of the regime).

The rest of the paper is organized as follows. Section 2 looks at what do we know about ICT diffusion? What is the role for the institutional and regulatory framework? Section 3 briefly reviews the related empirical literature. Section 4 presents the dataset we put together for this paper and investigates what we know about ICT diffusion and IRF dynamics in LAC. Section 5 reports our econometric estimates on the main determinants of ICT diffusion in LAC, with emphasis on the understanding of the relative role of IRF. Section 6 concludes.

2   REGULATION AND DIFFUSION: CONCEPTUAL FRAMEWORK

This section outlines the conceptual framework used for our empirical investigation. The regulatory framework has played a large role in mainstream thinking of technology diffusion since at least the early 1980s. Diffusion theory has been developed for the last three or four decades (see Geroski, 2000 for a review). International organizations (e.g., World Bank, 2006) have promoted the idea that regulation matters greatly for diffusion since the early 1990s in the context of the Washington Consensus policies, which may give the impression that this topic has received no attention previously. We argue here that this is clearly not the case (Mowery and Rosenberg, 1982 explicitly link regulation to diffusion) and in so doing we review the main theoretical ideas about the process of technology diffusion.

There are two important notions about technology diffusion. One is that, in purely economic terms, technology diffusion matters more than pure technological innovation itself. Of course, without innovation there is no diffusion in the same way that without invention there is no innovation. The economic (and productivity and welfare) effects of a given technological innovation are maximized once the diffusion process reaches its saturation stage. When a large fraction of the potential users of a given technology are exhausted, these effects reach their maximum. In other words, innovation matters, but diffusion matters much more.

The second idea is that, like invention and innovation, technology diffusion is a complex phenomenon. Rosenberg argues that one of the few things we can be sure about is that diffusion normally follows the 'stylized

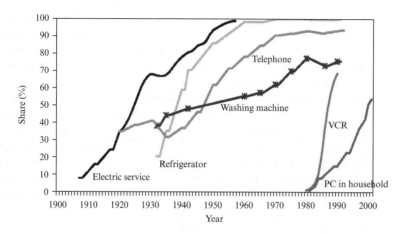

Source: Hall and Khan (2003).

Figure 10.1 Diffusion rates in the US for selected consumer products

fact' of the S-shaped pattern (very few users in the early stages followed by a rapidly increasing share of adopters in the total population, followed by a stage of saturation in which a plateau is reached in terms of share of adopters). Such S-shaped patterns seem to prevail albeit often coupled with an 'overall slowness' in the move from the invention to the diffusion (saturation) stage and, more worrisome, with observed 'wide variations in rates'.

Wide variations in diffusion rates are difficult to explain by single or simple factors. Figure 10.1 shows the diffusion of a few selected innovations (these data refer to the United States). Contrast the diffusion of the washing machine to that of the VCR (video cassette recorder). Both seem to follow S-shaped patterns, however the diffusion of VCRs is represented by an almost vertical line indicating that the saturation stage was reached rapidly (or 'thin-S' pattern), while the diffusion of washing machines followed a 'fat-S' pattern in which the share of potential adopters increases very slowly over time. Why does the share of US households that have at least one washing machine increase slower than the share of households that own at least one VCR? We argue here that three groups of reasons may explain differences in adoption rates (notice that these differences can also refer to the same technology in two different countries): demand factors, supply factors and regulatory or institutional factors. Demand factors are things like net benefits accrued to a potential adopter. Supply factors are, for example, how big and how fast are technical improvements in new technology. Regulatory framework relates to government actions that foster or hinder the adoption of a particular technology. For instance, mergers and acquisitions legislation may be used to stop or slow down the introduction of new technologies in a variety of ways. Before discussing these three general factors in more detail, we briefly present the standard models of technology diffusion.

The three standard theoretical models of technology diffusion are mostly concerned with the questions: how does diffusion start? What ignites the diffusion process of a new technology? Given the almost inevitable S-pattern (for successful innovations), what factors explain the take-off of the diffusion process?

Geroski (2000) summarizes the theoretical literature by arguing that there are three main approaches: one is based on the notion of adopter heterogeneity, a second is centred around learning and the third is the real option approach. Theoretical models based on adopter heterogeneity argue that firms or households are intrinsically different in terms of their expected benefits from adoption because of various reasons. To revisit the washing machine example, households may differ in the availability of and command over innovations that turn out to be complementary such as electricity and sanitation and sewage (which in turn depend on urbanization). If expected benefits are the same, then heterogeneity may arise because firms face different costs because they may have more or less skilled workforces.

The second standard theoretical model can be related to this first in that it argues that adopters are heterogeneous with respect to when they learn about the net benefits of a given innovation. As some firms are better connected or have better trained workforces or explicitly invest in information acquisition regarding new technologies, some firms adopt early and some firms adopt later. In this view, diffusion is a process almost analogous to invention in which luck and uncertainty can play a large role. The simpler learning models explain the diffusion process as an increasing share of potential adopters learning about the new technology over time. A few adopters discover a given innovation early on, with the rest of potential adopters learning later. In these models the S-shaped diffusion pattern is driven by the heterogeneity that can be restricted to 'when' (at which point in time) different firms learn about different innovations. If one considers 'what' and 'how' the potential adopter learns (firm, household, etc.) then a bridge with the adopter heterogeneity model can be built.

The third model differs from these two. The real option approach proposed by Stoneman has its roots in the investment under uncertainty literature developed in the 1990s by Dixit and Pindyck among others. The three central ideas in this case are: uncertainty, irreversibility and the option value of waiting. Irreversibility is the notion that various investment decisions involve a number of items with costs that are to be counted as sunk. Sunk costs are an important barrier to entry (and, we may add, to innovation) as these refer to costs an entrant has to incur even before starting production (the airline industry is an example of high sunk costs, while the software industry is one with low sunk costs). Investment decisions with a large share of sunk costs tend to be more irreversible where reversibility refers to changes in the investment project after it started that severely change the calculation of the expected benefits and costs. Everything else the same, the higher the sunk costs and the more uncertain the evolution of a given innovation, the more likely potential adopters are to exercise the option value of waiting (that is, the larger the value they attach to delaying the adoption of this innovation). If adopters are heterogeneous in the nature of the uncertainty they face and in the way they can spread sunk costs, then this model generates an S-shaped pattern of diffusion that is driven by different reasons than those in the two other models.

These models are useful to explain the take-off and saturation stages of the diffusion process, but do not explain why different technologies diffuse at different rates (or equivalently, why the same technology diffuses at different rates in different countries or in different regions in the same country). Moreover, these three standard models are of limited value if one studies the existing related empirical work. In this context, here we follow most of the empirical literature on diffusion and argue that there are three broad groups of factors that may be helpful in explaining differences in adoption rates: demand factors, supply factors and regulatory or institutional factors. Let us briefly discuss these in turn.

On the demand side, several factors may help or hinder the diffusion of a given technology. The adopter or potential user faces both benefits and costs from adoption that he/she takes into account. Benefits include increased productivity driven either by time savings for a fixed set of inputs and outputs and/or improved (value-added) outputs. Costs relate to the impact on all costs accrued with respect to the technology being substituted (that is, adopting a 'new' production method in the limit means to totally scrap the 'old' production method). Other costs of the adoption of a new technology are complementary investments or expenditures (in many cases, without which the new technology will not fully function). Rosenberg (1972) stresses the need for complementary skills and inputs as a crucial cost potential users consider. Another manifestation of such complementarities is network effects: a potential user will be more likely to adopt a new technology in time t the larger is the share of potential adopters that have adopted the technology in time $t - 1$ (e.g., video services in mobile phones).

On the supply side, some factors relate to the technology itself, chiefly, the nature and the extent of improvements in the new as well as in the old technology. If the 'new' technology improves fast, with prices declining and quality constant or increasing, then the likelihood increases of more agents (firms, households, regions, countries, etc.) adopting the new technology. ICT provide myriad examples in this case. Arguably, the better known is the price–quality ratio for personal computers, which has declined dramatically in the last 15 to 20 years. Adoption is also a positive function of the lack of improvements in the technology being substituted, that is, the less 'old' technology improves vis-à-vis the 'new' one, the larger are the advantages of adopting the latter and indeed the more likely we should expect it to be adopted. One recent example is the relative abandonment of watches because of their presence in mobile phones. A third supply side aspect is the availability of complementary inputs, which in turn determines whether a new technology will work at full potential (generating the maximum expected benefits or productivity improvements). Such availability can also indicate irreversibility in the sense that an increasing number of agents believe that the new technology is superior to the point of committing resources to the supply of its complementary inputs (which more often than not are innovations themselves; consider the case of PCs and printers) and as such should also contribute to the diffusion of the new technology and/or to the abandonment of the old technology. Finally, we suggest a link between these and the last of three standard theoretical frameworks discussed above, by positing that heterogeneity can arise by assuming different firms acquire, build or implement complementary inputs at different points of time.

The third group of factors thought of as influencing technology diffusion is institutions. This broad issue has received a great deal of attention in the economics literature recently. Institutions affect technology diffusion through market structure. Do firms with larger market shares innovate more or adopt new technologies earlier than firms with smaller market shares? This is a Schumpeterian question: is monopoly (or high market concentration) conducive or detrimental to innovation? Behind this is the contrast between, on the one hand, the large professional Research and Development laboratory owned by a large firm and an independent inventor, on the other. Larger firms have greater ability to appropriate the profits from adoption, have more resources (ability to pay/install new technologies/sunk costs), can more easily spread risks and exploit economies of scale. This is a difficult debate because there are also disadvantages (vis-à-vis technology adoption) of large firms: they tend to be more bureaucratic (slower and more layered decision process), less flexible (with inertia hampering implementation) and, in part for these two previous reasons, they have difficulties operating in the presence of networks that are not or have not been internalized by the firm.

Another factor that falls under the institutions heading is government regulation. Indeed, although Hall and Khan (2003) argue that these potentially have 'similar effects to the market structure/size . . . in that the effect of regulation is often to foreclose entry and grant fairly large market shares to incumbents, reducing incentives for cost-reducing innovation but also . . . increasing the benefits from innovation due to the small number of firms in the market', some authors have made a more direct link between regulation and diffusion much earlier, for instance, in the seminal Mowery and Rosenberg (1982) work on the civil aircraft industry, which shows that the role of first the Post Office and then of the Civil Aeronautics Board were both crucial in the definition of the technological trajectory of this particular industry.

3   BRIEF REVIEW OF THE EMPIRICAL LITERATURE

Although the second taxonomy ('demand–supply–institutions') discussed above maps quite nicely into the first taxonomy ('adopter heterogeneity–learning–uncertainty'), the former is often preferred in empirical analyses because it applies almost equally to households, firms and countries. In this section we present a brief review of the nascent econometric literature on the determinants of ICT diffusion (see Pohjola, 2003 for a more extensive survey).

Caselli and Coleman (2001) examine the determinants of the diffusion of personal computers across countries. Because most developing countries do not produce PCs domestically, the authors captured PC diffusion across countries through PC imports. They model PC imports empirically as a function of per capita income, investment in physical capital, the manufacturing share of GDP, the level of government spending, the extent of property rights protection, the fraction of the native population who speak English, the level of human capital and the level of general manufacturing (as well as of non-OECD) imports. The Caselli and Coleman sample has 89 countries and the time coverage of their estimation is from 1970 to 1990 (this period precedes the introduction of structural reforms around the world). One differentiating feature of this paper is the use of panel data estimation, a choice that is still not widespread in this literature. They find that the two most important factors in explaining the cross-country over time variation in the level of PC imports are levels of human capital and manufacturing imports from OECD countries. The rationale for the first factor is that there should be a minimum level of average education in a country to fully capture the benefits of PC adoption. In other words, absorptive capacity considerations make a minimum level of education in the importing country a required complementary input to PCs. One main concern in this analysis, highlighted by the authors themselves, is that PC imports are an indirect way of getting at the issue of technology diffusion as they may be unduly influenced by overall trade policy stance as well as degrees of preferential treatment for electronic products.

Canning (1999) investigates what the factors are that help explain the large variation in the number of Internet users across the globe. The data cover 44 countries between 1995 and 1999 and Canning estimates a basic equation in which Internet users across countries is a function of the countries' population levels, per capita income levels, the number of fixed telephone lines, the number of faults per fixed telephone line, the average price of a residential connection charge, the average price of a residential telephone subscription and the average price of a three-minute telephone call. This paper is an interesting example because it differs from Caselli and Coleman. The latter try to explain ICT diffusion focusing on macroeconomic, demographic and institutional variables, while Canning adds technology-related variables to income and populations levels. One advantage of the introduction of such variables is that it makes the link with the theories reviewed above much less tenuous as most technology diffusion theories posit that the interplay (or the direct comparison) between the new and the old technology plays a fundamental role in explaining diffusion. Canning's basic specification contains various important aspects of complementary technologies (or inputs) to Internet access, in particular the extent, reliability and cost of the fixed telephone line network (through which most Internet access takes place). The average cost of telephone charges and subscription is an indirect proxy for the effectiveness of the existing regulatory framework and as such would capture the important institutional dimension of the technology diffusion process many institutional organizations believe is key (as noted above). The econometric estimates reported by Canning support the notion that levels of population and per capita income are the most important determinants of Internet diffusion (which is the same as saying that technology-related variables play a secondary role in explaining technology diffusion across *countries*).

Dasgupta et al.'s (2005) paper differentiates itself from the former two in that it looks at the determinants of diffusion of three types of ICT, namely Internet subscribers/mainlines (their growth and level), fixed lines (level) and mobile lines (growth). The paper is slightly unclear about the motivation for focusing on growth rates of some ICT and levels for others, as well as for the varying number of observations in the case of econometric specifications that do not seem to vary correspondingly (some of the results are for 44 countries, some for 57 and some for 99 and the time window used in the estimation is between 1990 and 1999). A second differentiating feature of this paper is that in addition to demographic and macroeconomic variables, it is one of the first to include a direct measure of the institutional and regulatory framework in the form of a World Bank-developed competition policy index. Their basic specification therefore includes share of urban population, per capita income, economic growth rates, education, governance, the 1990 initial level of mobile lines and the mentioned competition policy index. Dasgupta et al. find that the relative importance of the various potential determinants does not seem to vary dramatically. Moreover, they find that the urban population has a positive and significant effect as does per capita income, economic growth rates and the competition policy index, while the initial level of mobile lines reveals a negative effect, which suggests that a convergence story is at play (countries that start out at relatively lower levels of technology adoption enjoy and take advantage of laggards in that the data do suggest that they catch-up with more advanced countries). Surprisingly, however, this study does *not* find equally strong support for the notions that governance and the levels of human capital are important determinants of ICT diffusion.

In sum, in this section we reviewed three examples of recent econometric work on ICT diffusion across countries. Caselli and Coleman use panel data estimation, but they are a minority (the other few panel studies use rather narrow time windows, say 2000 to 2003). Panel data are essential to understanding differences in technology adoption rates (which are large, as we show in the next section) across countries *as well as* over time. Another common feature of the above studies is that none of them focuses on four types of ICT simultaneously (indeed, to the best of our knowledge, the largest number of ICT covered in any one paper is three). Given the emphasis in the various theoretical models on the interplay between old and new technology, choosing a restrictive (in this sense) approach can be costly as omitted variables biases can turn out to be severe. The same concern applies vis-à-vis the types of factors one believes influences ICT diffusion. Existing work tends to focus on a limited number of areas (e.g., Caselli on macro and demographic issues, Canning on technology aspects and Dasgupta et al. on governance and reform). If one is interested in establishing the relative importance of the regulatory framework and its reforms as a factor driving ICT diffusion (as we are in this paper), then we can not afford to exclude factors that other studies have shown to be important, to greater or lesser degree. Actually, this can only be done in a framework that includes all factors. We know of no paper that includes all such factors. In a nutshell, our paper intends to contribute to this literature by using a panel dataset encompassing a large variety of ICT as well as a sufficiently large number of factors (economic, political, technological and institutional) that are thought of as important determinants of ICT diffusion. We describe the dataset we put together for this paper next.

4   DATA: WHAT DO WE KNOW ABOUT ICT DIFFUSION AND ITS DETERMINANTS IN LAC?

In this section we describe the dataset we put together to assess the relative importance of institutional/regulatory factors in the process of ICT diffusion. The time window covered by our data is 1989 to 2008, with yearly observations for a maximum of 35 Latin American and Caribbean countries. We first look at the dynamics of the adoption rates of four different types of ICT (fixed and mobile telephone lines, personal computers and Internet), after which we discuss the variables collected and constructed to reflect the potential economic, political, technological and institutional diffusion determinants.

To have an idea of how ICT are diffusing around the globe, Table 10.1, from the ITU Telecommunication Indicators Database, shows teledensity measures that are calculated by summing the number of fixed lines and mobile lines per 100 inhabitants at four points in time: 1990, 1996 2002 and 2008. These figures are central in the debate on the so-called 'digital divide'. The table shows the gap between the developed countries and different groupings of developing countries. One can see that East Asia (EAP), Eastern Europe (ECA) and Latin America (LAC) (and to a much lesser extent the Middle East and North African countries) have made great strides in trying to close this gap.

Next we use ITU data to measure the diffusion of the four ICT we are interested in here: fixed telephone lines per 100 inhabitants, mobile telephone lines per 100 inhabitants, personal computers per 100 inhabitants and Internet users per 100 inhabitants.

Figure 10.2 shows the data we use in the estimation below for fixed lines, averaged for the Latin American and Caribbean countries as well as for the OECD economies, while Table 10.2 reports OLS estimates for the diffusion rates of the four technologies for LAC. The figure seems to indicate that fixed telephones have reached the saturation stage. Indeed, the number of users declines after about year 2000 and this trend reversal in LAC mimics what we observe in the OECD countries, suggesting this may be a global phenomenon. The diffusion rates in the two groups are obviously similar, and we estimate that fixed lines have grown on average 7 per cent per year in LAC countries from 1989 to 2007. As shown in Table 10.2, this is the lowest diffusion rate, suggesting that this technology is a mature one and already showing signs of relative decline.

Table 10.1   Teledensity per region, 1990 to 2008 (number of fixed lines and mobiles lines per 100 inhabitants)

	1990	1996	2002	2008
Developing regions:				
Sub-Saharan Africa	1.1	1.5	5.4	34.8
East Asia Pacific	5.3	11.3	36.0	80.1
Europe and Central Asia	26.0	36.8	84.7	153.7
Latin America and the Caribbean	6.3	11.3	35.7	97.9
Middle East &North Africa	4.5	7.9	22.0	84.9
South Asia region	0.6	1.4	4.4	34.6
Developed countries	46.1	66.1	121.7	150.7

Source: Author's calculation based on ITU Telecommunication Indicators Database.

Figure 10.2b shows our data for the technology that is substituting fixed lines, namely mobile phones. In the case of the OECD countries, it is clear that the S-shaped curve predicted by theoretical models emerges with great clarity and indeed suggests that the diffusion of mobiles has already slowed down in the OECD countries. On the other hand, the diffusion of mobiles in LAC as of 2004 is pretty much just starting to take off. We estimate the diffusion rate of mobiles for LAC at 47 per cent on average per year, which is more than twice as large then any of the rates we estimate for any of the other four technologies. Of course, Latin America and the Caribbean is a large and very heterogeneous group of countries and it is be surprising that such heterogeneity appears when we look at individual countries.

Figure 10.3 shows the experience of selected countries. Argentina is the country in the region with the highest level of mobile penetration in 2007. The gap between Chile and Brazil (one of the countries with lowest penetration rates) is rather large, of almost 70 percentage points. The trends in mobile diffusion in Argentina and Uruguay follow almost identical trajectories in the period of analysis.

Figure 10.2c contains diffusion rates of personal computers (PCs) in Latin America and the Caribbean and in the developed countries (OECD). The diffusion process of the four technologies differs among themselves. For the case of PCs, we see an accelerating trend and an increasing gap between adoption rates in LAC and OECD. PCs are diffusing fast in LAC (at a rate of about 20 per cent per year on average), but much slower than, for instance, mobile phones. Figure 10.2d shows the diffusion of Internet

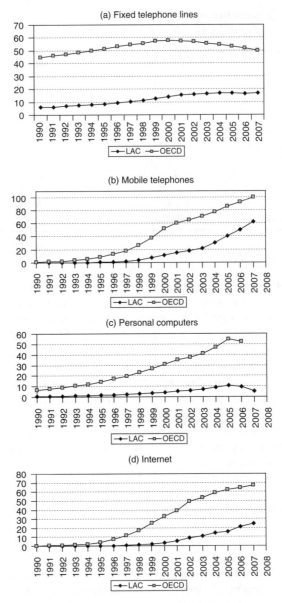

Source: Author's calculations based on data from the International Telecommunications Union.

*Figure 10.2   Diffusion rates of different types of ICT, 1990–2007
(connections per 100 inhabitants)*

Table 10.2 *Average diffusion rates, 1989–2004, OLS estimates for the OECD area and Latin America and the Caribbean*

	OECD Area	Latin America and the Caribbean
Fixed lines	0.02	0.07
		(0.002)***
Mobile lines	0.36	0.47
		(0.007)***
Personal computers	0.15	0.20
		(0.006)***
Internet diffusion	0.53	0.27
		(0.0135)***

Note: ***<0.01.

Source: Author's estimates.

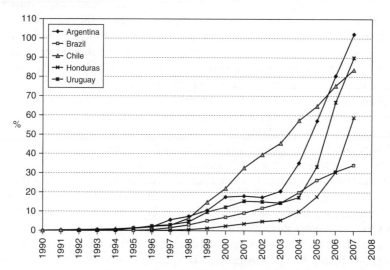

Source: Author's calculations based on data from the International Telecommunications Union.

Figure 10.3 *Mobile diffusion rates in individual countries of Latin America*

users and not surprisingly their patterns follow (albeit at faster rates) that of PC diffusion in both LAC and OECD.

In sum, the four ICTs we consider have followed different diffusion patterns depending on the technology, the region and the exact time period.

For LAC the one ICT that has clearly diffused fastest has been mobile phones, while for the OECD that seems to have been Internet users. We now turn to the potential factors that we use to try to explain the diffusion process of these four ICT over the 1989 to 2004 period.

Let us now discuss the data we collect and construct to capture the (potential) economic, political, technological and institutional ICT diffusion determinants. As our unit of analysis is the *country*, our economic variables are naturally all measured at the country level. This part of our data originates mainly from three sources: Summers and Heston's Penn World Tables (Version 6.2) for the macroeconomic variables; the Morley et al. (1999) structural reform indexes,[1] and Lederman and Saenz (2005) for measures of overall technological effort. Our dataset includes variables for total population, population density, share of rural population, real per capita GDP and government expenditures and investment expressed as shares of GDP. For education and technological effort more generally we collected data on gross enrolment rates in primary, secondary and in tertiary education, total number of patents granted, R&D expenditures, royalties, R&D in public and private sectors as well as that carried out by foreign-owned firms, and the number of R&D personnel. We also have data on high-tech exports (as percentage of total manufacturing exports) and on the manufacturing share of GDP. Finally, the Morley et al. structural reform indexes cover trade liberalization, financial development, tax reform and labour market liberalization. They also produce an index of privatization efforts (which we use as an admittedly less than perfect proxy for changes in the regulatory framework) as well as an aggregate indicator of structural reform combining all these components.

Some authors have started to examine whether a country's overall *political* characteristics can play an independent role in propelling ICT diffusion (e.g., Andonova and Diaz-Serrano, 2007). Such factors proxy changes in the regulatory framework. For example, in more democratic countries voters can express their dissatisfaction with poor public (telecommunications) infrastructure by selecting representatives that are keen on addressing such issues. In Latin America, the quality of the telecommunications infrastructure in the late 1980s (just before the onset of ICT diffusion) was widely perceived as broadly inadequate. There were long waiting times for fixed telephone lines, the quality of actual phone calls was poor and their cost was high. Indeed, anecdotal evidence for Brazil in the late 1980s is that fixed phone lines were treated as an investment with owners renting them out. To establish causality and precisely assess the linkages in this situation may be complicated, but we must also note that it may be no coincidence that the late 1980s is a period of extensive democratization in Latin America. Therefore, we also collected data for a series of political factors that have been extensively used in recent economics scholarship and follow this in taking the Polity IV dataset (2002) as the main source. We collected data on four dimensions: an overall democracy index, a measure of regime durability (the number of years a political regime has been in power, where the political regime is defined by the political scientists responsible from Polity IV following various criteria), the extent of constraints on executive power (which is the political dimension used by Andonova and Diaz-Serrano, 2007), and the degree of political competition. Because we also include measures of the quality of the institutional or regulatory framework in our estimations, it should not be surprising that such political effects turn out to be smaller than expected or smaller than previously found (because part of their effect will be captured directly by the regulatory variables). Yet our purpose here is to investigate whether there is an independent direct effect of political liberalization on ICT diffusion that can contribute an additional dimension to the current debate on the digital divide. To put it bluntly, a few underlying questions on which we want to throw some light here are: is democracy good for technology diffusion? Is faster or deeper ICT diffusion an extra benefit of democracy and a channel through which democracy may affect economic growth and development?

The third factor we believe is important in trying to understand ICT diffusion is intrinsically technology-related. Everything else the same, if the technical performance of given ICT improves, we expect more users will be likely to adopt these technologies. By technological performance we mean the quality to price ratio: if in one country personal computers are faster or more powerful than in another and their prices are the same, then we expect that PC usage in the first country will be more extensive than in the second (ceteris paribus). The same reasoning applies for comparisons over time: if this year's PC is faster than last year's and it costs the same, then we should expect the number of PCs in use to increase. Of course, what happened to personal computers, mobile phones and the Internet in the last decade or so is that not only did their price decline massively, but this was accompanied by substantial improvements in quality and performance.

One important feature of technological determinants of ICT diffusion is that for them to be of any use they have to be ICT-specific. In this light, we collected data for various technological characteristics of telephone lines (from ITU, 2005) such as the average price (in US dollars) of business, residential and mobile telephone connection charges; the average price in USD of business, residential and mobile telephone monthly subscription charges; the average price in USD, fixed and mobile prices of a three-minute local call (peak and off-peak rates), the number of telephone faults per 100 main lines per year (and the average time required to clear such faults), the number of days the average consumer spends on the waiting list for main lines, the mobile coverage as a share of population, total annual investment in telecommunications, and total telecommunications equipment imports.

We collected data for various technological characteristics related to Internet use (from ITU, 2005). In addition to the Internet average monthly price (in USD per 20 hours of use and as a percentage of monthly per capita income) we also have collected information on the average bandwidth, which determines the quality of Internet access (not the quantity) and is defined (ITU, 2005) as 'total capacity of international Internet bandwidth in Mega Bits Per Second (Mbps). If capacity is asymmetric (i.e., more outgoing that incoming or more incoming than outgoing), data provided is the outgoing capacity'.

Finally, with respect to personal computers, from ITU (2005) we collected a price index for private fixed investment in computers and peripheral equipment as well as a series for computer imports (in USD). We also have time-series data from the Mexican market (Lizardi, 2006) on average processor speed of a desktop PC (in MHz), the average Random Access Memory (RAM, in Mb), the average size of the hard drive (HD) of desktop PC (in Mb) and the price of an average desktop PC itself. We have few options in this regard as yearly time-series technical data for PCs is not available for all the 35 LAC. An often-used alternative in the literature to measure ICT investment (see OECD, 2005) is to use data from the US market, which are readily available. For our case, the assumption is that the technical specifications of the average PC are the same in the United States as elsewhere.[2] Given that all countries of LAC are developing economies, our assumption of the same technical specifications (and price) of the average PC in Mexico and elsewhere in LAC seems reasonable. Therefore, the technological factors for personal computers differ from the others discussed above because they do not vary across countries; they vary only over time.

Last but not least we turn to our regulatory framework variables. We have collected data on (1) the level of competition in DSL, mobile, cable and Internet provider markets; (2) year of creation of the regulatory authority and total staff of the regulatory authority (per capita); (3) a categorical variable reflecting the status of the main-fixed line operators (1 = state-owned; 2 = partially privatized; 3 = fully privatized); (4) year of privatization, percentage initially sold and percentage privatized. All these variables originate from the annual ITU Telecommunications Regulatory Survey and reflect answers to this survey supplied by national regulatory authorities themselves. We have also collected data on potentially relevant composite indicators such as the World Bank's Regulatory Quality Index (Kaufmann et al., 2005), the Morley et al.'s privatization index mentioned above and the United Nations' E-Government Readiness Index (2006). To differentiate the level of competition in the domestic computer segment, on the one hand, and fixed, mobiles and Internet, on the other, we use two additional series. One focuses on tariff levels for computer imports, which approximates regulation in the PC segment and yields consistent data (across 35 LAC countries, yearly between 1989 and 2004). Figure 10.4a shows that tariff levels declined rapidly from about 40 per cent in 1989 to about 10 per cent in 1992 and that this trend has continued throughout the 1990s. A second variable we construct to reflect institutional and regulatory factors is the level of competition in the telephone fixed line segment. In this case, competition refers to introducing competition among national service suppliers and/or foreign suppliers without limitations. Figure 10.4b shows that this variable trends upwards between 1989 and 2004, indicating an increasing level of competition in the 35 LAC countries under consideration, on average.

5   THE DETERMINANTS OF ICT DIFFUSION: ECONOMETRIC RESULTS

In this section we present our main empirical results. We model the diffusion of our ICT (fixed and mobile lines, Internet and PCs) at the country level as a function of (1) economic, (2) political, (3) technological, and (4) regulatory variables, covering a maximum of 35 Latin American and Caribbean economies, yearly between 1989 and 2004. We report panel estimates that control for time- as well as country-fixed effects.

Table 10.3 has our estimates for the case of fixed telephone lines. The country coverage is rather good, with 32 LAC countries in the actual sample. We have transformed all variables into logs: this transformation allows the coefficients to be interpreted in standard fashion as elasticities (percentage changes on percentage changes) and facilitates comparisons across the various factors we investigate. In column 1 we first test whether any of the economic determinants that have been widely used previously in the literature turn out to be of any help in explaining ICT diffusion in LAC. We find that the level of human capital and the level of real per capita GDP play massive roles in explaining fixed telephones diffusion in LAC. Surprisingly, aggregate investment seems to play a minor role and government spending seems to play none. This relatively simple model fits the data well as it explains almost two-thirds of the variation across countries and over time in fixed phones. Column 2 adds the share of manufacturing

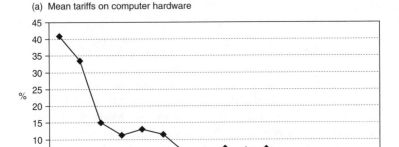

(a) Mean tariffs on computer hardware

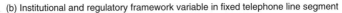

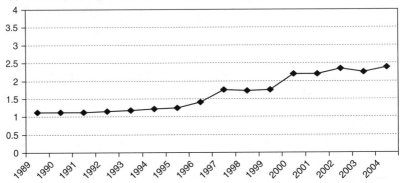

(b) Institutional and regulatory framework variable in fixed telephone line segment

Note: The vertical scale is an index ranging from 0–4 on Figure 10.4b. The higher the number, the higher the level of competition in local fixed telephone services. ITU's level of competition: 1 = monopoly; 2 = duopoly; 3 = partial competition; 4 = full competition. Competition refers to introducing competition among national service suppliers and/or foreign suppliers without any limitations.

Sources: Institutional and regulatory framework variable comes from the annual ITU Telecommunications Regulatory Survey (2005), supplemented by data from AHCIET (2003) and REGULATEL (2006).

Figure 10.4   Examples of tariffs and level of competition in ICT

in GDP. Treating the share of agriculture and natural resources as roughly constant, we expect the share of GDP to carry a negative sign because this means that the demand from the services sector is playing a positive role (the share of services is measured inconsistently across LAC countries over time). The result supports this view. In column 3 we add a measure of

Table 10.3 *Determinants of ICT diffusion – dependent variable: telephone fixed lines*

	(1)	(2)	(3)	(4)	(5)	(6)
Income per capita	1.025*** [0.16]	0.866*** [0.17]	1.394*** [0.20]	0.852*** [0.18]	0.801*** [0.19]	0.883*** [0.17]
Investment	0.215*** [0.074]	0.124* [0.067]	−0.329*** [0.058]	0.133* [0.071]	0.150** [0.075]	0.119* [0.063]
Govt spending	0.0954 [0.14]	0.00993 [0.12]	−0.0375 [0.091]	0.0221 [0.13]	0.0264 [0.12]	0.036 [0.16]
Human capital	1.054*** [0.062]	0.977*** [0.068]	0.732*** [0.059]	0.872*** [0.080]	0.733*** [0.092]	0.811*** [0.099]
Manuf./ GDP		−0.618*** [0.10]	−0.518*** [0.089]	−0.594*** [0.11]	−0.593*** [0.12]	−0.392*** [0.13]
Reform (general)			1.769*** [0.28]			
Durability of regime					0.0147*** [0.0041]	
Cost of connection (res.)						−0.077*** [0.024]
Competition level				0.116*** [0.033]	0.134*** [0.038]	0.0852*** [0.031]
Constant	−11.8*** [1.44]	−7.917*** [1.64]	−11.81*** [1.95]	−7.548*** [1.78]	−6.895*** [1.87]	−7.769*** [1.81]
Observations	340	316	211	306	254	264
Number of countries	33	31	17	29	22	29
R-squared	0.67	0.73	0.83	0.74	0.77	0.74

Note: Robust standard errors in brackets; *** p<0.01, ** p<0.05, * p<0.1.

Source: Author's calculations.

overall economic reform from Morley et al. and we can see that not only is this variable strongly significant, but it has a relative role much larger than all others discussed until now. One major drawback of these reform measures is that they are only available for 17 countries and therefore we must leave the full investigation of this issue for future research once such data for more countries is made available. Column 4 substitutes our main variable for the regulatory framework for general reform. The number of countries covered increases substantially again, and the coefficient on regulation has the expected sign and is strongly statistically significant. However, note that, according to our estimates in Table 10.3, its effects are much more modest than those of level of development or human capital. Notice also that once we control for the extent of actual competition, the age of the regulatory agency or whether it was implemented before the main privatizations does not matter.

Column 5 of Table 10.3 shows results suggesting that regime durability has a positive influence on the diffusion of fixed telephone lines (similar results hold for the democracy variable), while column 6 shows that the technical characteristics also play a significant role, albeit the smallest one in terms of the size of the effect in comparison with the three other factors. This should not be surprising because our data are not at the level of the sector or firm and thus we shouldn't expect these to play a major role in explaining ICT diffusion across countries and over time. We should also add that all these results are qualitatively similar if we estimate our diffusion models using random-effects instead.

Table 10.4 uses the same estimation strategy as before and the only change we observe regards the technological variables, which now relate to mobile phones. The results in columns 1 to 6 are in line with those discussed from Table 10.3. The one important difference is that investment now carries a negative sign, although its coefficient loses statistical significance once we control for our full set of factors. A second difference is that the individual effects tend to be larger than those for fixed lines but we believe this may be easily understood once one recalls that the diffusion rates for mobile phone are more than twice those for fixed lines (for LAC during this period). As the amounts explained by the models in Table 10.4 are surely not smaller than those from Table 10.3, one should not be surprised by the larger effects. The relative importance of the regulatory framework is almost the same as before.

Table 10.5 presents our results for diffusion of personal computers keeping the same estimation strategy and way of displaying our results. Although the number of countries declines, the amount of variation captured by our diffusion models in this table does not seem to differ greatly from those in the tables just reviewed for the other ICT. Two important differences in this case are that the role of services over GDP seems much larger than for the other ICT (and its relatively importance is surely larger) and that our measure of the level of competition 'government regulation-supported' in the domestic market does not seem to help to explain variation in PC diffusion. Note that our previous measure of regulatory framework does play an equally important role in this case, but we are not convinced it is appropriate to extrapolate its uses. It is difficult to capture regulation relevant for PC diffusion because, differently from the others, PCs can hardly be considered as public utilities. Further, serious efforts were made to regulate the computer industry in LAC (e.g., in Brazil the Informatics Law was in force until 1991) side by side with a very strong laissez faire stance by (arguably) the majority of the governments in the region, which

Table 10.4   *Determinants of ICT diffusion – dependent variable: telephone mobile lines*

	(1)	(2)	(3)	(4)	(5)	(6)
Income per	7.833***	7.233***	6.477***	6.895***	6.482***	10.61***
capita	[0.89]	[0.87]	[1.04]	[0.86]	[0.83]	[1.30]
Investment	−0.422	−0.819**	−2.148***	−0.751*	−0.863**	0.246
	[0.41]	[0.40]	[0.40]	[0.40]	[0.36]	[0.47]
Govt	0.555	−0.34	−0.987	−0.5	−0.722	1.980*
spending	[0.92]	[0.89]	[0.85]	[0.91]	[0.80]	[1.04]
Human	6.582***	6.360***	5.930***	5.709***	4.886***	3.475***
capital	[0.43]	[0.48]	[0.41]	[0.53]	[0.51]	[0.79]
Manuf./		−2.146**	−0.926	−2.048**	−1.562*	−0.465
GDP		[0.83]	[0.85]	[0.85]	[0.90]	[0.86]
Reform			7.289***			
(general)			[2.30]			
Durability of					0.0826***	
regime					[0.021]	
Cost cellular						−0.004***
connection						[0.00083]
Competition				0.600***	0.723***	0.488**
level				[0.18]	[0.17]	[0.21]
Constant	−96.44***	−80.30***	−74.70***	−74.62***	−69.04***	−111.1***
	[8.87]	[9.69]	[10.2]	[10.1]	[9.49]	[14.0]
Observations	272	255	172	246	200	150
Number of countries	32	30	16	28	20	25
R-squared	0.71	0.76	0.83	0.78	0.83	0.8

Note: Robust standard errors in brackets; *** p<0.01, ** p<0.05, * p<0.1

Source: Author's calculations.

makes capturing this factor both important and difficult indeed. One way we thought would be good to do this was to use the average tariffs for computing equipment, but unfortunately this variable does not seem to work in favour of our argument as is blatantly obvious from Table 10.5.

Finally, Table 10.6 shows our estimates for the diffusion of the Internet, captured by the number of Internet users over 100 inhabitants. In this case we obtain the poorest coverage in terms of both countries and time. Moreover, the fit of our diffusion models deteriorates considerably vis-à-vis those for the three ICT discussed above. Despite these drawbacks, our finding that levels of human capital are the main determinant of Internet usage across countries and over time in LAC can hardly be described as unexpected. However, note that once human capital and development level are accounted for, the next most important determinant of Internet

Table 10.5   Determinants of ICT diffusion – dependent variable: personal computers

	(1)	(2)	(3)	(4)	(5)	(6)	(7)
Income per capita	3.353***	2.888***	2.994***	2.945***	2.686***	0.930***	0.426**
	[0.41]	[0.42]	[0.35]	[0.55]	[0.50]	[0.33]	[0.21]
Investment	-0.409**	-0.418**	-1.111***	-0.861***	-0.495**	0.0372	-0.143
	[0.20]	[0.19]	[0.20]	[0.22]	[0.19]	[0.11]	[0.096]
Govt spending	-0.426	-0.355	-0.329	-1.021*	-0.248	-0.158	-0.0962
	[0.50]	[0.44]	[0.31]	[0.58]	[0.44]	[0.30]	[0.27]
Human capital	2.687***	2.220***	1.805***	1.817***	2.069***	0.403**	0.242*
	[0.17]	[0.21]	[0.17]	[0.20]	[0.24]	[0.18]	[0.14]
Manuf./GDP		-1.615***	-1.104***	-1.098***	-1.602***	-0.922***	-0.832***
		[0.39]	[0.28]	[0.41]	[0.43]	[0.19]	[0.12]
Reform (general)			6.731***				
			[0.91]				
Computer tariffs				-0.106			
				[0.069]			
Durability of regime					0.0248*		
					[0.014]		

	(1)	(2)	(3)	(4)	(5)	(6)	(7)
PC speed						0.377***	0.158***
						[0.027]	[0.030]
Price PC							−0.002***
							[0.00025]
Constant	−37.21***	−27.05***	−30.99***	−24.13***	−25.11***	−8.082**	−1.181
	[4.34]	[4.90]	[3.62]	[5.50]	[5.68]	[3.44]	[2.27]
Observations	223	220	148	116	177	220	220
Number of countries	28	28	15	21	19	28	28
R-squared	0.7	0.74	0.85	0.83	0.77	0.88	0.92

Note: Robust standard errors in brackets; *** p<0.01, ** p<0.05, * p<0.1.

Source: Author's calculations.

Table 10.6   Determinants of ICT diffusion – dependent variable: Internet users

	(1)	(2)	(3)	(4)	(5)	(6)
Income per	2.289*	1.783	3.307	2.480***	1.672	1.844***
capita	[1.16]	[1.11]	[2.95]	[0.88]	[1.10]	[0.64]
Investment	−0.204	−0.418	−0.271	−0.132	0.175	0.239
	[0.33]	[0.30]	[0.51]	[0.26]	[0.39]	[0.34]
Govt spending	−0.0239	−0.601	−0.29	−1.195*	−0.529	−0.408
	[0.66]	[0.71]	[0.94]	[0.68]	[0.69]	[0.48]
Human capital	1.878***	2.317***	3.391	2.177***	2.954**	3.065***
	[0.63]	[0.82]	[2.04]	[0.72]	[1.38]	[1.11]
Manuf./GDP		−1.566**	−1.313	−1.157*	−0.766	−0.303
		[0.69]	[1.29]	[0.65]	[0.84]	[0.55]
Reform			−8.541			
(general)			[7.20]			
Competition				0.613**	0.611**	0.326*
level				[0.24]	[0.29]	[0.19]
Durability of					0.0496	−0.00493
regime					[0.040]	[0.019]
Bandwidth						0.000123***
						[0.000028]
Constant	−27.41***	−18.36*	−31.22*	−24.27***	−25.58***	−28.17***
	[9.41]	[9.93]	[17.6]	[8.44]	[9.48]	[7.07]
Observations	122	113	69	112	85	64
Number of	26	25	14	24	18	16
countries						
R-squared	0.24	0.37	0.43	0.45	0.5	0.67

Note: Robust standard errors in brackets; *** p<0.01, ** p<0.05, * p<0.1.

Source: Author's calculations.

diffusion is the quality of the regulatory framework, with technical characteristics a somewhat distant third, and political stability having an almost negligible role to play in this instance.

6   CONCLUSIONS

This paper tries to provide a comprehensive assessment of the determinants of ICT diffusion in Latin America and the Caribbean. We study the diffusion processes of four types of ICT (fixed and mobile phones, personal computers and the Internet) and examine a comprehensive set of potential determinants (i.e., economic, political, technological and the institutional and regulatory framework dimensions) using a unique yearly panel dataset of 35 Latin American and Caribbean economies between 1989 and 2004.

Our estimates support a ranking of determinants with levels of human capital and per capita GDP generally as the main factors, followed in decreasing order of importance by the effectiveness of the regulatory framework (degree of competition in the domestic market and various characteristics of regulatory agencies), technical aspects (e.g., average price of call for phones, bandwidth for Internet and speed for computers) and political variables (democracy and durability of the regime). This ranking varies slightly depending on the type of ICT. The general ranking holds for fixed and mobile lines (although human capital is more important than per capita income for the latter), while in the case of PCs the share of the services sector on GDP is more important than level of human capital, technical factors are more important than regulatory and political aspects. Finally, the rise in Internet users seems to depend on levels of human capital, per capita income, regulation and technical aspects, while political factors matter little.

NOTES

*   I would like to thank Mario Cimoli, Nelson Correa, Alvaro Diaz, Giovanni Dosi, Joao Carlos Ferraz, Fabio Freitas, Dale Jorgenson, David Kupfer, Gaitzeen De Vries, Marcio Wohlers and seminar participants at the ECLAC Workshops 'Growth, ICT and Productivity' in Santiago on 30 November and 1 December 2006 and 29–30 March 2007 for valuable comments on a previous version of this paper. Mariela Dal Borgo provided superb assistance with the data. The views expressed in this paper are my own and do not necessarily represent those of ECLAC.
1. We are grateful to Roberto Machado of ECLAC for sharing the updated version of these indexes.
2. This may be less strict than the assumption that the relationship between PC prices and PC technical characteristics is the same in the United States as elsewhere, which is also commonly found in this literature.

REFERENCES

Andonova, V. and L. Diaz-Serrano (2007), 'Political Institutions and the Development of Telecommunications', IZA Discussion Paper No. 2569.

AHCIET (Associação Hispanoamericana de Centros de Investigación y Empresas de Telecomunicaciones) (2003), *Handbook of ICT Related Public Policies in Latin America*.

Canning, D. (1999), 'Internet Use and Telecommunications Infrastructure', Harvard, CAER II Discussion Paper No. 54, December.

Caselli, F. and W. Coleman (2001), 'Cross-country Technology Diffusion: The Case of Computers', *American Economic Review*, **91**(2), 328–35.

Dasgupta, S., S. Lall and D. Wheeler (2005), 'Policy Reform, Economic Growth, and the Digital Divide', *Oxford Development Studies*, **33**(2), 229–43.

Geroski, Paul (2000), 'Models of Technology Diffusion', *Research Policy*, **29**(4–5), 603–25.

Hall, Bronwyn and Beethika Khan (2003), 'Adoption of New Technology', in D. Jones (ed.), *The New Economy Handbook*, San Diego and London: Elsevier/ Academic Press.

International Monetary Fund (IMF) (2001), *World Economic Outlook*, Chapter 3.

International Telecommunication Union (ITU) (2005), World Telecommunication Indicators Database, Geneva: ITU CD-ROM.

International Telecommunication Union (ITU) (2006 and various previous issues), *Trends in Telecommunication Reform*, Geneva: ITU.

Kaufmann, Daniel, Aart Kraay and Massimo Mastruzzi (2005), 'Governance Matters IV: Governance Indicators for 1996–2004', The World Bank.

Lederman, Daniel and Laura Saenz (2005), 'Innovation and Development around the World, 1960–2000', World Bank Policy Research Working Paper No. 3774.

Lizardi, Carlos (2006), 'Una aproximación al sesgo de medición del precio de los computadoras personales en México', *Economía Mexicana*, **XV**(1), 97–124.

Morley, Samuel A., Roberto Machado and Stefano Pettinato (1999), 'Indexes of Structural Reform in Latin America', ECLAC Serie Reformas Económicas No. 12.

Mowery, D.C. and N. Rosenberg (1982), 'Technical Change in the Commercial Aircraft Industry, 1925–1975', in N. Rosenberg (ed.), *Inside the Black Box: Technology and Economics*, New York: Cambridge University Press.

OECD (2004), 'Regulatory Reform as a Tool for Bridging the Digital Divide', Paris: OECD.

OECD (2005), *Guide to Measuring the Information Society*, Paris: OECD.

Pohjola, M. (2003), 'The Adoption and Diffusion of ICT Across Countries: Patterns and Determinants', in D.C. Jones (ed.), *New Economy Handbook*, San Diego and London: Elsevier/Academic Press, pp. 77–100.

Polity IV (2002), 'Political Regime Characteristics and Transitions, 1800–2002', available at http://www.systemicpeace.org/polity/polity4.htm; accessed 29 March 2010.

REGULATEL (2006), 'Proyecto de Acesso Universal para Telecomuncaciones en América Latina: Informe de Paises', September.

Rosenberg, Nathan (1972), *Technology and American Economic Growth*, New York: Harper & Row.

United Nations (2006), *UN Global E-Government Readiness Report 2005: From E-Government to E-Inclusion*, New York: UN.

World Bank (2006), *Information and Communications for Development 2006: Global Trends and Policies*, Washington: World Bank.

Index

Lederman, Daniel 250
Leontief, Wassily 208, 229
Levine, Ross 140
Lipsey, Richard 3, 6, 181
Lithuania *see* Eastern Europe and the
	former Soviet Union
Lizardi, Carlos 102, 252
Lokshin, Boris 188
Louçã, Francisco 160
Lucas, Robert 182
Lundvall, Bengt-Åke 45, 51
Luxembourg 75, 86, 88
Luzio, Eduardo 102

machinery 53, 77, 86–8, 94–5, 103, 109,
	218, 220
	computing 98, 217
	of electronic system 227
	equipment 125
	iron 53
	office 218
macroeconomic
	drivers 140
	impacts 13, 140, 154
	instability 13, 130, 134, 136
Madagascar *see* Sub-Saharan
	Africa
Maddison, Angus 46
Makepeace, Gerald 140
Malawi *see* Sub-Saharan Africa
Malaysia *see* developing Asia
Mali *see* Sub-Saharan Africa
Mankiw, Gregory 144–5
manufacturing 80–84, 86–8, 94, 139,
	165–6, 168, 173, 218, 220, 243,
	253
	formal 175
	imports 243
	widening 164
	workers 61
marginal products 3, 77, 105, 125, 144,
	182, 185
Marques, Felipe 229
Mauritania *see* North Africa and
	Middle East
Mauritius *see* Sub-Saharan Africa
McCombie, John 208
Melchior, Arne 47
Meliciani, Valentina 48
Metcalfe, John 177

Mexico 9, 12, 21, 25–7, 33, 60, 63–4,
	121, 123, 127–9, 175, 193–4,
	199–200
MFP (multi-factor productivity) 3–5,
	10–13, 76–7, 79, 85, 88, 90,
	118–19, 124–6, 128, 130, 133,
	135–6, 205
micro
	computers 102
	electronics devices 2, 54
	processors 1, 175
microeconomic
	behaviours 172, 175
	theory 160, 172
microeconomics 6
Milgrom, Paul 56, 187–8
Miller, Ronald E. 230
Minges, Michael 155
mining 53, 85, 95, 165–6, 168, 220
Miozzo, Marcela 64
Miravete, Eugenio 188
mobile 150–54, 247, 252–3
	phone 13, 16, 61, 131–2, 136–7, 139,
		142–3, 145–7, 149, 154–8, 175,
		237, 241–2, 244–51, 256, 260–61
Mohnen, Pierre 188
Morley, Samuel A. 130, 250, 253, 255
Morocco *see* North Africa and Middle
	East
Morrison, Catherine J. 108, 111
Mortimore, Michael 173
Motohashi, Kazuyuki 96
Mowery, David 238, 243
Mozambique *see* Sub-Saharan Africa
Mulder, Nanno 96, 136–7

Namibia *see* Sub-Saharan Africa
national accounts 79, 96, 98, 104, 204,
	214, 232
National Classification of Economic
	Activity (CNAE) 216
National Institute of Statistics and
	Censuses (INDEC) 108
National Statistics Institute (INE) 108
natural resource endowment 172
Nelson, Richard 45, 51
neoclassical approach 7, 206
Nepal *see* developing Asia 21
Netherlands 11, 20–21, 50, 60, 62, 75,
	79, 85, 88, 90–91, 162, 209